GRANTA 80

The Group

ICA Films - Unmissable Cinema

Institute of Contemporary Arts, The Mall, London SW1

020 7930 3647   www.ica.org.uk

From 29 November
OUR FATHER (ABOUNA)
Dir Mahamat-Saleh Haroun (Chad)
'A life-affirming and optimistic work.' *Variety*
A richly coloured, beautifully shot tale of two brothers searching for their lost father.

Opens 15 November 2002
Sans Soleil
Dir Chris Marker (France)
'Cinema's greatest essayist sums up a lifetime's travels, speculations, passions'
Time Out
A new print of Marker's masterpiece – graceful, exhilarating and endlessly fascinating.

Opens 24 January 2003
THE MAN WITHOUT A PAST
Dir Aki Kaurismaki (Finland)
'Sublime' *Observer*
'A life-affirming joy'
The Times
Winner of the Grand Jury and Best Actress prizes at Cannes.

Opens Spring 2003
MON-RAK TRANSISTOR
(A Transistor Love Story)
Dir Pen-ek Ratanaraung (Thailand)
'the film's cheery energy and spirit prove contagious'
Variety
A colourful Elvis Presley-style musical.

JONATHAN FRANZEN

Passionate, independent-minded non-fiction from
the international bestselling author of *The Corrections*

HOW TO BE ALONE

GRANTA

GRANTA 80, WINTER 2002
www.granta.com

EDITOR *Ian Jack*
DEPUTY EDITOR *Sophie Harrison*
ASSOCIATE EDITOR *Liz Jobey*
EDITORIAL ASSISTANT *Fatema Ahmed*

CONTRIBUTING EDITORS *Diana Athill, Gail Lynch, Blake Morrison, Andrew O'Hagan, Lucretia Stewart*

ASSOCIATE PUBLISHER *Sally Lewis*
FINANCE *Geoffrey Gordon, Morgan Graver*
SALES *Frances Hollingdale*
PUBLICITY *Louise Campbell*
SUBSCRIPTIONS *John Kirkby, Darryl Wilks*
PUBLISHING ASSISTANT *Mark Williams*
ADVERTISING MANAGER *Kate Rochester*
PRODUCTION ASSOCIATE *Sarah Wasley*

PUBLISHER *Rea S. Hederman*

Granta, 2–3 Hanover Yard, Noel Road, London N1 8BE
Tel 020 7704 9776 Fax 020 7704 0474
e-mail for editorial: editorial@granta.com

Granta US, 1755 Broadway, 5th Floor, New York, NY 10019-3780, USA

TO SUBSCRIBE call 020 7704 0470 or e-mail subs@granta.com
A one-year subscription (four issues) costs £26.95 (UK), £34.95 (rest of Europe) and £41.95 (rest of the world).

Granta is printed and bound in Italy by Legoprint. The paper used in this publication meets the minimum requirements of American National Standard for Information Sciences—Permanence of Paper for Printed Library Materials, ANSI Z39.48-1984.

Granta is published by Granta Publications.
This selection copyright © 2002 Granta Publications.

Acknowledgements are due to the following publishers for permission to quote from:
Camera Lucida by Roland Barthes, translated by Richard Howard, reprinted by permission of Vintage, and Hill and Wang, an imprint of Farrar, Straus & Giroux © 1981 Richard Howard; 'For Richard Turner' from In These Mountains, by Peter Sacks, reprinted with the permission of Scribner, an Imprint of Simon & Schuster Adult Publishing Group © 1986 Peter Sacks

Design: Random Design
Front cover photograph: courtesy of Georgina Buxton; hand-colouring by Andy Dark
Back cover photograph: Susan Meiselas/Magnum

ISBN 0 903141 56 6

⩵ISTORY IN T⩵E MAKING

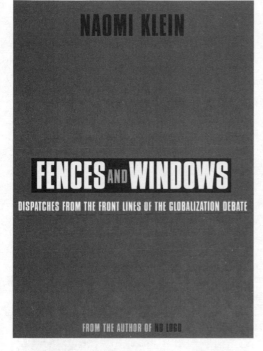

NAOMI KLEIN's *No Logo* revealed the uneasy struggle between corporate power and its opponents.

Fences and Windows reports from the front lines of the globalization war.

Booker prize winner **ARUNDHATI ROY** has always attracted worldwide attention.

The Algebra of Infinite Justice is a stunning collection of her most controversial journalism.

FLAMINGO

www.fireandwater.com

PAST MASTERS
PERFECT PRESENTS

A wonderful and immaculately researched novel that brings Dr Johnson, his friends and his times to life

The biography of an extraordinary and influential eighteenth-century figure

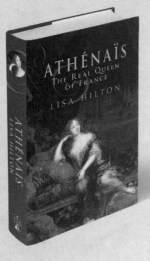

'Lisa Hilton has rescued Athénaïs from her underserving obscurity. Here she lies before us in all her glory and pain – one of the most compelling women of her age' Amanda Foreman, author of *Georgiana, Duchess of Devonshire*

The revolutionary adventures of the two scientists who inaugurated the metric system

War and the British people – from the Roman military occupation to the Gulf War two thousand years later

 ABACUS   Imprints of Time Warner Books UK

USED TO BE GREAT FRIENDS

C. J. Driver

A Chinese restaurant, Cape Town, 1962

This is a photograph of a twenty-first birthday party in the late winter of 1962. The parents of one of the young men in the photograph have taken him, his girlfriend, and seven other young people to dinner in a Chinese restaurant. Two—including the birthday boy—are wearing dinner jackets; the other men are in suits (I am fairly sure two of them are even wearing waistcoats, though only one is visible). Three of the young women are wearing evening dresses of the kind usually worn to dances in those days; the other—who is holding a wine glass—is so well wrapped up against the cold that she won't relinquish her overcoat to a waiter. It was surprisingly often useful to own an overcoat, even in Cape Town.

Yes, it is South Africa; and, yes, there are no blacks visible in the photograph. Some of us in the photograph did have black friends; but in those days there were perhaps only two restaurants in Cape Town to which blacks and whites could go together, and this wasn't one of them. Yet, of the nine (white) youngsters, two were to serve prison sentences for their active opposition to apartheid, and one to do a short spell in solitary confinement under the Ninety Day Detention legislation before leaving the country and becoming, for more than twenty years, a prohibited immigrant. Another of the young men would be assassinated, shot through his own front door by someone who has never been brought to justice, but who was almost certainly either in, or employed by, the South African security police. Most of those others in the photograph have since then lived much of their lives outside South Africa—though, paradoxically, the two who served prison sentences have spent much time in recent years back in southern Africa, and one of them is living there permanently. Those who have chosen to continue in exile have, in general, had very successful working lives. One, at least, might be described as a star of some magnitude. Almost none of us sees much of each other any more, to an extent that one might suppose us to have fallen out; yet I don't think we have done so actively: it is simply the way things have worked out.

Let me begin to attach names to the faces. On the far left is Alan Brooks, the man in the group to whom I was, in those days, closest. He was the son of a doctor in what was then Salisbury (now Harare), who had come down from what was then Rhodesia (now Zimbabwe) to the University of Cape Town in the same year as me. He had taken an Arts degree, and was beginning to specialize in law.

We had both for three years been rebellious members of the same deeply right-wing university residence, Smuts Hall. Very much the intellectual—he played the violin, he taught the rest of us more advanced forms of bridge than Culbertson advocated, he had no interest in other games at all—and in those days still heavily Methodist in religion and attitude, he could at times be rather forbidding. I still remember two 'put-down' remarks he made to me: 'The trouble with you, Jonty, is that you think your father is God—and you know what that means you think of yourself,' and (after I had confessed that I didn't much like Brahms) 'You'll know better by the time you're forty.' The second remark was wholly true. We were both passionately anti-apartheid, and our opposition was already not merely verbal: we were active in campus politics, particularly in the National Union of South African Students (NUSAS), and had worked off-campus for the Liberal Party. Alan Brooks was however already more radical in his politics than I was, though I am not yet sure if he had begun the shifts of direction which were to lead him, first, into the ranks of the African Resistance Movement (the ARM)—the first organization, though it was mainly white and (in the Cape at least) almost entirely liberal, to use sabotage against the apartheid state—and (very soon afterwards) away from liberalism into socialism, and from socialism into the South African Communist Party (in those days, deeply Stalinist).

It was for his work in the ARM (blowing up railway lines and electrical pylons) that Alan was sent, a few years later, to jail for two years. Ironically, by the time he was arrested, he was struggling to extricate himself from the ARM because of his commitment to communism. Ironically, too, although he had moved further, faster and harder to the Left than any of us, it turned out that he was entirely unknown to the security police. When Alan was betrayed by the person who had recruited him, Adrian Leftwich—as were most of his companions in the ARM—it turned out that the security police had no record of Alan at all, no photographs, no secret recordings, no copies of letters; they went back to Leftwich for more information on this mysteriously unknown person of whom they could find no trace. By then, Alan had gone underground and was living under an assumed name. 'Oh, he's easily recognizable,' Leftwich is supposed to have said. 'He has a habit of pushing back into place a strand of hair that flops over his forehead.' Raiding some unconnected premises in search of someone entirely different, the security police failed to pick Alan out from among the others there until, just as they were leaving, he made that most characteristic gesture, and one of the more vigilant policemen remembered.

In detention, Alan was as stalwart as the most committed of the members of the ARM, even though he was savagely beaten up. (After his release from jail, he had a settlement from the Minister of Justice in recompense of the injuries caused—though the police tried to pretend he had 'fallen down some stairs'). Immediately deported from South Africa on his release, he went to England, where he took a degree from the University of Sussex, worked for the Defence and Aid Fund (which looked after the legal costs and families of political prisoners in South Africa), became a committed member of the Anti-Apartheid Movement, and—one assumes—continued to be a member of the South African Communist Party (SACP). Though he came to my wedding in 1967, and I went to his, a little time later, our different attitudes to communism had already begun to separate us; I remember hardly believing my ears when he sang the praises of an Eastern European country he had gone to for his summer holiday—was it Romania?

Occasionally since the weddings, I have heard something about Alan: that his marriage produced two daughters, of whom Alan is both proud and protective, though the marriage failed; that he went to work in Mozambique after its liberation from the Portuguese; that he is still committed to communism. Once, by chance, we bumped into each other on Hampstead Heath, and exchanged a few desultory words before walking on. There are other friends of our generation with whom I fell out politically, but with whom I am still friends— South Africa was (probably still is) such a politically divided society that, to have friends at all, one had to learn to ignore some of what they seemed to believe in; one came to judge people by the way they acted, not by what they said they thought. Alan was always a person who tended to follow his line of reasoning to a logical conclusion, even when the conclusion was uncomfortable; moreover, he had the kind of intellectual rigour which likes to pretend head comes before heart, even though everyone who knows him knows too that his particular heart is as deep as his passions are narrow.

Sitting next to Alan in the photograph is John Clare's father, the host, who died in 1976; I propose to leave him—and John's mother, just visible at the opposite end of the table—out of my reckoning. They were generous parents, and made much of their son's friendships; if it hadn't been for them, we shouldn't have been dining out to celebrate a birthday, but would have been holding a cheap and noisy 'bop' in someone's flat, with each guest bringing what drink he could afford. Going out to a restaurant was a real treat.

Sitting next to his father is John Clare, boyish in his dinner jacket. He is now the education editor of the *Daily Telegraph*, and the man who first applied to schools the principle of league tables based on success in public examinations. People in England are sometimes surprised when I tell them that John is—was—a South African. (Actually, he was born in China and spent three of his earliest years in a Japanese prison camp outside Shanghai.) Physically, he has worn very well and is still recognizable from the photograph. I suppose many would typify him as 'right wing', though actually he is much more in the mould of the radical reformer, happiest when he is pointing out that the emperor is quite naked. When he was a journalist on *The Times*, John Clare upset Alan Paton by asserting that Paton's support of Chief Buthelezi of the Zulus made it seem that he was supporting the Bantustans and thus apologizing for apartheid—Alan Paton was as bad as most of us are with anything which looks like criticism. John is still capable of giving offence, because, in pursuit of the unpalatable truth—or perhaps even a good story—he can be singularly awkward. It amuses me that, once upon a time, when I was editor of *Varsity*, the weekly newspaper of the University of Cape Town, John was 'my' news editor—and, if I taught him nothing else, I did teach him something about punctuation. Nowadays, I write occasional articles for him and he cuts them down to an appropriate length.

Next to John Clare in the photograph is Stephanie Kemp, his girlfriend at the time—or is it more proper to say that John was Stephanie's boyfriend, because she was a very lively girl? I remember once talking to Steph about 'being wild'; 'If you think I'm wild,' she said to me, 'you should meet my sister, the air hostess. If half the things she says the aircrews get up to are true, you'd know wild.' I never met the sister, and Steph always seemed a few steps ahead of me. She is the subject of a book, Albie Sachs's second volume of autobiography, *Stephanie on Trial*, published in 1968. While it is not as brilliant as Sachs's *Jail Diary* (still one of the most lucid and vivid accounts of what happens to someone who is locked up in solitary confinement), it too bears rereading, more than thirty years after the events it describes—and even though the author was so obviously in love with his subject it should surprise no reader that, by the end of the book, Stephanie Kemp has become Mrs Albie Sachs. At one stage of her detention, Steph was beaten up by a security policeman called 'Spyker' van Wyk (Spyker means nail), who held her hair and beat her head on the floor until she was unconscious—bruising her so much that, in her own words to me, her blackened eyes extended to her chin. She was another of those who, despite being convicted— she was sentenced to five years, three of them suspended, though she served only a year before release—later got a settlement from the Minister of Justice for her injuries in custody. She was a tough person, Steph, as well as very attractive.

I haven't seen Stephanie for years, though I know that, after she and Albie parted, she and John Clare were for a time together again. I have been told that she disapproves of me as much as I do of her irrational attachment to 'dialectical materialism'. I don't know when she became the lover of Joe Slovo (the white *éminence grise* of the ANC and the SACP), though I know she had a child by him. After the end of apartheid she chose to go back to South Africa and lives there now, first practising physiotherapy in a clinic in Alexandria township in Johannesburg and then teaching it in the University of Natal. Joe's untimely death from cancer deprived South Africa of one of its most able cabinet ministers, and Stephanie has written in newspapers of her disillusionment that, after years of what she would see as commitment and self-sacrifice, she is apparently cold-shouldered by those now in power. Albie Sachs was working in Maputo when he was badly injured by a car bomb put in place by the South African security police; he lost an arm and an eye as a result. He is now one of the eleven judges of that remarkably liberal institution, the South African Constitutional Court.

On Stephanie's left in the photograph is Roger Jowell. I've always been rather surprised that we have hardly seen each other since we both came to live in England. I see his elder brother sometimes

(Jeffrey Jowell, sometime president of the Oxford Union and now a celebrated academic lawyer) and I send affectionate messages to Roger, but nothing happens—no doubt this is as much my fault as his, though I have wondered if I did something somewhere along the line which offended him. We (and one other in the photograph) shared a house in Cape Town for most of a year, and I was a regular visitor to his parents' wealthy and hospitable Jewish home. Roger's sardonic humour made him an entertaining companion, though perhaps it was only his relative wealth which made me think he was sophisticated, too. He has made a name for himself in England as the head of a research institute concerned with public policy—and he gave his name to someone better known than himself: Tessa Jowell, now a minister in the latest Labour government, though no longer married to the man whose name she still carries. In one of the Honours lists of 2001, Roger was made a CBE.

Next to Roger Jowell in the photograph is Sally Frankel; I have to confess that I didn't remember even her first name, and so asked John Clare if he remembered. John said he thought it was someone called Naomi, but it wasn't. Of Sally Frankel all I know is that, after leaving the university, she—like many of our contemporaries—emigrated to Australia. (The 'Naomi' John Clare thought he remembered must have been Saone Barron, who was Roger Jowell's girlfriend both before and after the time of this photograph. I mention this mainly because Saone is now married to the celebrated American politician, Chester Crocker—yet another thread in this peculiar web.)

Half hidden behind Sally Frankel is John Clare's mother, still alive, but now in a nursing home in England and very forgetful.

On her left, on the edge of the photograph, is me, hair brushed back slickly, and the other one in a dinner jacket. It surprised me to remember that I owned a dinner jacket in those days, because I was poor by the standards of white English-speaking South Africa. In fact, I had worked all through one summer holiday in a miserable wholesale warehouse in the Eastern Transvaal to make the money to get the suit made for me—for most of my life I have been too tall and too oddly shaped to buy suits, jackets or even trousers off the peg; and, because I knew the dinner jacket would have to do long service, I went to a good tailor who found me a very expensive and lightweight Italian cloth. It was a good buy, and in due course served both my sons, slightly adapted to their more usual shapes. I hope my happiness shows: after a rather frustrating career at school where I had never seemed to achieve quite as much as I wanted—or felt able—to do, I was having a blissful time at the University of Cape Town: acting, debating, editing the student newspaper, committed to student politics, writing occasionally for Patrick Duncan's liberal newspaper, *Contact*, editing the official university literary magazine, co-founder of another literary magazine called *The Lion and the Impala*, and in between times doing enough work to have taken one degree and to have started on two more. Sometimes, looking back, I feel almost guilty—and then I reprimand myself for silly liberalism. Why shouldn't I have been happy? Just because I was surrounded with so much cruelty and injustice? How fortunate I was to enjoy such privilege.

One of the main causes of my happiness was the person sitting next to me. Her name was Jann Parry, and I had fallen totally in love with her soon after her arrival at the University of Cape Town, when I was in my third year. Her father was the director of broadcasting in Rhodesia, though Jann had been sent to boarding school in Johannesburg. Very unusually, she had then spent a year in a finishing school in Switzerland; she was thought to be pretentious by some of the other girls in Fuller Hall, the women's residence opposite Smuts Hall, because when she first arrived she was supposed to be putting on a French accent; I couldn't hear it myself, but she made herself unpopular with some of the other students by emphatically refusing to have anything to do with the very childish forms of initiation first-year students were then expected to undergo. She was a ballet dancer, though she was technically too tall; I don't suppose one would have called her beautiful, but she was the most intensely alive person I had ever come across, graceful as a gazelle, short-sighted and clever—most dancers are too bound up in their bodies to pay much attention to their intellects. She was also extraordinarily unpunctual: I would wait for (literally) hours in the porch of Fuller Hall or outside the ballet school for her to emerge. She fell in love with me too, for the time being at least, and we were as inseparable as university rules permitted—in those days, people 'went out' with each other; they didn't 'live together' nor even 'go to bed together'. We did however work together on literary magazines and the newspaper, and we were asked to act opposite each other in Peter Ustinov's *Romanoff and Juliet*, she as the Russian sea-captain, me as the American baseball-player, Freddie; a review in *Varsity* said that 'Jann Parry and Jonty Driver played Jann Parry and Jonty Driver'. When I went to stay with Jann's family in Rhodesia, her father gave us both parts in a radio production of one of Dorothy Sayers's versions of the Christmas story. Jann had a big role (the Virgin Mary, I think); mine was as a porter or soldier or something, but, as John Parry savaged in rehearsal my lack of competence, I began to realize that he didn't much approve of me as suitor. Jann had been invited to a dance at the Governor General's residence; I hadn't. Her parents insisted she went. I drove her there in her little car, and waited outside for the dance to end; there were young men with sports cars at the dance, and I thought one of them might have tried to take her home.

After three years at Cape Town, Jann took her degree, with distinction. She had won a Commonwealth Scholarship from Rhodesia to Girton College, Cambridge, and I had failed to emulate my father by winning a Rhodes Scholarship to Oxford, despite having been shortlisted twice. Our plan to go to England together was further complicated by the fact that I was now deeply involved in the national affairs of the National Union of South African Students. I had been elected vice president in July 1962; within a few months, the president elect, who was training to be a Methodist minister, had been forced by his church elders to step down, and I took over as president in January 1963. My parents supported me loyally, though I knew my father felt I should be making a start on a career as a schoolteacher, which I was now qualified to do. I was by no means sure I wanted that—I wanted to be a writer, a poet in particular, though clearly I couldn't also be a husband (and a father) on what a poet would earn, even in England. To be sure, I was paid to be president of NUSAS, but it was scarcely enough to live on, and—whether I was travelling or not—I relied on friends for housing. Jann and I wrote to each other every week, or more frequently, though there were other women, in Cape Town and elsewhere, and I tried not to think that there might be other men in Cambridge.

Then, in the English summer—South African winter—of 1964, when I was in my second year as president (and in trouble with most of white South Africa, including most of the members of NUSAS, because I had made a speech, now described in histories of the time as 'prescient' but then as 'inverted racialist', saying—among many other things—that, though we were hardly likely to become 'the student wing of the liberation movement', which some of our wilder members wanted, we still needed to look to black students for leadership), Jann came back to South Africa with a troupe of actors from Cambridge. The tour happened by chance to coincide with the national congress of NUSAS at the university of Natal in Pietermaritzburg. I had seen Jann briefly and rather unhappily in Johannesburg soon after the Cambridge troupe had arrived; when we met in Pietermaritzburg a week or two later she announced to me that she had fallen in love with one of her fellow actors.

Life was desperate enough already for me without that. The year before, my father had had two heart attacks, and had been told he must give up being headmaster of Uplands Prep School (he was also the unpaid vicar of two parishes in the area). The warning had come too late and, in January, just as my parents, brothers and sister completed the move to Bloemfontein, where my father had been appointed temporarily a curate in the Anglican cathedral, he died, aged only fifty-one. Although one brother was working, my sister was still at university, and another brother was at school. The last letter my father wrote before his death was to Jann in Cambridge, as if to a daughter-in-law. It was clear, too, that NUSAS itself was in the deepest possible trouble, even without the trouble I had made for it with my outspokenness; my immediate predecessor as president, Adrian Leftwich, had been arrested in a police raid, and there had been other arrests, including that of David ('Spike') de Keller from the NUSAS congress itself. I, and a few others, guessed that we knew the reason for the arrests; Adrian, Spike and others had been running the organization called first the National Committee of Liberation and then the African Resistance Movement, and we supposed all the arrests to be associated. There was also a strong rumour that Adrian Leftwich himself, a central figure in the ARM, had cracked very quickly under police questioning, and had told the police everything they wanted to know. Although he had made an effort to recruit me to the ARM, I had refused, in anger at his lack of judgement in asking someone who was already too much in the public eye—and therefore much too much in the eye of the security police. I had already learned to distrust Leftwich—we had shared a house for six miserable months, and I had discovered a great deal about his psychological frailties—having previously admired many of his qualities, including his brilliance in political debate and his skills as an organizer. Still, even I was surprised at the speed of his capitulation in solitary confinement. I was also sure that, tactically, the project was premature. It was true that I had several times carried messages (the content of which I didn't know) between Adrian and other members of the ARM; and, more than a year before, Jann and I had been persuaded to open a post office box in a Cape Town suburb under false names, for what we knew were clandestine purposes. We knew that now we had somehow to keep NUSAS clear of the ARM, despite the obvious overlap of membership; for instance, those who wanted the NUSAS congress to take to the streets to demonstrate against the arrest of an ex-president and other members had to be headed off. It was obvious, too, that I needed to extricate myself from South Africa swiftly, partly because NUSAS would be safer without my presence, partly because I thought that if I could get to England I might still be able to persuade Jann to marry me.

We were fortunate in having as an ally Robert Birley, formerly headmaster of Eton, who had come out to the University of the Witwatersrand as visiting professor of education. Maeder Osler, the vice president of NUSAS—and more than that to me, because he is still my closest friend—talked to Robert on my behalf, and he said he would find me a teaching job in England from September. Maeder—who had already been elected as the next president of NUSAS—would take over at once, rather than in December. Almost immediately, I was offered not one but two jobs in England: one at Marlborough College, one at Sevenoaks School. Which should I take? I telephoned to ask Professor Birley. Sevenoaks, he said. I accepted the job by telegram, booked myself on a Union Castle liner leaving Cape Town in early August, alerted the various affiliated centres of NUSAS, prepared a press statement—and, the night before I was due to sail, with my trunk already on board the liner, the security police arrested me under the terms of the Ninety Day Detention legislation, which allowed for suspects to be held in solitary confinement, without access to lawyers, for as long as the police chose (if one were released after ninety days, one could be immediately rearrested to be held for another ninety days).

Five weeks later, I was released. It would probably have been sooner, but until I knew who had given my name to the police I had no idea how much they knew about my activities: were they interested only in the ARM, or were they trying to connect NUSAS to the ARM specifically? Eventually, a fellow detainee told me who had given my name; it wasn't Adrian Leftwich, though I had little compunction in telling the security police that he had tried to recruit me to something which sounded very dodgy, and that I had turned him down. The person who had named me knew nothing about anything I had done which was remotely illegal—we had known each other since prep school days, and my fondness for him didn't extend to trusting his judgement. I gave the police a couple of bits of information about people I knew were safely out of the country and, despite a few anxious days before my release—the police did say they were considering a charge under the Suppression of Communism Act, though I was known to be anti-communist, and that carried the possibility of up to five years in jail—I was released. Two days later I was on a flight to London, and within a week I was in a classroom, teaching English, Latin and History. I'm told I went into my first class scowling and then growling, 'I take it you are aware that I have just been released from jail. I'm not going to have any trouble with you lot, am I?' I have little memory of any of that time, now. One does not do even five weeks in solitary confinement without some damage—and I was lucky, because I was not beaten up or tortured; the worst I went through was to stand for ten hours while a team of policemen questioned me. One of my Sevenoaks friends told me, a year or two later, that I had been quite mad that first year in England; and a long poem, 'Through Tall Fires', published in the *London Magazine* in 1965, seems to me to confirm that view.

The break-up of Jann's relationship with her Cambridge actor did not restore her to me. For the next two years (at least), I went on hoping that she might change her mind back again, and I saw her whenever she would agree to meet me. In the end, a girlfriend of hers told me that I was wasting Jann's time, my time, and her own time. Only then did I accept that persistence would not succeed. Though I went on seeing Jann, it was only very occasionally and it was many years before I could see her walking towards me without my heart lurching.

Some years later, when Jann was living with the journalist and broadcaster Richard Kershaw, she was on her way to work at the BBC African Service when she was knocked off her motorbike by an articulated truck, and fell under a back wheel. The wheel ran over her pelvis, crushing it. That she did not die was the result of various chance circumstances. First, the accident happened not far from a London hospital. Secondly, there was a junior doctors' strike in progress. No regular operations meant that there was plenty of blood available (Jann needed ninety-eight pints) and that the surgeons and consultants were free to devote themselves to saving her. Thirdly, because she had never stopped dancing, she had an unusually powerful heart, and lungs to match. The doctors patiently rebuilt her innards. I was not brave enough to visit her in hospital, though Richard Kershaw had taken the trouble to telephone to tell me of the accident; a photograph of her, when she was out of danger but still in hospital, shows her as thin as a prisoner coming out of a concentration camp. She told me in a letter, many months later, that she had been taught to walk again by a physiotherapist who was an RAF sergeant—and that she therefore walked like an RAF sergeant. She used to sit in a deckchair at cricket matches, watching not the cricket, but women walking past—and then, later, in front of a dancer's mirror, she would imitate the way women walked. She stayed on with the BBC, though in due course took early retirement and devoted herself to writing about ballet, particularly as the dance critic of the *Observer*. She and Richard Kershaw are now married.

I turn again to the photograph. Next to Jann, head turned to smile at the photographer, is Rick Turner. The photograph doesn't show his red hair, of course. He was the third of those in the photograph who shared the White House in Claremont; we rented it for relatively little because it was due to be demolished to make way for a block of flats. Rick had the nicest room, although there was a penalty for that: because it was the tidiest too, we always used it for our public entertaining. We had some uproarious parties there. In those days, Rick didn't seem particularly political, at least not in any active sense, though he was very interested in political philosophy, and always ready to talk about it. In the end, however, he became the most involved in politics of any of those in the photograph. After his return from the Sorbonne, where he had written a thesis on Sartre and absorbed some of the radical excitement of the 1960s student movement, he taught politics in various universities and finally at the University of Natal, the Durban section. At a time when police repression was at its most savage—a speech in opposition to apartheid was enough to earn a banning order, and even the South African Congress of Trade Unions was lying as low as it could—Rick Turner argued that African workers could and should be organized into effective unions. Views like these were possibly one reason for his murder, though there were other rumours: that he had seduced the wife of a policeman; that his influence on the young was pernicious; that he had uncovered 'dirty tricks' either in the sugar industry or in the police force. Whatever the reason, late one night early in 1978 someone called him to his front door and shot him. He died in front of his children. No one was ever tried for his murder, though the most persistent rumour of all was that he had been killed by a police assassin. This is one of the many tributes to him, from a poem by Peter Sacks, 'For Richard Turner', in his collection *In These Mountains* (1986):

> You sat among us on the floor,
> Translating Althusser,
> Barefoot, jeans, a pale blue shirt,
> Your black-rimmed lenses doubling
> The light, the red shock of your hair.
> At some slight turn of argument
> Your freckled hands followed
> The actual phrasing in the air.
> 'I know it's difficult in this country,
> but we've got to think more clearly
> than the State allows.'

When I showed John Clare the photograph of his own twenty-first birthday party, he called the young woman next to Rick Turner the 'star of the show'—and I suppose she is: she is now Barbara Follett, MP for Stevenage since 1997, a specialist in management training, 'style consultant' to New Labour, and often credited with having helped make the Labour Party more attractive to the urban middle classes, to women, and to the young. She was one of the founders of 'Emily's List', which promotes the election of Labour women to Parliament. Her present husband is the thriller writer, Ken Follett, and they own homes in Stevenage, Chelsea, Antigua and Tuscany. Gossip had it that they were among the closer friends of Tony Blair and his wife, though there was a public falling-out in 2000. At the time of the photograph, Barbara was Rick Turner's girlfriend, pretty, bright, at once young and sophisticated. Born in the West Indies, she had lived in England and in Ethiopia before coming with her family to South Africa in 1957. A few years after this photograph was taken, she and Rick married—the ceremony was in the garden of John Clare's Cape Town flat, and it is a nice touch that twenty-two years later John was called to be a witness of what Barbara said was to be her 'last marriage'. Barbara and Rick had parted and divorced some years before he was murdered, but she has written movingly of having been called to help by their distraught children after the murder.

Were we wrong to leave South Africa, those of us who did? Are those who have gone back right to have done so, even if they now find themselves sidelined? Some of those in the photograph didn't have much choice. Alan Brooks, for instance, was deported from South Africa when he had served his jail sentence. Rick Turner, on the other hand—who could easily have chosen to stay abroad after his years of study in France—chose to return; apparently he never even considered the alternative. After Rick's murder in 1978, Barbara Turner chose to leave—and who would blame her for that? John Clare's then wife, Sheila Robertson, had been briefly a member of the ARM, though she had baulked at the sight of actual explosives; betrayed to the police by Adrian Leftwich, she was arrested just after the birth of her daughter and told she would have to give evidence for the State; she left on the next Union Castle liner out of Cape Town, managing to do so without her name appearing on a passenger list. John Clare, who had a British passport, followed a few months afterwards. When he applied for a visa to visit his dying father a few years later he was refused.

When I left, after my detention in 1964, I intended to return to

South Africa. My plan was to teach at Sevenoaks for a year, then go to Oxford (probably to Trinity, my father's old college) for two years, and then back to South Africa. In the event a decision was forced on me sooner than I had planned. Halfway through my time at Oxford, my South African passport expired (I had managed to hide it away from the security police when they arrested me, by leaving it in a jacket which I changed and put back in a wardrobe after they had finished searching; sometimes, meticulous efficiency may be its own downfall). I applied to the South African Embassy in London for the renewal of my passport. The request was referred to Pretoria. Months later, there came a refusal. I took the letters and went to the South African Embassy. The clerk at the passport counter seemed mystified by the correspondence I showed him, but he was friendly and helpful. He would find out what was going on, he said, and disappeared with my papers. A few minutes later, a man whom I recognized as a security policeman arrived in the office and stared hard at me. He went away, and shortly afterwards the clerk reappeared, no longer friendly. I could, he said, apply for a re-entry permit to South Africa; no, he didn't know how long that would take to come through. He would answer no more questions.

Perhaps I could have tried to go back without a passport, though I'm not sure an airline would have accepted me on board; but it would have meant abandoning Oxford, halfway through my MPhil, and who knows what welcome would have been awaiting me? I was, I realized, effectively stateless.

Once that decision was made, I used to object when people said I had been 'forced into exile'. 'No,' I would answer. 'I wasn't "forced"; I chose.' I remember a protracted disagreement in London with Alan Paton on this subject; always competitive in argument, he was determined to win his point. My definition of 'forced' was too narrow, he maintained; there was more than one kind of force. Detentions, banning, loss of passport, warnings that I would be unemployable, particularly if I chose to be a schoolteacher (for which, I was beginning to realize, both nature and heredity had designed me, and for which I was certainly trained), all these were a kind of force. The argument was made more awkward because my insistence that I had chosen exile was meant as a compliment to people like Alan Paton himself, to whom considerable force—in his sense—had been applied, but who refused to leave South Africa permanently, even though he would have been fêted abroad, wherever he had gone. More than that, too many of my friends never had any choice in the matter. Some of my black friends—Templeton Mdlalana, for instance, who had been the NUSAS representative at the University College of Fort Hare and then our so-called 'literacy officer' in the Transkei— didn't have the means; there was no wealthy friend to pay for an air ticket out of the country, as I had been fortunate enough to have, no mentor to find a post abroad, no place at Oxford nor scholarship money to fund that place. Others were in jail, for a few years or even longer: Stephen Gawe, Spike de Keller, Hugh Lewin. One could say that they were being forced to stay, though actually most of them had made an earlier choice. If one had served a jail sentence, and had then been released only to be banned—often in terms which precluded one's earning a living—one could perhaps be said to have been forced out. People like me had chosen.

There was also the fact that, just as my ancestor, Edward Driver, had managed to settle—aged twenty-two or -three—very successfully in the Eastern Cape in 1820, so too I—aged twenty-five—was young enough to settle somewhere else—probably in England, though other South Africans were going to Canada, Australia, the USA. I can't remember quite why now, but I had a romantic hankering for the West Indies; was it because the South African writer, Peter Abrahams, had settled there? Was it because it seemed a society in which all races lived together in apparent harmony? (Isn't it odd to recall that, in the 1950s and 1960s, when apologists for apartheid used to ask us to cite any example in the world where people of different colours, backgrounds, religions and classes, lived together in amity, we used to talk about—of all places—Lebanon?) I know that, early in 1967, I was still talking about going to live in the West Indies. However, the reality was that I would probably settle in England, though I liked to think of myself as one of the 'new internationals'—stateless in fact, stateless by nature.

Is 'diaspora' too grand a term for the dispersal of white South Africans from the country we were born in? Most white South Africans didn't 'go into exile'; very few 'escaped from oppression'; nearly all emigrated to resettle in countries where they thought their future would be more secure. A common reason was that they did not want their sons to have to serve in the South African armed forces. Sometimes the émigrés found they didn't settle where they had landed and they went back again, or tried another place. More often, they settled perfectly well: in Australia, in Canada, in the USA, in England—and went back only for family weddings and, in due course, funerals until, eventually, they (and their children more especially) became part of the new culture, except for the oddly ineradicable accent. The end of apartheid hasn't meant the end of that process. If it was hard to get money out before, now, with the collapse of the exchange rate, what money may be got out doesn't convert to many dollars or pounds.

Do I still think of South Africa as 'home'? Well, not consciously: it is where I grew up—and where my mother and brother (and, until very recently, my sister too) still live, and some of my dearest friends. Home is England now, and in England; when I have been abroad, and the ferry docks or the aeroplane lands, I feel I am back where I belong—whereas I know that, when I land in South Africa, and take out my British passport to join the queue of foreigners, there is still a degree of resentment in me, even though I know the country is utterly unlike the one which locked me up and turned me away.

There is therefore in me a sense of something lost—though I know too, in actual terms, what good fortune I have had since I chose to leave South Africa. When apartheid came to an end, and the restrictions on my return were lifted (in the topsy-turvy language of the bureaucrats, 'your visa exemption is restored'), I flirted with the idea that I might return permanently to live and work in South Africa, either as a schoolteacher or as a writer (even an attenuated English pension would go a long way in the new South Africa). I mentioned this to my mother, and drew an immediate and typically cross response: 'Don't be so silly,' she wrote. 'You're out now, and you must stay out. By all means come to visit as much as you like; but you're English now.' Well, she's right: I have an English wife, three English children, an English cottage, my portraits on the walls of two English schools, an entry in *Who's Who*, my birthday noted annually in the *Daily Telegraph* and *The Times*, a nodding acquaintance with some of the great and the good, and several friends in high places; and only occasionally will someone say to me,

'Of course, you were born in South Africa, weren't you? One still hears the accent a little.'

And so I turn back to that photograph of forty years ago, to try to remember our innocence and our excitement—because they were exciting times, and we were quite certain we were prepared to risk everything. Perhaps it is true that no one should be judged until he or she is dead, because the possibility of choice remains open, and the last choice may change everything which has happened until then, though every choice along the way has its consequences. So, when I look at those nine lively faces, it is Rick Turner's I see most clearly, and I imagine again the moment the doorbell rang, and he got up from the sofa where he had been sitting to walk to the front door, behind which stood a shadowy figure carrying a gun. Did he realize, I wonder? Did he hesitate? No answer is possible; neither is one necessary. □

SNAPS
Liz Jobey

There is a photograph of my mother, taken on the beach at Robin Hood's Bay in Yorkshire when she was nineteen, during a holiday with girlfriends from her training college, that suggests to me something of how happy she must have been in those days—the days she talks about often now, since she's over eighty, and lives alone. Although she's totally compos mentis, I think those girlfriends are closer to her than the people she sees in Tesco and the greengrocers', and her neighbour from whom she maintains a polite distance. The photograph is of a young woman with an Eton crop wearing a backless cotton sunsuit with a polka-dot halter neck that leaves her shoulders bare and divides into baggy shorts just above the knee. You can't see her face, because she's bent right over, hands on knees, head down, legs apart, braced for a person running in from the left of the frame to leapfrog over her. You can just see the hands and the feet of the person who's already in flight, preparing to land their hands on her back and jump—my mother is small, five-foot nothing (and shrinking, she'd say now), but what's so attractive about the photograph is how noticeably young and strong and smooth-skinned she is, and how physically active the photograph is as a whole. You know this person just out of the frame is going to catapult over my mother's sturdy frame in the next split second. On the back it says, 'Vicky was a bit early in taking this.'

She was quite athletic as a young woman, my mother, good at the high jump, because she had a low centre of gravity, her gym mistress said, that carried her up and over easily. She cleared great heights in proportion to her own. I was always envious when she told me about it. I was as hopeless at the high jump as I was at all athletics. The sound of a metal pole on concrete and cinders is one of the bad memories of my teenage summers, because I was a fat child and I dreaded games and I knew I'd never get much past the lowest bar-height which was something like two feet ten inches. Once I jumped three feet eight inches, but I never managed it again.

But my mother loved games and loved training college, so much so that she sent me to a boarding school in Yorkshire in the belief that I'd like the countryside and the walks and the girlfriend camaraderie just as she had. But of course I didn't. I hated the walks and the countryside and those friendships forged out of proximity and loneliness rather than genuine affection. For years I believed my parents sent me there because it was cheaper than keeping me at home—though of course this wasn't really the case. I didn't think they were cruel: I knew my mother thought she was giving me a treat, access to possibilities I would otherwise not have had, and that my father would have gone along with her decision because she had been a teacher, and was more educated than he was. Later I found out that she had made a huge sacrifice sending me away. It shocked me when she told me how she had cried and cried the night they had left me there—particularly because when they came to say goodbye to me I'd been comparing tuck boxes with my new room-mates and had hardly noticed she and my father were leaving.

My mother wanted me to have a good schooling because she felt she'd missed out on her own. She'd desperately wanted to go to university, but my grandfather couldn't afford it. Her brother, my uncle, had read classics at university and become a senior schoolmaster; but my mother wasn't considered in the same way— as girls' careers weren't, then—and she supposed she was lucky to go to training college, though she said she never wanted to be a teacher. But teaching had been one of the first professions which single women could take up with a measure of respectability. There had been so many unmarried women and widows left economically stranded after the First World War. It was one of the most acceptable routes to female independence. And my mother wanted to be independent. She says if she had been born into my generation she might never even have got married, but I think she says that now to make me feel better about my disastrous record in that area (two marriages, two divorces; no children).

I found the picture of my mother in the Black Magic box, still with its red satin ribbon, which for as long as I can remember has contained most of the photographs of our immediate family. There was a second, larger, shallower lilac-ribboned chocolate box with a ruby-cheeked girl with a bonnet and muff on top where we kept the larger photographs, many of which documented the history of our farm, rather than our family: aerial pictures of the new pig shed, a particularly fine sow with her litter, the South Yorkshireman express steaming over the twenty-six-arch viaduct that crossed our fields, a new combine harvester, a clay-pigeon shoot. The Black Magic box was where we kept the smaller snapshots, some of them no more than three inches by two, of my mother and father with one or both of us as toddlers at the seaside, Yorkshire resorts such as Scarborough or Filey, my dad with his trousers rolled up, my mother with my brother poking in a rock pool with a scarf in her hair; or of my mother in her early twenties, sharply dressed in a striped blouse and knee-length skirt, sitting on a wall, one leg elegantly crossed over the other, swinging (as it were) a brown stack-heeled court shoe. The same shoes that, twenty years later, I would clunk dangerously around the house in, aged six or seven, wearing her old navy-blue nip-waisted suit, a pair of black-framed sunglasses with the lenses punched out, clutching a would-be clip-board, playing secretaries—Della Street, from the TV courtoom drama series *Perry Mason*—or, adapting the costume slightly, acting out one of the characters from my favourite series of books—*Jean Becomes an Air Hostess*; or *Susan Becomes a Nurse*.

Even at that age, getting out these two boxes made me feel slightly sick, and it still does. For years this complicated mixture of nostalgia and dread had a lot to do with the fact that I feared coming across an unexpected photograph of myself at my ugliest, around ten, with the short back and sides that succeeded the loss of the long, thick plait which had hung to my waist (and which I whisked out of the way with a toss of my head when putting on my raincoat weeks after it had been chopped off), the slightly protruding second teeth, the face composed of small plump cushions of fat placed one against the other into which my eyes seemed to disappear. Over time I destroyed any of these photographs as I found them, and now, when I discover any I had overlooked, I can still remember that feeling of a life doomed to unhappiness because of a bad case of puppy fat.

Most of these pictures were taken with my mother's early Kodak camera that opened up like an accordion with a delicate metal button on a stalk which you pushed to open the shutter. When I looked into the boxes as a child there always seemed to me to be many more pictures of my brother than there were of me, due largely to his interest in his miniature car, which he washed, polished, careered about in grinning at about the age of four or five, while one or other parent clicked away. It never occurred to me that by the time I was born five years later, both my parents were too busy working on the farm to which we moved in 1949, and which my father learned to manage from books and the kind advice of local farmers, to have time to photograph either of us very often. I was always keen to distinguish myself from him in photographs of us as babies, and I always got it wrong ('Is this one me?' 'No, your brother.'). Quite long periods of my own life as a toddler seem to have been spent either riding on, or sharing a kennel with, our black labrador, Jet.

My mother was the third and youngest child in her family. She always said she had been an afterthought, that she hadn't been planned. She was named Elizabeth, after her mother, 'Lizzie', as I was. Lizzie had a weak chest, as did my aunt Phyllis, ten years older than my mother. Harry came in between. I never really warmed to my uncle, though I know he was a kind and clever man, but he was too severe for me, too much like the schoolmaster he was, and my father used to ridicule him gently for his pedantry, which I now realize was probably my father's defence mechanism for feeling his own lack of university education. So much competition about that, even then. My father was neither uneducated nor stupid but he was made insecure somehow by 'artistic' learning. Perhaps it spoke to something in his emotions he couldn't quite cope with. He didn't like novels, he hated dramatized serials on TV, and as for poetry—my mother said Rupert Brooke was the only poet he knew, and then only because Rupert Brooke was her favourite poet when they met, and my father learned '...some corner of a foreign field' to woo her with. It hurt him, I think, that I wasn't good at, and didn't like, the subjects he was good at: he was very quick at arithmetic and could add up long strings of figures in his head, and into old age his most prized gift was an enormous *Times* atlas my mother bought him, which he pored over with a magnifying glass, making imaginary journeys to places he'd never visited and planning a return trip to the Middle East, where he'd been spent four years during the Second World War in the Royal Artillery. My mother and I liked English and history and music and art, though art wasn't considered a serious subject at my school. My brother was good at languages, but he read geography at Oxford, partly because he was told it would be easier to get a place, and partly, I suspect, because he knew it would please my father. But it was never his subject. He spent his years at university trying to keep up—not academically, but socially; a not-very-rich direct-grant boy from a South Yorkshire farming family, in with the public school boys, the rich boys, and desperate to impress. My parents were proud when he got his place at Oxford. But he didn't have the self-confidence, or the money, to survive it. When he died, at forty, it was as if the legacy of that life had caught him up.

By today's standards, we were not a much photographed family. When I look at the total accumulated photographs from my immediate family, including the meticulously catalogued sets of colour slides my brother took during his serious 35mm camera phase—that is, between the ages of ten and fifteen—they represent only a tiny fraction of the hundreds of sleeves of colour snapshots my friends collect of their children at every stage of their growing up, to say nothing of the camcorder tapes and videos of weddings and christenings and even mothers giving birth that they seem to have collected over the years. I haven't yet been invited to watch someone's dying moments on film, but I can't believe it will be a taboo for much longer. Whether this exhaustive and mostly banal documentation is, in the end, any more precious than the relatively few black-and-white snapshots most of us have salvaged from our parents' and grandparents' lives I don't know. There is a time—probably around forty, when our own children are growing up and we're asking ourselves what character traits we've passed on to them for better or worse, and whether they are hereditary, or learned—when family photographs, and the past in general, becomes more precious to us than it has ever done before. Our parents die. We are the new repositories of family history. We want to find out more about where we've come from, to make sure of the details, so we'll know more about why things turned out as they did.

For those growing up after the 1960s, family photographs serve another function. It is not only the technology of snapshot photography which has been radically altered, but the structure of family life. Families no longer live in the same towns and villages for generations; children move away from home. Wives and husbands separate; children are stretched between two estranged parents, sometimes losing touch with their grandparents altogether. All this fragmentation contributes to a loss of family identity: we need some sense of the past, a sense of continuity. Photographs, like the telephone and email, have replaced the network of the extended family. No wonder we record banalities. Photographs are how we keep in touch.

I have a friend in California who every year sends me as a Christmas card a photograph of her daughter, who I haven't seen since she was born. Now she's eight. It always says, 'Come visit.'

Photographs provide at least a visual record of our past. Looking at our parents and grandparents and even our great-grandparents; looking at their dress, their surroundings, their class and aspirations, fixes us in society, in England particularly, it still fixes us in our class. And in this photographs also provide us with a collective identity, a sense of shared experience at a particular time and place in history. Photographs can evoke a collective emotion—a generalized, rather than specific identification with the past—and this is the power that at the end of the twentieth century found itself harnessed to contemporary art.

Since the 1970s, the 'found' photograph has been a popular accessory for conceptual artists, and in 1990 I found myself in the Whitechapel Art Gallery in London, at an exhibition of works by the French artist Christian Boltanski, standing in front of a wall of small black-and-white photographs not unlike the ones of my own family. In Boltanski's case he had taken them from the albums of a family identified only as family 'D' (later revealed to be that of his dealer). It was impossible to be unaffected by these small re-photographed snapshots of uneven quality which showed mothers and fathers and small children in all the groupings, formal and informal, familiar to anybody who had grown up, like Boltanski, in the immediate post-war period. I believe none of the visitors I stood next to at the Whitechapel at that point knew of the existence of family D, let alone had any relationship to them. But there was a sense of recognition that brought with it a powerful mix of emotions: love, fear, sadness, amusement, dread. Boltanski understood the effect these photographs would have. It was a shared experience—we recognized our own childhoods, we recognized a past when the future was full of promise, people we had lost and would never find again, times and places we had been happy, times when we had believed we would be safe, or successful, or were blessed. They reminded us of when we believed that friends and marriages and principles would endure for a lifetime. And they told us that once we had been loved unconditionally, and now those unconditional guardians and their protection were gone for good. It was a simple device, but at the end of the century Boltanski had identified its subjects: memory and death.

I was very affected by the exhibition at the time—by how simple it was, and yet how powerful, when so much contemporary art was cerebral, rather than emotional (or so it seemed to me). A few years later, I took my mother to see a Boltanski installation at the Henry Moore Foundation galleries in Dean Clough Mills outside Halifax. Halifax was at the centre of the Yorkshire textile industry and Boltanski had used an old register of mill employees from the last century as the basis for his installation. We went down into a cold, damp, whitewashed basement room in the middle of which was assembled over a hundred old rusting biscuit tins, the tall kind that stand about eighteen inches high. Each tin was labelled with one of the names from the register. The idea was that their descendants should bring anything—any small piece of clothing, jewellery, picture—that had belonged to their dead relatives and place them in the tin that bore their name. In this way, each tin, though we couldn't see what was inside, once more represented an individual life and symbolically linked the past to the present. I wondered if my mother understood.

She went round quietly, and afterwards said she'd found it affecting, even if it was a bit bleak. And I thought how patronizing I'd been, showing her 'my' kind of art, expecting her to humour me by going round it, but not to understand it. But of course she understood it. She understood it better than I did. She had lost not only her parents and a husband, but also a son. She knew more than I was ever going to about memory and death.

All photographs are about the past. For years I didn't read Roland Barthes's *Camera Lucida*. I was probably afraid I wouldn't understand it. When I did, I discovered not only the clearest analysis of photography, but also a painfully moving account of parental love, growing old and parental death. This was his last book—published in 1980, the year he died. Barthes describes his love for his mother without any sense of embarrassment.

When he finds the particular photograph that keeps her memory alive, he wants to enlarge it to see her better.

> Lost in the depths of the Winter Garden, my mother's face is vague, faded. In a first impulse I exclaimed, 'There she is! She's really there! At last, there she is!' Now I claim to know—and to be able to say adequately—why, in what she consists. I want to outline the loved face by thought, to make it into the unique field of an intense observation; I want to enlarge this face in order to see it better, to understand it better, to know its truth (and sometimes, naively, I confide this task to a laboratory). I believe that by enlarging the detail 'in series' (each shot engendering smaller details than at the preceding stage), I will finally reach my mother's very being.

This idea—that photographic enlargement makes visible details which otherwise would remain hidden—reminded me of a visit I once made to the Magnum photographer, Elliott Erwitt, in his New York apartment. It is a large old-style place, and to get to the kitchen you have to walk down a long corridor past the sink for washing prints which is opposite his darkroom. On this particular evening he was in the process of making very large—about six feet by four feet—prints of some of his more famous black-and-white pictures. Not every print had come out well in the developer, and one or two were ripped up into pieces in the sink. Which is why, when I walked by, I caught sight of a triangle of torn paper roughly six inches long on which I could make out an eye and, in its corner, a newly formed tear which hadn't fully left its tear duct. And I knew that eye. It was Jackie Kennedy's eye, and the torn-up print was a famous photograph taken at John F. Kennedy's funeral at Arlington Cemetery, just at the point when Mrs Kennedy was handed the American flag that had covered her husband's coffin. On a regular print, the size most often reproduced in books or magazines, her face is crumpled, she looks distracted with grief and next to madness, but there is no sign of the teardrop. The photographer told me he had never realized it was there until he had enlarged the print. But it had been there all along. It explains part of the magic of photography—not only to copy what we can see with our eyes, but to make visible that which we can't.

I always loved looking. Long before I loved looking at paintings and drawings and photographs I loved just looking at the world. But even when I was quite small I always wondered whether I saw the same things other people did. Did they see the same colours—I don't mean were they colour-blind, I mean did the trees appear to them the same or a different shade of green? Did they feel the same response in the pit of their stomach when they stood in front of, say, a Degas pastel, or a Cézanne apple, or a Rothko, or the Picasso Minotaur in the collection at the Beaubourg in Paris? Why was I so affected by pictures when others were not? I have a physical, as well as a psychological need to have them around me, and when they're missing, it affects me physically. I feel the blankness inside. Where did this come from? When did it start? I never went to art galleries as a child. We didn't have pictures on the walls at home save a couple of old nautical oils bought from a house sale. We didn't have books on art. I had a Brownie 127 like most children my age, with which I took a few black-and-white snapshots, but none were memorable. Photography was not generally considered an art form in England in the mid-1950s, nor was it collected for posterity except inside a few institutions such as the Museum of Modern Art in New York. I loved photography as a child because it showed me places and people and events I would otherwise never have seen. And for that I believe I have to thank Mr Biltcliffe.

Mr John Thomas Biltcliffe owned the photography studio in the small town where I grew up. It was little more than a lean-to wooden shack tacked on the front of a house and painted red. It stood on the corner where the lane to our farm turned off the main road from town, which meant the shop had three windows—two at the front and one down the side where our lane began. All three windows, from top to bottom and side to side, were lined, edge to edge, with postcard-sized black-and-white photographs showing the history of the town taken by Mr Biltcliffe and his father before him.

The business had been started by Mr Biltcliffe's father, Joshua, and some of the photographs dated back to before 1900. I would press my face on the glass trying to decipher the captions: the High Street, c1895; Saturday Night market in 1891; the Cattle Market in 1910; market day, even into the mid-Fifties, was when the pubs stayed open all day.

Because of those pictures I knew about what people referred to then as 'The Big Snow' of 1947. It was the year my brother was born, at the beginning of February, and my father had to dig my mother and the baby out of the snow when the car got stuck on the way back from the hospital. I knew about it from the whole series of photographs that showed the town sinking under a giant blanket of snow with people tunnelling their way through six-foot-high drifts from their houses to the street.

I was particularly keen on the local disasters. I also knew that on February 2, 1916, the second and third arches of the viaduct which carried the Lancashire and Yorkshire railway line collapsed, taking a tank engine with it. The train plunged headfirst down the embankment and left a yawning gap across which the two thin twisted metal tracks still stretched. For years after seeing this photograph I would go and examine the viaduct for cracks, or signs of re-pointing. I imagined a similar tragedy was waiting to happen. But all that was left was a slight variation in the stone where the arches had been rebuilt. The viaduct was chiefly famous in my childhood for its echo. If you stood under the highest arches and shouted, your voice would ricochet spookily around the fields, over and over until it faded away.

Mr Biltcliffe died in 1987. Though we'd left the town by then, I know the photographs were rescued because a local historian published a pictorial history of this small town in the Pennines using photographs from Mr Biltcliffe's collection. In the book there is a picture of his studio taken in 1964, looking just as I remember it. Apparently the small red hut had once stood next door to a local pub, but Joshua Biltcliffe had brought it by horse and cart to form the studio part of his house. 'The showroom, picture-frame workshop and darkroom were added later and the business became firmly established.' I have no memory of ever going inside, though my mother tells me I had my first passport photo taken there sometime in the 1950s, presumably by John Thomas himself. What I do remember is the growing familiarity it gave me with what might be termed 'world events'—at least the world outside the very narrow confines of my childhood.

I was born in 1952. It was the year Henri Cartier-Bresson published *The Decisive Moment*, and I should love to be able say that my first love of photographs comes from seeing old copies of *Life* or *Picture Post* hanging around our house, but it wouldn't be true. Apart from a nursery book entitled *Look Mummy!* in which you had to identify particular objects and shout 'Look Mummy—a dog!' or 'Look Mummy—a cat!', one of the first books of photographs that fascinated me was entitled *The Queen and Princess Anne*, by Lisa Sheridan.

I was very interested in the Queen. She had, after all, the same name as I had, and she had been crowned in the year I was born. (I firmly believed this for years. I thought that, since George VI died in 1952, the crown must have been taken from his head and immediately given to the Queen. I finally had to accept that the Coronation was a year later, in 1953.) There were all sorts of coincidental similarities between the Queen's family and my own. She had married her husband in 1947, the year my brother was born. Her son was called Charles, like my brother, and his sister Princess Anne was only a couple of years older than me. What's more, my mother looked like the Queen. (This was not a childhood illusion, she still can look remarkably like the Queen in some photographs, just as my paternal grandmother looks a lot like Queen Victoria in hers.) And in particular I had seen photographs of the Royal Family sitting on a tartan rug in their garden (at Balmoral), surrounded by their corgis, that looked just like photos we had of my father and mother and my brother and me, sitting on a tartan rug on our lawn, surrounded by our cats and dogs, my mother in a tweed skirt and twinset and pearls, with her dark hair set back from her face, just like the Queen. And I knew Anne had a pony, just like I did. She called it Greensleeves.

Lisa Sheridan was a photographer By Appointment to Queen Elizabeth the Queen Mother—and the book was the nearest the Windsors came in 1959 to a public snapshot album. At a time when they were keen to advertise themselves as a modern popular monarchy, the aim of the book was 'to share the ordinary every-day pleasures of a mother and daughter who are also Queen and Princess'.

I was riveted to see what smug little Princess Anne got up to. Partly she seemed to do many of the same things I did—she had a pony, she went to Brownies, her mother had one of those shirtwaister suits with a blouse and matching dirndl skirt in printed cotton, just like my mother's, and Anne even had a pair of those thick yellow cotton-knit riding gloves and a tweed hacking jacket like my father had insisted on buying me. Her pony, like mine, had belonged to her brother before her. But her pony was a delicious sounding 'Strawberry Roan' while mine was a shaggy black Welsh mountain pony called 'Beaut'.

The photographer's brief had been a tricky one. She had to stress the informality of royal family life, but remind us they were still Royal (they needed to keep the crown). In her introduction to the pictures she is at pains to stress the strength of the family unit, its sense of family history and tradition, and to emphasize the relaxed way in which the young prince and princess were being raised.

Pets, apparently, played an important part in the lives of the Royal children. Charles and Anne kept a pair of lovebirds, called Annie and Davy. Greensleeves followed Princess Anne wherever she went, as did the 'nursery' corgis, Whisky and Sherry—cocktail cabinet names, though it didn't strike me then. And sport played an important part in her physical development:

In my photograph on page twenty-one it is particularly interesting to see Princess Anne's straight back...the taut little body is doubtless due to the various healthful recreations in which the child is encouraged. There is a weekly dancing class at the Palace; there is riding at weekends in Windsor and many a quick spin on her green bicycle round the garden-paths of Buckingham Palace. Then, in summer and winter alike there is swimming, for the swimming-pool at Buckingham Palace can be heated when necessary. Prince Philip teaches her to play tennis correctly. The Princess also attends a gym class once a week and now the Brownies are beginning a variety of physical exercises. This lively little girl enters into all such activities with her customary vitality and enthusiasm.

But the real message came with the final paragraphs, and, considering what we know now, they can be read only with irony.

The Queen and Prince Philip are devoted to an ideal of family life and have as closely-knit a united life with their children as one may find in any family in the land. They wish their children to grow up as naturally as possible without undue evidence of their important status. This educational policy is being most successfully developed, as those who have had the privilege of meeting the Royal children in their home always testify.

Some years ago when I photographed the Queen and Princess Margaret as children, I was impressed by the informality of their home lives and by their unaffected charm. When asked, as I often was asked, 'What are the Princesses really like at home?' I always felt I should reply: 'Really natural children. Children privileged by a sense of security in knowing themselves each a treasured part in an affectionate united family.'

Certainly the same words would serve today in describing the home life of our present Royal Family where Princess Anne is growing up and is now nine years old.

Sunshine, roses, dogs, and a sense of history. That was England in 1959. Mother and daughter pose arm in arm in the gardens of Windsor, climbing roses against the old stone, a snoozing corgi at their feet. The Princess wears a striped cotton dress, white ankle socks and white buckskin buttoned pumps. The Queen is in her sprigged dirndl suit with navy court shoes and three rows of pearls at her neck. She is thirty-three years old. There are two more children, Andrew and Edward, still to come.

In 1959 we took our first family holiday 'abroad'. We didn't go to France or Italy, places that were just being developed for tourism, but sailed—the arrangements courtesy of a friend of my father—in a cattle boat to Eire, or what we called 'Southern Ireland'. I have a recollection of being taken down into the hold by my brother to visit rows of steaming bullocks in metal pens, warm and sticky packed together in the dark with their wet pink noses pushing through the bars, the smell of manure. Really it was just a concentrated version of what I was used to at home, and I stuck my hand through the bars to let the calves suckle my fingers. I could feel their rough tongues and hard gums pulling my hand further inside their mouths. But my brother jerked my hand away and said these bullocks were too big and we weren't meant to be down there and should go back up on deck.

We stayed the first night in Youghal (pronounced Yawl, which I remember because the spelling was so different from the sound), in a hotel that smelled of must and was cold and we sat on a horsehair sofa covered in leather with spiky bits of hair poking through and scratching the underside of my thighs for ages until they said the room was ready, then we came back down for peppery soup and white sliced bread. My mother found bedbugs when she turned back the sheets that night and the next day we left and drove off in a green rented VW Beetle to find another hotel, which we eventually did, in a village called Ardmore, and there the holiday began to be a happy one. For some reason I remember more about this holiday than I do about any of those that followed, some far more luxurious and spectacular by comparison, and perhaps it was because I was small and it was the first proper holiday, apart from the seaside, in my memory. But also because it was photographed religiously by my brother, who not only had his new 35mm camera, but for the first time was photographing us in colour.

The writer Julian Barnes, describing his own family holidays in France when he was a teenager, said that it was hard, if he was honest, to know exactly how much of those holidays he remembered from the actual events, and how much he remembered because he had subsequently revisited those events through family snapshots. For a lot of people of my generation, the first beneficiaries of cheap colour printing technology, photographs constantly supplemented our recollections of real events. And usually they were the happy ones. Only professional photographers specialize in tragedies.

My brother was supposed to share the 35mm Kodak camera he had been given for his birthday that year with my father. The sharing part was because it had been such a lavish gift. In reality my brother was the one who had control of both the photographing and the developing. The films had to be sent off by post to the manufacturers, and they came back in yellow or orange boxes, depending on whether the film was made by Kodak or Agfa. These transparencies in turn required a whole new apparatus for viewing. We had both a manual slide viewer, into which you slotted a slide and held it up to the light, and—inaugurating another family ritual that has become part of the collective memory of children of my generation—a slide projector and screen. From the age of seven to seventeen (when I went on my first holiday without my parents), these transparencies, which recorded summer holidays both successful and disastrous, were required viewing at least once, gathered round the projector in the sitting room to inspect ourselves on film.

Now when I look at these slides I scarcely recognize the people in the pictures. I can see facial similarities between myself and my mother when she was the age I am now. But trying to find signs in the child I was then of the person I am now, there is little to go on. My father and my mother look like two people coping with a family holiday. My father looks happier than my mother—he put family life at the top of his list of values. And my brother appears rarely. He was usually behind the lens. The colour has that lovely old faded quality that does much to crank up the nostalgia value of the viewing experience, but quite honestly, so little of what we all imagined the future would be for ourselves and each other turned out to come true that I find it hard to look at the pictures with much pleasure.

For two or three years at the beginning of his teens my brother, spasmodically methodical, catalogued all his transparencies in specially designed boxes, numbering and captioning them; it was around the same time that he enjoyed collecting stamps, before all this taxonomy grew boring. I still have all the transparency boxes, beautifully fitted out inside in wood, with a hundred little slots, each one numbered at the side and every slide still in its correct slot. And in the corresponding booklet, every slide is accounted for, 1 to 37 for each film, with all the captions written out in capitals.

Ireland 1959. We joined the boat at Liverpool: 'The docks', 'Family on boat', 'Docks', 'Sea loch', 'Floating crane'—all my brother's slides have a heavy emphasis, encouraged no doubt by our father, on any sort of engineering or military installation: not for nothing were we a family raised on Dumpy Books and Observer guides to trains and boats and planes. Then to 'Roche Point', 'Cobb', 'Black Rock Castle', me with dog ('Ardmore'), my mother with dog. My mother would have been just forty; she looks fine, slim, in trousers and the suede jacket she once told me in a fit of honesty about her own clothing excesses cost a month's teaching salary and which I've borrowed and given back according to the ins and outs of fashion over and over again. My father, only in the earliest stages of corpulence; my brother already at senior school (I can tell by his socks with the yellow and black band and the green garter tabs) and all of us, the perfect family, healthy, innocent, together. No wonder, I think, looking at a photograph of my father and me, his hand resting lightly on my shoulder; my mother and me hugging a black dog here, a yellow dog there; the four of us, posing for the delayed action shot. No wonder we grew up thinking nothing bad was going to happen.

Like Julian Barnes, I'm not sure where my memory of photographs departs from my actual memory, but looking at these pictures for the first time in thirty years, I'm amused, even gratified, at the accuracy of my pictorial recall. Perhaps it's because these events were often discussed and became the stuff of our collective family legend: the day I paddled determinedly in the freezing Irish Sea in my navy-blue school gaberdine with breakers crashing behind me; the day I said 'Adios Amigos'—as I'd heard cowboys say on Hopalong Cassidy on television—to the Spanish trawlermen at Bantry Bay; the horrible day I refused to kiss the Blarney Stone after making such a fuss about getting to Blarney Castle.

The events of that day are played out in a sequence of pictures which, in the expanse of grass surrounded by bushes, in the random distribution of the three figures in each of several frames—my mother, brother and an increasingly tearful me, and in the over-saturated colour and eerily bucolic atmosphere, reminds me now of the sequence of photographs in Antonioni's Blow Up. I cried because my brother wouldn't let me have the ball we were playing with. I cried even more when I discovered that to get to the Blarney Stone meant hanging upside down, held by my ankles, and being lowered down head first to kiss the stone. I refused absolutely, despite complicated feelings of cowardice and disappointment, and despite my father's assurances that he wouldn't drop me. It had been the same with my first trip down a playground slide. 'All those other children are doing it, so why can't you?'

And what did Ireland look like? Like a toy country, an over-green landscape with mossy stone walls and wave after wave of mountains. The roads were narrow, lonely, and cars were few. There are carefully composed folkloric shots—an old woman sitting on the back of her horse-drawn cart; a man pulling scrap with his horse and cart; a street scene in Blarney which it took me a while to discern the point of. Our green VW is parked outside a pawnbrokers' shop, there's a man reading a newspaper on the street corner, a little old woman beginning her slow crossing, a Morris Minor and an Austin A30 coming down the hill—then, on the left-hand side of the road, I finally made out a procession of little girls in their communion dresses, a column of little brides of Christ, almost hidden and—like the couples in those photographs of French country weddings—bizarrely out of place. 'Catholic Parade' reads the caption. There are several photographs of roadside shrines, portrait studies of an obliging, and presumably 'typical', petrol pump attendant and local farmers showing my father how to cut peat. In Killarney I registered the aesthetic qualities of landscape, probably for the first time: Killarney's lakes and hills reaching to the horizon. And there they are in a photograph, my father and me standing at the roadside, and behind us, a view like the backdrop in a Renaissance painting.

If colour film recorded what I could already see, colour television recorded quite a lot of what, previously, I couldn't. I remember the first boxing match I saw on colour television. Until that point it had seemed a rather glamorous boys' sport, hedged about with legends and heroes, and in reality I never took much notice until one day I saw blood. Blood. Oozing from puffy purple bruises; red blood and purple bruises, most often on black skin. Blood coming from cuts above the eyes, from nicks along the cheeks, from noses, mouths. Once I could see blood, I saw other nasty things, saliva, gum shields, vulnerability, insanity. Where once boxers had seemed to be little more than chiaroscuro figures without any connection to me, now they were very definitely flesh and blood, and the realities of the sport came home to me as they had never done in black-and-white. When photographers talk about black-and-white reducing a picture to its essentials, I'm never convinced. Black-and-white seems to me to make pictures more stylized, more formalist, more detached, perhaps more aesthetically pleasing, but not more true.

I had this discussion with one of the twentieth century's most famous black-and-white photographers, Henri Cartier-Bresson, when I interviewed him just before his ninetieth birthday. He explained why he never used colour film. It wasn't, as was often believed, because he disapproved of it on some kind of moral grounds, but because chemically manufactured colour was so very limited in its range. He was, at heart, a painter, and the natural world contained so many more shades than photographic chemicals could even begin to formulate. He gave me an example. One of his friends, a *pastelliste*, had told him that at the shop where he bought his artists' materials in Paris—the shop Degas used—which was owned by three old ladies, they stocked 300 shades of green. *Three hundred.* Could I imagine it? The old ladies, he said, were going to die with their secret and the implication was that some of those colours would disappear forever. But his point was that all the colours in nature are relative to each other, and there are hundreds of them. Colour photography, he said, was an insult to nature. Chemically produced colour was the visual equivalent to junk food: harsh, reductive, untrue.

Once my brother stopped coming with us on holiday, our supply of family photographs dried up. None of us had the same urge to photograph each other, except for the obligatory couple of family groups. Perhaps we became blasé about foreign travel, staying in European hotels, driving through whole countries in one day. (My father was a dedicated driver: our holidays involved the shortest possible sea crossing, and we never went by plane.) Maybe we didn't have that sense of family any more. Like most of that first post-war generation, we were proudly breaking up, moving out, living far from home, never to move back. □

LIFE AT TILTY MILL
Christopher Barker

Back row, from left: Christopher Barker (with bike), Sidney (W. S.) Graham, Robert Colquhoun, Robert MacBryde, George Barker, John Fairfax, Paul Potts, Cedra Osborne
Front row, from left: Georgina Buxton, nee Barker, Sebastian Barker (looking though tyre), Damon Osborne (behind him), Elizabeth Smart, Rose Barker

I love this snap. It is the only photograph I know of my father, mother and three siblings together and like all team photos in my life it has its own tale to tell. Inevitably, because of its age, the tale does not have a happy ending.

Strictly speaking, it's not a snap at all. It was the result of a formal photocall by my mother, the writer Elizabeth Smart, for her weekend guests at Tilty Mill, the house in Essex where we all grew up. It seems odd now, looking at them, to think that I am much older than they were then; they were the colossi at whose feet we played. In the years since then I have seen most of them grow old and die, and none, I'm sad to say, went 'gentle into that good night'. Saddest of all was my sister Rose, the youngest here, who died before her time, and so could not be the last to unravel all our tales.

Still, here they stand in their prime. My father, the poet George Barker, is the balding adult, fourth from the left, who glances down at his progeny with amused tolerance (this was a rare visit so we probably seemed taller to him). My mother squats at his feet, smoking nervously, solicitous as always of her younger daughter next to her. My brother Sebastian, the blond chimp wearing a cap and tie specially for the photo, rolls the tyre. My sister Georgina tosses her ball and I'm the one sounding the horn on my bike. The little boy shying from the camera behind my brother is Damon Osborne whose mother, Cedra Osborne, is on the far right of the photo. I think we bullied him.

As for the rest, this was the wild bunch that peopled my childhood nightmares. The first adult on the left is Sidney—the poet W. S. Graham—wearing what look like distressed stonewashed jeans. This is 1952. He must have daringly prepared them with a bottle of bleach to fit his slim hips. I can see him later in life, massive fist banging the table, gimlet eyes skewering me to my chair too terrified to answer back. He had had a passionate affair with my mother. Was it happening here? In front of my father?

Next to him are the Scottish painters, Robert Colquhoun and Robert MacBryde, who lived with us at Tilty Mill. They were devoted to each other, despite their frequent feuding, and stayed together until Colquhoun's death, only ten years after this picture was taken. The self-conscious young man to my father's left was a cousin, John Fairfax, known as 'Young John'. My father had dubbed him 'Fairfax' to lend him a revolutionary touch, but his real surname was Jackson. He was an aspiring poet and must have been thrilled to be among this heady artistic crowd.

The balding yeoman next to him is Paul Potts, a writer whose output was sparse but effective. Often a figure of fun as he grew older, he would eventually be barred from Soho pubs for incontinence as he bummed his drinks.

Cedra Osborne, propping up the fence to the far right of the picture, was a kindly soul who periodically visited us with Damon. I can remember little else about her. I know Damon was less robust than we were and his mother fought a losing battle to stem the tide of snot from his bubbling nostrils. He was far too slow to keep up and once, when he did, we were perched high on the mill roof. From there we quickly doubled back, leaving him stranded on the slates, paralysed with fear.

Typically, every Friday my mother would trawl the watering holes of Soho, gathering a weekend party for our tumbledown house. This photo celebrates a fine catch—my father. His visits were awaited with great excitement by all us children and with not a little longing by me. He contributed nothing financially to our existence. It was left to my mother to support us all. But to us children he was always 'George', the human god who sent out important messages into the world from Soho (wherever that was). There, we were told, he mixed with a set of wonderfully queer folk: the half-blind poet John Heath-Stubbs, for example, who much later I watched fumble with a curtain in a pub for ten minutes before I realized he was trying to find the door; or the huge-headed, stone deaf David Wright, who by a combination of lip-reading and a foghorn voice exercised his dry sense of humour. Dylan Thomas was another Soho regular, but he and my father rarely met. Though my father was a lifelong admirer of Thomas's verse, the feeling was not mutual, and Thomas's acerbity in print was guaranteed to keep them apart.

So this photo records a special gathering for my father's sake, and who better to have taken it than John Deakin, my mother's deliciously camp photographer friend from *Vogue*. 'Just a quick snap,' I can imagine Mum saying, before they all set off on the two-mile trek to the Rising Sun.

Later, when I took up photography as a profession, Deakin

sometimes approached me for surprisingly simple technical advice. His Rolleiflex had been a gift from the painter Francis Bacon, and on this weekend must have been out of hock, where it often languished. We children loved Deakin's visits because he was the only adult male to come to Tilty who was small enough for my brother and me to co-wrestle to the grass while he squirmed with delight. I never understood why he seemed to be weeping with pleasure as we bounced in victory on his chest.

One thing I do remember about this photo was that after it was taken, before they left for the pub, my father came to my bedroom. He'd decided to show his buddies how he could exercise paternal discipline. Never mind that he was an absent parent or that I'd done nothing to be punished for, he tried to put me over his knee and spank me. Well, I was far too old for this caper and would have none of it. As I flailed about in a desperate attempt to escape I grabbed at his balding pate and pulled out a clump of precious hair. He let go suddenly and I scuttled off to a corner, seething with hurt pride, but brandishing a fistful of his last remaining wisps. His chums hooted with glee and they all ambled off to the pub, leaving me feeling violated by a man who was little more than a stranger, but who I still yearned for as a dad. Those thin strands between my fingers gave me grim comfort.

In 1950, to keep our domestic ship afloat, my mother took a job in London as a copywriter in an advertising agency, thereby successfully subjugating all her literary ambitions. The book that would eventually make her famous—*By Grand Central Station I Sat Down and Wept*, the story of her meeting with my father—was already published. Her next was twenty-eight years away. In her absence she left Colquhoun and MacBryde, the two starving Scottish painters, in loco parentis. They weren't the most likely couple to spring to mind as babysitters. But it seemed to work happily enough.

Although you wouldn't know it from the pose—cool shades, shirt tails out, fag flapping—MacBryde was the one who usually played the housewife. He would tease and cajole us children, cook for us, clean and make us take our medicine. He could iron a man's shirt with the back of a heated spoon in seconds. In the evenings we would all gather round a wind-up gramophone and sing along. The most

Christopher Barker

popular record in our pile of old seventy-eights was 'The Three
Lovely Lasses from Banyon' and MacBryde would delight us all—
especially Colquhoun—by capering and preening to the music while
we children roared out the words. It usually ended in squeals of
laughter when we all aped MacBryde's limp wrist, hooting out the
last line in unison '…and I shall be dressed like a *queen*!'

As a youngster I never understood why the two of them slept
together in the same bed. Equally I could have no idea why, when
drunk, Colquhoun could send MacBryde into a frenzy. Colquhoun
had treacherous liaisons with both sexes. His bisexuality underlined
to MacBryde the perilous nature of their relationship and brought
out the worst in him—often after a night at the Rising Sun.

I would lie awake in my bedroom, my ears cocked for the clatter
of their return. At first they would settle down in the sitting room,
and the distant murmur was briefly reassuring. Perhaps, I'd think to
myself, tonight it won't happen. But soon enough the rumble of their
conversation would rise in volume until, like an underground train
bursting through the frightening dark, a door would crash open,
followed by the sound of shattering glass and splintering wood, and
Colquhoun's bellow would resound off the stone-flagged corridors,
'…befaaahkn' *Jeezus* … ye snivin' *shite*… I'll faaack'n *keel* ye!'

I prayed that the thing I dreaded wouldn't happen; that once again
the latch on my bedroom door would save me. I lay there shivering
as the tumult passed my door and the clattering of feet on the
wooden stairs signalled a troubled retreat.

Not surprisingly, one of the side effects of these terrifying nights
was a recurring nightmare. When I was fast asleep and all was serene
across the wooded Essex countryside, those human cries would be
replaced by the howling of a lonely wolf that turned my heart to
ice. The sound came nearer and nearer, louder and louder, until the
skittering of claws across the yard outside heralded the lifting of my
brave little latch and in through the door would crash a small fox
with piercing eyes that ran in circles around my bedside carpet and
with which I would be engaged in furious combat.

Next morning the trauma of these nights would be hard to recall
as MacBryde pattered round the kitchen making breakfast on the
coal-fired range. (To our everlasting shame among our peers, our
house had no electricity and was lit by oil lamps.) He would sing

quietly to himself, the 'Banyon girls' having been replaced by a troop of Irish dragoons '…marching down from Fife-ee-oh!'

For us children, however, those wild nights had their compensations. We would comb the battlefield that was last night's party gathering up armfuls of empties to be returned to the pub. The Rising Sun was halfway up the steepest hill in Essex, and because of this every self-respecting boy racer in the neighbourhood had a home-made, greased, state-of-the-art soapbox trolley. Ours was the envy of the hill because a local carpenter had made it, incorporating a real car seat, a steering wheel and a hand-operated chain drive into its design. It was very heavy and never ran as well as the other boys' carts. But on these occasions it made up for its failure as a racer. If we took out the car seat we could double or treble the number of empties we could pack into it. When we reached the Rising Sun, Harry Tann, the publican, would sort through our cargo, rejecting any bottles that lacked the right brewery label. We came dancing home triumphant with handfuls of coins.

When they were working, the two Roberts used a creaking wooden shed at the back of the garden as a studio. It had a large window on one side. I remember the wild mess of the interior and my eyes still smart at the memory when I smell paint. An easel stood in one corner with a work in progress clamped to it. The palette was a square of plywood besmirched with streaks of colour. Among the tangle of dirty brushes, the dull lead tubes lay curled up like winded toy soldiers with different coloured gore oozing from their necks.

Colquhoun spent most of his time in there while MacBryde tended to our needs, but sometimes he would emerge, beaten back from his work by the weight of his hangover. We would then all sit around the kitchen table and compete to see who could draw a perfect circle. Although his circle was usually frilled, as if inked by a trembling Richter stylus registering an aftershock, Colquhoun always won.

Sometimes, when he'd finished cleaning, MacBryde would put on a special spread for tea. On one particular occasion it brought out the devil in him—to my cost. We were gathered round the table when MacBryde sprang his treat: a plate of cakes. Among the more familiar shapes and sizes, the biggest and most toothsome was a meringue, nestling in a frilled paper cake-cup. MacBryde thrust the plate under my nose and asked me to choose. He'd guessed correctly which cake

I'd pick. As I bit into the glazed sugar carapace, instead of the soft chewy centre I had anticipated, my teeth cracked on a lump of rock that MacBryde had gleefully baked inside. He collapsed in fits of laughter, and the whole table fell about at my gullibility.

Mum, meanwhile, had begun to make real money in advertising. Eventually she decided to send us all off to boarding school, and we left Tilty and moved to London. So the Roberts had to relocate, too. After that they largely disappeared from our lives, but we heard that their careers had gained a momentum, and then declined as their antics grew wilder. Their infamy extended to the quiet London suburbs where one night neighbours called the police to visit the party next door after glimpsing a naked and livid Colquhoun chasing a naked and laughing MacBryde through the shrubbery with an axe.

Sometimes they would be invited back to parties at our Paddington flat. By this time I was much bigger than either of them. But still, as the evening wore on, Colquhoun's voice, thickened with whisky, would rumble and explode, followed by the crash of a breaking bottle, and for a second I would be back in my childhood bed, transfixed with horror, praying for a miracle to save me.

Colquhoun died suddenly from a stroke in 1962 and MacBryde was inconsolable. My mother gave him a small room in our flat and when he left for Dublin we cleared it out. There, under the bed among the dried excrement and crusty food, we found dozens of empty whisky bottles, some brimming with piss. We had often heard him sobbing uncontrollably into the small hours: we dubbed this room 'the Wailing Room'.

Four years later, he stepped under a Dublin taxi and was killed. My mother wept silently when, on a trip to Scotland, we failed to find their twinned graves in a vast cemetery in Ayrshire under a slate-grey and spitting Scottish sky.

She's dead too, now. But in this photo she is still incandescent. The spark you see between her fingers eventually engulfed her, as she knew it would. She had written her soaring appassionata for the man she loved and when he proved faithless and penniless, she had cared for his brood. He couldn't handle her need for independence and in the end it drove him away. But he was her lodestar until she died.

Paul Potts survived until 1990. I went to see him when he was housebound. He had narrowly escaped death the night before after setting his bed alight with a cigarette. His rank dressing gown flapped open to reveal glimpses of flaccid naked flesh that made him seem both pathetic and vulnerable. While we talked he rubbed his back against the charred wall to cure an itch that wouldn't go away. I'd brought him a takeaway curry and a half bottle of whisky. He wolfed down the curry. Then, as he was tipping back the bottle, he suddenly stopped and, calm as you like, vomited a column of biriani on to the bed. He wittered on unabashed while I cleaned it up.

He died two years later from smoke inhalation. This time he had been too slow to escape the flames.

And then there was Rose, my mother's last child. Rose Emma Maximiliane Roberta—she scooped up all the leftover names my mother and father loved. But she was a sacrifice to the gods: too innocent, too open, too loving. Without a father, she needed a firm voice to restrain her, and when no one spoke she just tried it on. Her wildness grew more extreme. She was moved from one 'progressive' school to another, was even sent to a Steiner school in America in an attempt to curb her behaviour. But the school gave up and sent her home when she desecrated the American flag during a graveyard prank.

Even then, at fourteen, she had begun taking drugs. At first it was recreational, but then their influence began to take hold. Moved from school to school, she lost interest in her education and finally abandoned it with no qualifications. She drifted into the Soho her mother and father had been part of. A taxi driver twice her age introduced her to hard drugs. She became pregnant by him. She and the baby moved from squat to squat. Once I was staying at a posh friend's family house when she appeared on the doorstep with the baby asleep in her arms. She came into the kitchen and asked if she could sleep on the floor. But it wasn't my house, and she couldn't stay, so she lurched off into the night sobbing, her baby still asleep. She never blamed me. Although she fuelled her drug habit by prostitution (she told me that she was once gang-raped in a squat), she never lost her wicked sense of humour. It had developed directly from her ordeals. Her punchlines were always perfectly timed, so I'm sure that the irony of her death would have amused her. At the age

Christopher Barker

of thirty-six, when she had kicked her habit at last, her liver gave out after she took a few paracetamol to ease a party hangover.

When Rose fell ill that last time, I ferried our father across England to be at her bedside. When I picked him up he was full of banter about the quirky design of the Citroën I was driving, but this slowly tapered off and gave way to more serious introspection. He knew his daughter had been dying for some time, and he knew this call might be to her death. When we got to the hospital, we all gathered outside the operating theatre. My brother had been speaking hopefully of recovery when his voice trailed away. A white coat was among us.

'Rose is dead. Would you like to see her?'

We shuffled in, and as we did so a strange family division took place. Clutching an arm, I went in with the women, and soon the corridors of King's College Hospital, Camberwell echoed with their cries. But my father could not bring himself to view the corpse. □

GRANTA

ORANGE PEOPLE
Tim Guest

Children of Medina Rajneesh, Suffolk, 1982

In the late Seventies and early Eighties, a group of the most devoted of the British 'sannyasins', disciples of Bhagwan Shree Rajneesh— my mother's Indian guru—published the *Rajneesh Buddhafield European Newsletter*, an irreverent compendium of news from Rajneesh's ashram in Pune, India, and the latest sannyasin gossip. Somehow a stack of these newsletters have ended up in the British Library archives; and in the March 1980 issue, sandwiched in between predictions for the coming spiritual revolution ('The entry of Pluto into Scorpio heralds a new age and the transformation of society') and beauty tips written by my mother ('Whether windows to the soul or communicating that you fancy someone across the disco, beautiful eyes need taking care of!'), I found this advertisement announcing the birth of a new British commune:

MEDINA RAJNEESH: A RAJNEESH CITY TO BE BUILT IN BRITAIN
No longer is the Buddhafield restricted to six small acres in an Indian town; the seed is being scattered to the four corners of the earth. In every country, our master has said, there is to be a city of sannyasins, a Buddhafield, a self-supporting alternative community modelled on the ashram in Pune.

The city is to be a strong and potent availability, an offering up of the creativity, awareness and love we have received through our sannyas. It is to be a model city through which can be glimpsed the possibility that is open to all. It is to be an energy field so that all those who, knowingly or unknowingly, are seeking Bhagwan can find him.

The city has been given an Arabic name—Medina Rajneesh. The sacred city. The holy city. The marketplace. We have already started looking for a large suitable property.

Medina Rajneesh was nearly two years old when the photograph on the left was taken. It shows a group of us—children of the British sannyasins, a ragtag bunch, disciples by default—in the grounds of £350,000 worth of 'large suitable property': Herringswell Manor, a four-storey mock-Tudor manor set in fourteen acres of Suffolk countryside.

Medina Rajneesh. Never in history had so much orange gathered together to say 'Beloved' so often. Three hundred adult sannyasin gathered here to whoop and cry, to shout and whirl, to dance and embrace, to cook wild rice and buff the wooden floors. At Medina, even the signs in the toilets loved you. BELOVED...PLEASE WASH YOUR HANDS.

This photo is one of very few I have from the commune. We have been dressing up. You can't see it, but even this tattered collection of clothing, gathered for us from across the commune by Sharna, the school leader, has been dyed various shades of orange and maroon—orange at first, and later maroon after being washed time and time again in the communal laundries. We have been auditioning for *Grease*, the first Medina Kids Players production.

In the photo you can see our mala necklaces, symbols of our devotion: nylon cords strung with 108 polished rosewood or sandalwood beads (one for each of the sacred meditations). We all wore them: baby malas, with smaller beads, for the kids. The malas would snap once or twice a week, popping in the hands of some other kid as you slid past, a rain of sandalwood to be gathered up as best you could and taken in cupped handfuls to the mala cupboard to be restrung.

To separate us from the visitors during the frequent celebrations, the commune kids got special beads for our malas: green to show we were residents; yellow to show we were allowed up after eleven; and, when we were older, silver and gold to show our Aids status: silver for tested-and-waiting, gold for an all-clear. (When I got my gold bead I ran, barefoot and elated, from the kids' hut to the main house to tell my mum. It was the first time being negative had ever been good news.) Dangling at the bottom of each of our malas you can see the little lockets, framed in wood, each with the same black-and-white photo of Bhagwan.

Most of these children's parents would have heard Bhagwan on tape, or read his books, before going to visit his ashram in Pune to take a new name. My mother first heard Bhagwan's voice in the winter of 1978. She was sitting in our living room in Leeds, smoking a joint in her dressing gown. At the end of the tape, she cried. A friend gave her the address of the ashram, and she wrote a letter to Bhagwan. 'I felt you were speaking to a part of me that has never been spoken to before,' she wrote. 'I have heard that the way to learn from you is to become a "sannyasin", one of your followers. I would therefore like to take sannyas from you and go deeply into all that this may mean.'

The three commitments of a sannyasin were—and still are—to meditate daily; to wear the mala; and to wear clothes only in the colour of the sun. Because of this last vow, sannyasins were known as the Orange People, and after my mother took sannyas, everyone who came round to sit on the beanbags in our living room wore orange: orange dungarees, orange drawstring trousers, orange sandals, orange robes. By this point there were so many sannyasins in Leeds that the Woolworths on the high street was permanently sold out of orange dye. Despite the shortage, my mother got hold of some. She dyed all her clothes in the bath, then hung them by the fire to dry—to my delight, they left permanent orange stains on the fireguards—and she and her new friends began to hold meetings in our living room, from some of which I was carefully excluded. She put photos of Bhagwan up all over the house, including one on the slanted wall above my bed.

I still played with the local kids in the street, but in our games of 'superhero' I began to be Bhagwan along with Zorro and Spiderman. Most of my clothes had already turned orange in the wash. In the late autumn of 1979, with my mother's help, I too wrote a letter to Bhagwan.

My mother got hold of a baby mala for me. I wore it proudly in the street, my new orange costume the envy of all the kids in the neighbourhood. Georgie, my best friend, asked his mum if he could join in too, but she said no. He was sad, though, so when no one was looking I pretended to be Bhagwan, waved my plastic sword, and gave Georgie sannyas anyway. I was four years old.

'Dear Yogesh,' Bhagwan wrote in reply, 'I give you sannyas because I love you.'

Bhagwan Shree Rajneesh. My mother's guru—mine too, in a way—who, in the eight years I spent in his communes (in India, Germany, Suffolk and Oregon) I saw just twice.

Bhagwan, collector of ninety-three Rolls Royces (all Corniche models, because, he said, the Silver Shadow hurt his back); Bhagwan, the superstar guru. Bhagwan, who was never there but always there: in his books and tapes; in the songs we sang—'Disappearing into you, oh Bhagwan, the sun and the moon...'—wrought in miniature round all our necks; writ large, too, on the walls above our heads, in the laminate photos that were sometimes six feet wide.

Bhagwan, who gave us all new names. Who gave me my new name: Yogesh, a Sanskrit word for God.

He gave new names to the buildings, too: the main house was 'Kabır', 'The Great One'; the shop was 'Muti', 'The Provider'; and the health centre, where my mother worked as a therapist, was known as 'Hadiqua'a', 'The Walled Garden of Truth'. Each name was lovingly carved and hand-lettered on varnished wood.

I had trouble with the adults' names, but I will always remember the names of the children in this photo. Just to the right of centre, her head cocked to one side, is Rani. She looks like her mother, Poonam, the leader of the commune (all the commune leaders were women, by Bhagwan's decree). It is Poonam who, in the first Medina promotional video, fixes the camera with a determinedly honest stare—I have to bite my tongue to let the video play on—as the voice-over declares: 'The family sits by the fireside, gathered together in bliss for the first time...'

At the back, on the left, is the luscious Purva—you can just see her eyes, which were gorgeously blue. I fancied Purva and, after we had watched a pirate copy of *E.T.* in the kids' hut living room one day, I gave her every piece of *E.T.* merchandise I could lay my hands on. I gave her my *E.T.* stickers, my *E.T.* lunchbox, my *E.T.* pen; she gave me a kiss on the cheek.

In the front of the photo, arms wide, hamming it up for the camera, is goofy, affectionate Saoirse. She looks sweet now, but back then Saoirse was the awkward one, easy to tease, the one at whom we chanted, *Champak and Saoirse,/ Sitting in a tree,/ K-I-S-S-I-N-G!*

In the middle, at the back, baring her teeth, is Rupda the Terror. The week before this photo was taken, Rupda stopped me at the back of the kids' hut, by the smoking hut, and told me that unless I did what she ordered, she and Champak would wake me in the middle of the night, hold my mouth shut and burn the inside of my arm with a cigarette. Champak nodded, and rolled his sleeves up obligingly to show me his own burn. As we stood there, though, for a long minute or two, it grew clear that Rupda didn't have any actual ordeals in mind.

That's me, standing in front of her in the photo, to the right, hiding behind Saoirse's outstretched arm. Yogesh, the commune space-case ('Hellooo! Earth to Yogesh! Do you read me?'). The non-embracer. The anti-whirler. Saoirse's arm seems to be hiding my face; but look at my elbow. I'm hiding myself, too, just to be sure.

I remember the day this picture was taken. After that moment of clowning for the camera we all dispersed. We were going on a group outing later in the afternoon, to have a picnic on the beach. On the way there a tractor crashed into the side of our minibus. We rolled off the road and into a ditch, where I awoke from my customary doze to find everything upside down. We've been moved to another van, I thought, until across the bus Viragini—the girl on the right of the photo, pulling her eyes out wide with her hands—reared up, covered in ripe bananas, and began to wail.

We were taken to Ipswich Hospital, where the doctor announced Viragini has broken her collarbone. I remember playing stick-in-the-mud in the park opposite, when a car full of panicked mothers rolled into the hospital car park. This time my mother was around, but other times she was not. Many times my mother would be elsewhere: on tour round the country, running sannyasin therapy and meditation groups to raise money for the British Buddhafield; living in Cologne, pressing sheets in the laundry at Wioska Rajneesh Commune on Lütticher Strasse; in Pune, India; in Oregon, USA; in the belly of a 747; almost anywhere, it seemed, but home with me.

But not this night. This night—with us, the kids, safe and sound—was a celebration night, and this was the evening my mother and Poonam called Rani, her sister Soma, and me into the commune's head office, and gave us our first taste of lemon sorbet and champagne.

The children of Medina Rajneesh. Children of the Buddhafield—but Buddha wasn't around. In summer we played on the lawns, climbed trees, ran across flower beds. We trekked across fields and along B-Roads to the heath, where we chased imaginary adders, swam in the river and slid down a concrete waterfall. We went swimming at the public pool in Mildenhall, then made our own way back to the van; slunk down the back streets so we could stuff our

Tim Guest

vegetarian mouths with the battered sausages never served up in the commune's dining hall. In winter we crunched over frosty grass in our moon boots, picked up sticks and had play fights, or gathered chestnuts to roast in bulk over the fire in the Main Hall. When the lake froze over we slid across it or played basketball on the ice, fleeing when it cracked: occasionally some of us would get marooned on the island in the middle, until someone could stop laughing and fetch a plank. In winter, the adults in meetings, we sat in a circle in the kids' hut playing spin-the-bottle, with the sky through the little window above the piano growing dark.

Nowadays I occasionally bump into one of the Medina kids. Our paths cross, or our mothers' paths cross, and phone numbers are exchanged. I met up recently with Bindhu and Majid, two of my good friends from that time. We used to jump out of the first-floor window of the guest house together, strapped into the new rope-pulley fire escape—the one we had been told explicitly never to touch unless the whole place was definitely burning down. We met on a weekday evening for dinner at Majid's house in Brighton. Bindhu is a software engineer now, living in Boulder, Colorado. Sitting on Majid's sofa, Bindhu told me he remembered me being picked on a great deal at Medina. 'Really?' I asked. 'Why's that?'

'Because you were young,' he said, 'and scrawny, and detached.'

Sannyasins wanted us to let go. They kept telling us: Let Go! It's that simple! But all we had ever done was let go: of our past; of our parents; of our Lego.

Bhagwan always said his adult sannyasins were beyond help: they were too far gone to understand what he had to say. It would be the kids, he said, who would get it.

My mother told me that. 'When you do get it,' she added, 'would you let me know?' □

64

GRANTA

PRINCE STREET GIRLS

Susan Meiselas

I was riding a bicycle through my neighbourhood in Little Italy nearly twenty-five years ago. Suddenly, a blast of light flashed into my eyes. Its source was a group of kids standing with a mirror, focusing the sun on my face, nearly blinding me. That was the day I met the Prince Street girls, the name I gave the group that hung out on the nearby corner almost every day. I was the stranger who didn't belong. Little Italy was mostly for Italians then.

The girls were from small Italian–American families and they were almost all related. Sometimes they would reluctantly introduce me to their parents if we met in the market or at the pizza parlour, but I was never invited into any of their homes. I was their secret friend, and my loft became a kind of hideaway when they dared to cross the street, which their parents had forbidden.

I started photographing them in the spring of 1975. At that time, I was completing a project about carnival strippers, which would later become my first published book. The Prince Street girls began as a series of incidental encounters. At the beginning I was making pictures *for* them. They'd see me coming and yell, 'Take a picture! Take a picture!' By 1978 they were changing, and I wanted to capture them growing up. Yet my focus was shifting. I had joined Magnum Photos and my work was taking me away from the neighbourhood. When I landed in Central America, I found myself in the middle of a war and part of another community.

By the time I got back to New York nearly ten years later, the girls were long past their teens, beyond the boundaries of our streets, and beginning families of their own. Looking at these pictures now reminds me of how difficult it was to integrate my two lives—family and friends at home, and my life as a journalist on the road. It was often a painful separation, though not one I regret having chosen.

I still live in the old neighbourhood, though it has changed enormously; it's filled with young models and dot-com-ers, chic cafes and expensive shops. It's almost impossible to imagine the streets as they once were. The girls have moved away, but Frankie, the only boy in the group, is still here. He keeps in touch with them. Through him we all got together for dinner a few years ago. We passed around the pasta and the pile of old photographs I'd brought. It was a delight to watch them rediscover themselves, and think about how my neighbours, who became my subjects, now feel like old friends. □

From left, back row: Pina, Carol, Lisa, Frankie; front, Lisa, their dog 'Peaches', Denise (Dee), 1975

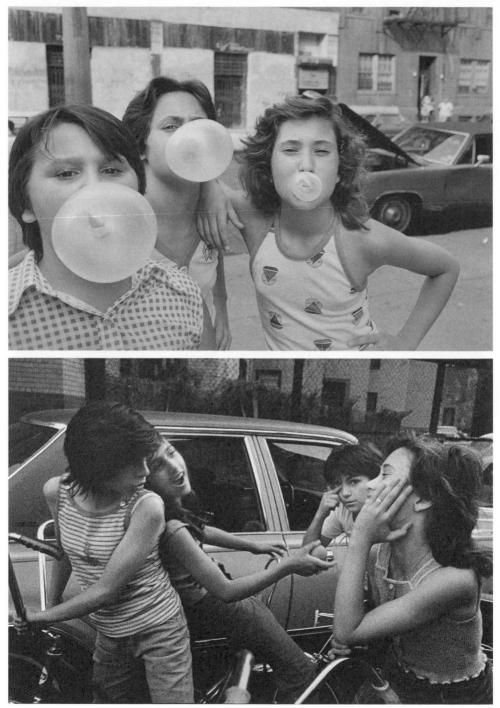

1976

Mott Street, New York, 1976

1976

On the corner of Prince Street and Mott Street, 1976

1976

On the way home after St Patrick's Cathedral School, NY, 1976

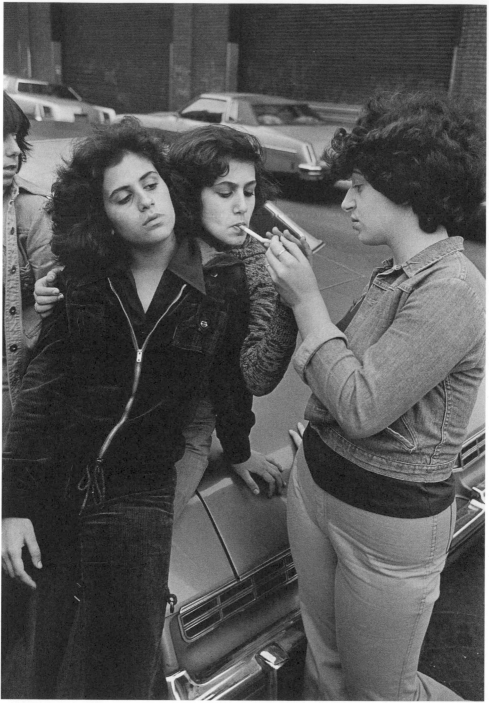

1978

Opposite: Pebbles, Jo-Jo, Ro; top Pina, Phyllis, Jo-Jo, Lisa; above, Tina with her arm round Julia, 1978

1978

On the A train, 1978

1978

Rockaway Beach, NY, 1978

1979

Baxter Street, 1979

Julia's wedding, St Patrick's Old Cathedral, Mott Street, 1992

Lisa and Frank on their wedding day, Mott Street, 1990

Lisa and her daughter Lindsay, Staten Island, 1996

"KAMIKAZE SPIRIT"

** TROLLEY **   www.trolleynet.com

NEW INDEPENDENT PUBLISHERS, DISTRIBUTED WORLDWIDE BY PHAIDON PRESS LTD.
IMAGE BY MASAYUKI YOSHINAGA FROM THE BOOK BOSOZOKU, ON SALE 31ST OCTOBER

MUMMY
Angela Lambert

The Lambert family with friends: Angela (far right); her mother (next to her);
Monica (in kilt) and her father (centre)

If I free-associate around the word *Mummy*, what comes up? Smoking. Showily crossed legs. Good ankles. Laughter. Cocktail parties. Gin and It. A Ewbank squeaking over the carpet. Lay the table for me—here, knives and forks. Toast and dripping, beans and bacon, eat the fat up it's good for you, don't be cheeky, I give up, go to your room. Acrid smell of warm wool or summer cotton. Sunday afternoon walks. Boredom. Tennis, me as ball-boy. Butterfingers! Warm milk, night-night sweet dreams, give your Mummy a hug. Downstairs, cigarette smoke, whisky and soda siphon, card games, radiogram: Jerome Kern, Charles Trenet, Jean Sablon, *la vie en rose*; dancing, laughing, not here, somewhere else, outside, absent, grown-up...

Well, she's dead now and Daddy's dead and most of their friends are dead, so I can write about her openly; she crops up in several of my novels as a noisy, vain woman, trampling over her daughter's delicate adolescent emotions. I resented her from the age of seven and gave up trying to love her by the time I was twelve, yet my younger sister Monica (known as Monilein, Minna or Minnachen) adored her and they were close for more than fifty years.

I didn't mind that she was German; in fact it was one of the best things about her. It meant I grew up bilingual, steeped in the German poetry and *lieder* she loved. She sang to me when I was little; sang to us both, I suppose, although you never spoke German as well as me, did you Minna? *'Erl-König'*, *'Sah ein Knab' ein Röslein stehen'*, *'Alle Vöglein sind schon da'*, *'Die Lorelei'*, the plangent mediaeval German carol *'Es ist ein' Ros' entsprungen'*. I don't even need to hear them—just their names bring tears to my eyes.

But it is possible to know the poems of Goethe, Heine and Schiller by heart and still be insensitive and stupid. All her life she called Jews 'Jew-boys' and black people 'niggers' and Down's syndrome children 'mongrels' (she meant mongols) and working class boys 'gutter-snipes' and when I tried to correct her she would insist, 'But darling, they *are*!' Once a prejudice had lodged in her head nothing could shift it. As I child I absorbed them all and didn't find it easy to get rid of them when I grew up.

It was decades later, when I saw a *Timewatch* programme about the early Nazi years, that I realized how much my mother was a product of her time. The female equivalent of Hitler Youth was the *Bund Deutscher Mädel*, the League of German Girls, and surely my mother, twenty-one in 1933 when Hitler became Chancellor, would have belonged to that? She personified the Nazi ideal of young womanhood—although she wasn't blonde. Those healthy girls swinging their arms and singing in unison as they strode across the Lüneburger Heide—that was her. Those excited flag-wavers, eyes sparkling at the nearness of their Führer—that was her too. She took British nationality when she married my father in 1936 but she loved and admired her own country and never stopped deploring the English lack of efficiency, punctuality and above all, domestic hygiene.

I wrote down a fragment of our conversation in August 1995, after she'd spent a night with me in London. Next morning over breakfast, I asked, not to bait her, but out of real curiosity:

'Mummy, were there any Jews in your family?'

Expression of shock, quickly veiled.

'What?'

'Were there any Jewish members of the family?'

'No-o—because I suppose they must have been, tested, you know, to see if they were…pure. And they passed.'

Pause. Then she asked,

'Were there in *your* family?'

'Mummy, my family *is* your family.'

'Oh yes.' Pause. 'I had some very good Jewish *friends*.'

Another time, when I asked her what had happened to her Jewish school friends in Hamburg in the Twenties and Thirties, she said,

'They were from rich families, you know, and when the war came, they went away on holiday.'

'And did you see them again?'

'No. They never came back. They could afford not to, you see.'

She was born in Hamburg on March 5, 1912 and named Edith Paula Alice, though she was always called Ditha—pronounced Deeta. She was the third of four sisters. Hilde, the youngest, died of measles aged three. Perhaps this had something to do with it; perhaps it was the growing hostility between her parents; but for some reason my mother never grew up. All her life she was like a teenager—lively and petulant. Her parents divorced when she was twelve—a source of such shame that she didn't tell me about it (not even when my own husband left me) until I was in my fifties. My grandfather, a jeweller called Wilhelm Schröder, went on supporting not only his ex-wife and daughters but also his elderly parents-in-law until they died. Nearly twenty-five years later, when he was in his seventies, he told my mother he wanted to get married again. 'Who to?' A waitress—but a very nice girl. 'Don't expect *me* to call her Mutti!' said my mother; and that was the end of the waitress. My grandfather remained alone until his death at the age of eighty-four.

My grandmother ('Oma') visited London a couple of times before the war. She might even have seen me when I was a baby, but I have no memory of her except from photographs—a large, amply corseted lady in black, her hair parted in the centre and pulled into a bun. Apparently my grandmother was a paragon of sweetness and generosity, adored and praised by all—which was also how my mother saw herself, and my sister after her. Oma died of cancer during the war and my mother never stopped missing her: '*Oh for the touch of a vanished hand/And the sound of a voice that is still!*' she would recite in a special voice. I discovered only the other day that the lines are by Tennyson and not, as I had assumed, Patience Strong.

My mother had a hunger for praise and affection that my father and I could never satisfy. I learned to praise her as soon as I could talk but it didn't come easily to me. When my sister was born five years later the two of them formed a happy and satisfying mutual admiration society. Monica, my sister, nicknamed first Monilein (little Monica) and later Minnachen or Minna (meaning, more or less, mother's little helper), took after her. They both put a lot of effort into being winsome and feminine. Brushing my mother's hair had been my job but my sister took over as soon as she was old enough. They both loved having their hair brushed, and would take it in turns to groom each other, preening and admiring as they did so: ('Your hair's so *thick!*'—'*blonde!*'—'*shiny!*'). People didn't wash their hair as much in those days, and my mother's hair was often greasy and smelled somehow wiry, sour, *womanly* in a way I didn't like.

She had her family's tendency to indulge in sweet things and was usually overweight. She had a big nose and a habit of stroking it downwards between her index finger and thumb, which she believed would in time reduce its size. She had brawny hands and arms but she had good legs, which my sister—though not I—inherited. They liked to display them by wearing short, tight skirts and sitting with their legs angled sideways.

In 1947 when I was six and a half and my sister still a toddler, my mother went back to Hamburg for the first time in ten years. My father was attached to an organization called the CCG—the Control Commission for Germany—whose purpose was to put the Germans back on their feet and repair their shattered infrastructure. He had gone on ahead and we were on our way to join him, travelling with several other English families.

Our arrival in Hamburg and what we saw when we got there is the fiercest memory of my childhood. We started out by taking a boat, to the north German port of Wilhelmshaven I think, where we changed to a train for the last stage of the journey. The three of us had a compartment, not a carriage, to ourselves. I had my back to the engine and on the opposite seat were my mother and Monica. It was January or February of one of the coldest winters on record and the temperature outside was well below freezing. As the train approached Hamburg Hauptbahnhof and slowed to a stop before entering the station, a horde of small boys ran between the tracks next to it, hands reaching towards the passengers, jumping up and down to attract attention. I remember them all as being naked, though they can't have been or they would have frozen to death. At any rate they only had rags to cover their pale blue-and-white bodies and they were desperately thin. Even if I leaned back, trying not to look, their upstretched hands still flashed into view beside the window. I'd never seen such a dreadful sight; these skinny, icy children begging for money, food, anything.

Both my parents were heavy smokers and my mother had bought some cartons of Player's Navy Cut, perhaps from a NAAFI shop on board ship or even on the train. She shoved the window down, tore open a Player's carton and threw handfuls of cigarettes out to the boys, who caught as many as they could and scrabbled in the snow for the ones that had fallen on the stones and clinker of the track. A railway worker who was hosing down an empty train nearby noticed what was happening and turned his hose on the boys. A thick jet of ice-cold water engulfed them and they scattered. He yelled and shook his head furiously at my mother but I don't remember her answering back. She was shocked into silence. I'm sure the reason I felt it so keenly was not just because the action was barbaric and the boys pitiful but because I was still so closely bound up with my mother that her reactions were my reactions, her feelings my feelings. I felt the full measure of her suffering and it cut a groove in my memory.

We were billeted with other English families in the Streits Hotel, on the once elegant Jungfernstieg. The only good thing about the nine months we spent there was a broken chandelier in the attic. It lay strewn across the filthy roof beams and I and some of the other children would sneak up to play with it, jangling and making patterns with the dusty faceted crystal pieces that drooped from our fingers like giant earrings.

We got three meals a day in the hotel dining room and a food parcel once a week. My mother gave this to her father and her aunts. She also distributed what she could scavenge from the hotel kitchen to the starving people on the streets. Some had no clothes left and walked about wrapped in shaggy grey blankets. She often cried when she saw what had been done to the glamorous, cosmopolitan city of her youth.

This was when I met my grandfather ('Opa') for the first time—a large, musty-smelling man in a heavy coat and dark grey Homburg. We liked each other at once.

In about 1944, when it must have seemed as if the war would never end, he had written the story of his life in longhand and dedicated it 'To my beloved grand-daughter, Angela Maria, because I cannot hold her in my arms.' Those words still make my eyes well up. He was nearly seventy then and wanted to leave some record of his life. It was a story of hard work and enterprise. He was the son of a Schleswig-Holstein peasant farmer. By the time war broke out in 1939 he had built up a successful business as a jeweller and diamond merchant and made a modest fortune. When Hitler told the Germans to give him their gold for the war effort, my sceptical grandfather buried his stock in the back garden and dug it up intact after the war.

My mother kept his memoir from me for nearly forty years and only very reluctantly allowed me to read it. She had translated his account into English and inserted rose-tinted comments of her own, chiefly in the form of constant references to Oma; 'my dearly beloved wife' or 'my wonderful wife'. She then lost—or destroyed—the original. She always preferred her mother's way of looking at things, editing out the rough, tough reality and replacing it with compliments and prettiness.

Getting to know my grandfather and my two great-aunts was good for me. For the first time in my life I was spoiled and adored. My grandfather, a worldly man with a bone-dry wit, was delighted to find that I was an avid reader. He encouraged me—then about seven—to read Charles Dickens, his favourite author. *Bleak House* was the book he liked best. The great-aunts, with whom I sometimes stayed for a few nights, loved indulging me. My German had always been as good as my English and Tante Lidy told me stories out of her head. During the war she had earned a pittance writing an on-going story for the *Hamburger Echo* about a mischievous Scottie dog called Mohrle. Tante Anni, the youngest of my grandmother's many siblings, had Down's syndrome. ('Poor Tante Anni's not right in the head. She's a mongrel, so you must be extra-nice to her,' said my mother.) The things Anni said and her sense of humour were childlike and conspiratorial. I loved all three of them. It makes me sad now to think how lonely they must have been at the end of their lives. My mother, their one remaining relative apart from me and my sister, spent little time with Opa, perhaps out of misplaced loyalty to her long-dead mother.

Eventually we left Hamburg and went to live in the local CCG base at Bad Salzuflen, a spa town near Hanover. About this time my name changed. My sister was beginning to talk, and because she couldn't say 'Angela' she called me 'Lala', like the first two syllables in 'lullaby'. To my family and my parents' friends I've been Lala ever since, though I never liked it. We lived in a house with a garden at number 62, Roon Strasse. My mother had a seventeen-year-old maid called Annelore who collected *Maikäfer*—large, crackly brown beetles with a rapid wing action. She used to hide them in matchboxes inside my bed or under my pillow, where they buzzed furiously. I've hated bugs ever since. Annelore did most of the housework, freeing my

mother for tennis, bridge and 'Housey-Housey'. A friend of my
mother's from that time told me the other day, 'Our generation took
it for granted that we were more important than our children. If they
got in the way of us doing something we wanted—in my case having
a good time and lots of lovers!—we ignored them, or sent them to
boarding school.' My mother did not, I think, have lovers but she
did have a good time. Parties were what she liked most of all.

In between parties she played with us. I had a square face framed
by lank dark hair held back with a kirby grip, badly fitting glasses,
a square body, stocky legs and a closed expression, bookish and
judgemental. My sister had a mop of golden curls, a sunny smile and
an open, affectionate nature that hid a genius for teasing me in ways
that no adult ever spotted. Of course I hated her. She and my mother
formed a tightly knit unit which I defended myself against by bullying
Monilein and being 'cheeky' to Mummy. Cheekiness would reduce
her to pretend tears, which became real as soon as my father got
home. He would take me next door, to the dining room, out of sight
though not out of earshot. Here he would smack me, sometimes on
the palm of my outstretched hand, sometimes my bottom, depending
on what exactly I'd said to upset Mummy. He went on until I cried,
and once I realized this I never cried. My mother didn't smack me
herself but she was capable of sulking for days. This reduced me to
a state of anguish and guilt. I would beg forgiveness, but she would
turn her head away or look at me in silence, soulful and wounded.
Eventually she would relent and I would be given to understand that
I was one of the family again. Her behaviour taught me never to sulk
or take any notice of those who do.

What was my mother really like? As a small child I couldn't have
answered that question; she was my Mummy and I loved her.
She never took me seriously. Children were teased or passionately
cuddled, fed or frightened or tucked up, often for the benefit of an
adult audience, but did not exist in their own right. Like many
parents at that time, my mother thought teasing or deliberately
misleading children was funny and she would answer my questions
with a joke or a lie.

'Why can't I eat the cherry stones?'

'Because if you do a cherry tree will start to grow in your tummy and force its way up your throat and come out of your mouth and you'll die.' For years I had a picture of tree roots spreading round inside my tummy and branches bursting through my mouth. My mother loved describing the freaks she had seen exhibited at Hamburg's Christmas Fair when she was a child: 'A woman with the head of a rabbit!' 'A man with two heads!' 'The fattest boy in the world!' Even as an adult I think she still believed in these rabbit-women, proving herself as gullible as we were. She made up bedtime stories about pain and torture, about police with fierce dogs pursuing a murderer through black pine forests. 'They hunted him down like a fox to its hole,' is one phrase I remember. Then, to chase away the images she had conjured up, she'd sing a tender German lullaby— 'Schlafe, mein Prinzchen, schlaf' ein' or 'Guter Mond, du gehst so stille...'. The stories gave my younger sister nightmares and she would wake up screaming.

My mother's inability to realize that small children are highly impressionable was due partly to her lack of imagination. I knew she wasn't clever but I didn't see her stupidity as a fault; cleverness was a handicap—and quite unnecessary in a girl. She was a show-off, which even before going to boarding school I knew you weren't supposed to be. She was manipulative, though lacking the word itself, I don't think I knew that then. I often thought she was unfair, but unfairness is the chief complaint of every child against its parents. She was vain and shallow, she could be spiteful, and she was always self-obsessed.

Vitality was her great virtue. She was not pretty but she was always flirtatious: both men and women found her charming. She was kind and extravagantly generous, though she had to be showered with gratitude in return. She was warm, outgoing and friendly and great fun at parties. She was a good dancer, a moderate tennis player and lousy at bridge...not that she knew *that*. When she and my father went out to 'play bridge' (I pictured the sort of activity shown on willow pattern plates, with people endlessly crossing bridges) there would be loud arguments later about how badly my mother had 'played the hand'.

Above all, she had a blooming physical vigour that galvanized us into long walks every Sunday afternoon, during which she sang German *Wanderliede* in her strong, beautiful voice and tried to get us to sing too. Her liveliness was the perfect foil to my father's mental and physical laziness. He was a thoroughly decent and conscientious man who didn't stir from his armchair if he could help it. To the rest of the world he seemed timid and over-deferential but for the first twenty years of their marriage she worshipped him. Her first fond nickname for him was 'My Lord and Master', said without a trace of irony. Later she shortened it to 'Master' and continued to call him that till I was about thirteen. These were the years she looked after him with a gusto and devotion that must have swelled the stunted heart of a neglected, undersized youngest son. By the time they'd been married for twenty years she had switched to 'Deddy'. Later it became 'Grandy', which is what my children called him. When she was annoyed he was, curtly, 'John'.

My mother used the word *fleissig* a lot, meaning busy, industrious, house-proud. She thought a woman's home should look like an illustration from Alison Uttley's *Little Grey Rabbit* books or Kenneth Grahame's *The Wind in the Willows*— neat, orderly and *gemütlich*: cosy. We would pore over these books and admire the well-polished windows, spotless starched tablecloths and kitchen cupboards laden with home-made preserves. My mother couldn't make jam. She was totally impractical. Apart from knitting me pale yellow jumpers (not a good colour with my sallow skin and pink-framed National Health glasses) and darning my father's socks, she had none of the so-called female skills. She couldn't garden, dressmake, or even cook well, yet she regarded most English housewives as sluts.

She didn't know the names of any flowers, trees or birds— forgivable, I suppose, in someone brought up in the middle of a big city speaking a different language. I grew up able to identify a robin and a buttercup but not much else. Neither she nor my father could paint a room or put up a shelf. Hard up as they were, they had to employ 'a little man' to carry out the simplest repair. For most of her life she couldn't drive either, though she did eventually pass her test when she was seventy—yes, yes, quite an achievement—and spent a few lethal years on the road. Most of these inadequacies were passed on to me and I have never learned to drive (I failed the test five times) or even operate a sewing machine. My sister is much more practical; on the other hand she too belongs to the *Little Grey Rabbit* school of interior decoration; miniature china boxes called 'nicky-noos' clutter every surface. Just right for Toad and Ratty and Mole.

My mother, in my vitriolic teenage phrase, had 'natural bad taste'. She dressed herself and us badly. She had no sense of colour or how to arrange flowers or a room. Her favourite paintings were of the sun-slanting-through-autumn-woods and falling-leaves variety.

I was a judgemental, precocious brat, I recognize that, but my parents *were* philistines. My mother cared nothing for my intelligence and my father, I think now, was intimidated by it. It's hard when you're not praised for the one talent you *do* possess. 'Lala's nose buried in a book as *usual*!' was their constant reproach. Since they only possessed about fifty books and I'd read all the easy ones, it was quite likely to be Toynbee's *A Study of History* or Churchill's *The Second World War* in six stout volumes with pale grey jackets; books they'd been given as presents and stashed away unread in the chevron glass-fronted bookcase. I didn't understand them, but at least it was paper and print. I got hold of Arthur Mee's *Children's Encyclopaedia* and worked my way through that. One December when I was about nine and drooping with boredom, my mother reluctantly agreed to let me have a book she'd intended as a Christmas present. (We were scrupulous about not opening presents before Christmas or birthdays, and despised weak-willed families who did.) Bursting with impatience at the prospect of at least a couple of hours' absorption, I tore off the wrapping paper, to find inside a soppy *Story of Jesus*, which I read in less than ten minutes. My mother was furious with me for being disappointed; I was furious with her for choosing such a useless book. It could have been worse. After my ninth birthday party had produced an exciting pile of book-shaped presents from my little guests, I unwrapped six copies of that year's *Rupert Annual*.

It was high time I was shipped off to England and boarding school. My parents sent for brochures and chose a school called Wispers. I was to start in May 1950, the summer term, just after my tenth birthday. I dreaded it. My surname was Helps. At my present school (the British School in Bad Salzuflen), I was called 'Helpless'. What would be my nickname at the new one? A few days before term started my mother came with me to England to kit me out and see me off. We spent hours in Kinch and Lack, the official school outfitters, where I was measured by stout men in navy blue suits. In the evenings we sewed on name tapes: ANGELA HELPS. Sitting opposite each other on twin hotel beds, we attached them to liberty bodices, a dark green Jantzen swimming costume, six pairs of white cotton socks, four pairs of white knicker linings, two pairs of dark green outer knickers, three cotton night dresses, sponge bag with flannel (both marked); all of which were packed into my school trunk ('Everything new! Just like a little princess!' said my mother) and dispatched to Sussex via Messrs Carter Paterson. While we sewed my mother talked about her weight. She had realized she was too fat, she said, and while I was away she would go on a diet. She promised that by the end of term I'd be amazed how slim she was. 'You won't recognize your glamorous new Mummy!' I didn't mind her being fat. She was plump and soft and warm, no sharp bones, just rolls of woolly twinset against which I would be pressed in moments of sudden affection. She and her clothes smelled strongly of sweat. She thought deodorants unhealthy and never used them. I didn't mind until my teens, when the older girls in my dormitory reached the Odo-ro-no and Cussons Apple Blossom talc stage and became self-conscious about 'personal hygiene'—what the advertisements called 'daintiness'. After that I was embarrassed by her unwashed smell.

She wept on the platform at Waterloo as the school train drew out. I watched dry-eyed. Boarding school had been presented as a privilege for which my parents were paying a great deal of money. I was a lucky girl and should be very grateful. I sat in the long train carriage with thirty other juniors ('squits'), all wearing the same green-and-white striped cotton dress (22/6d), emerald green cardigan (14/6d) and regulation Clarks sandals with five teardrop shapes cut into the leather over the toes. If I'd been a really lucky girl I would have been lost in the new *Dandy* or *Beano*, but my mother thought comics would make the other girls look down on me, so I sat in silence as the train chuffed through the Home Counties, telling myself that when I got home, whatever happened I mustn't forget to praise my mother for having lost weight.

She wrote to me conscientiously once a week; chatty letters about how much 'We Three'—the holy trinity of Helpses from which I was excluded—were enjoying the summer. I spent the term in a state of miserable homesickness. When it was over I took the school train from Sussex to Waterloo, then travelled on to Harwich, by boat to Hook of Holland, and by train again across Holland and Germany (all this aged ten, unescorted, struggling with my heavy suitcase). As soon as I saw my mother standing on the platform at Bad Salzuflen I said, 'Goodness Mummy, aren't you *slim*! I hardly *recognized* you! Gosh!' I wasn't going to risk the holiday starting badly.

We left Bad Salzuflen at the end of that summer holiday. I had been in love for the past two years with a boy whose name I still can't bring myself to spell out, though I wrote a novel about him. I also had one friend; a girl called Evelyn Falconer. It was one of those odd, desperate friendships based on a conspiracy of dare and counter-dare that easily tips into deliberate cruelty. One day she dared me to walk along the top of the stone wall surrounding their garden. It was about six feet high with trees and shrubs at its base. I set off on tip-toe, arms outstretched for balance, but the top was uneven and I fell into a hydrangea bush. It had sharp dried-up stems in the centre and one of these drove deep into my right arm near the elbow. It hurt and bled a great deal and I left Evelyn without making her do a counter-dare and ran home, up Roon Strasse, straight past the two Alsatians that usually terrified me, desperate for comfort. We were due to leave in a couple of days and my mother was too busy sorting and packing to take much notice. Over the next forty-eight hours the arm throbbed and swelled and grew more and more painful.

Eventually the house was cleared, suitcases, trunks and family driven to the station and we began the long journey back to England. By now I was in agony, but my mother was too absorbed in saying good-bye to her friends and her country, and my father too burdened by the responsibility of getting us and our luggage home safely, for either of them to bother about me. I walked up and down the corridor of the train, holding my arm and groaning. When I finally got my parents to listen they told me to look for the guard's van and ask him if he had a First Aid kit. My sister, pretty as a picture and happy as a clam, still believes we were a loving family. She was five then, with lots of new people on the train to charm and do her little curtsey to. She doesn't remember this incident but I know it happened. I walked the length of the swaying train, found the guard's van and the guard, and asked if he had a First Aid kit. He rummaged about and produced a rusty tin, which he prised open. Inside were two cigarette stubs.

By the time we got back to England the arm was badly poisoned. My mother took me to Purley General Hospital where they X-rayed it—no bones broken—and removed a hydrangea twig about four inches long. After that it healed quickly, though the scar lasted for years. If I twist my arm and peer behind my elbow I can still just about make out a pale sliver of skin that marks the spot.

We were hard up in the early 1950s. Middle-ranking civil servants didn't earn much, and in any case 'throwing money away' was seen as vulgar. In the holidays from boarding school I had two changes of clothes—one for wearing and one for the wash. I wore them with my brown Harris tweed school overcoat, beige knee-high socks and Clarks lace-ups. We only spent money on food, which we bought from an early supermarket called Pay-&-Take. We lived on baked beans, macaroni or cauliflower cheese, scrambled eggs, rice pudding, a joint on Sunday, shepherd's pie (my favourite) on Mondays. Roast chicken was the most sophisticated food my mother cooked. Garlic never passed her lips. This was before Elizabeth David, and such exotic foods weren't available but even when they were she would make a great pantomime of disgust and refuse to eat anything unfamiliar. As a diplomat's wife in Finland during the mid-Fifties, when entertaining was part of my father's job, the first time the cook brought asparagus home from the market my mother made her cut the tips off and throw them away.

We returned to England from Helsinki in 1957, still poor. My grandfather died the following year. He bequeathed my mother a 1920s-style bracelet encrusted with diamonds that spent most of its time in the bank; a heavy, flexible gold armband that she passed on to me when I was twenty-one; and the deeds to a block of flats in Hamburg. My fanatically honest father declared the proceeds from its sale to the German and English tax authorities—both of whom took a generous cut—and to the Bank of England when he imported the Deutschmarks. The Bank took its cut, too. My mother ended up with a few thousand pounds, which were invested with such extreme caution that they never grew much. She was furious, her one chance for a really good spending spree lost. 'Deddy's *hopeless* with money!' she said.

Towards the end of her life I think she began to realize that she hadn't been the ideal mother for me. She said so to my daughter Marianne, and told her she wanted to say sorry, but by then it was too late. When she could no longer speak, or recognize me, or perhaps even hear, I wanted to say sorry to her, and did, on what turned out to be my last visit. She gave no sign of understanding. Too late.

Several nights a week I can't sleep. I go to the study and write, search the Net, read old emails, till my eyelids are dropping and I'm writing nonsense. Or I wake at two, three in the morning, a sleepless child. I do what my mother used to do: brew up some hot milk (she would have made Horlicks) and sit in the kitchen for an hour or more. I churn like a washing machine, pointless thoughts flapping round after one another, usually about my children—now all over thirty. Will my daughter do this, my son cope with that? Have I bequeathed my own unhappy marriage to my children, for whom I wanted only happy, stable, permanent lives?

That's what my mother achieved: one husband, one marriage, one family, maybe even happiness. And finally, a legacy—not a large sum but enough—for which my father had saved all his life. That's why he was mean, denying us treats, always looking for the cheapest of everything—to ensure that his scatty, extravagant wife wouldn't die penniless. His prudence meant that my sister and I didn't have to have her living with us. I never did although my sister tried for a few weeks. It didn't work so my mother went into one Home and then, when she became aggressive, another.

In all she spent seven years in Homes, exactly as long as I spent at boarding school. She ended her life among the faded remnants of gentlefolk in Weymouth. Her raging will to live kept her going till she was ninety, her north German heart and lungs pulsing steadily long after she was decrepit and insentient and should have died.

I went to her funeral but not to the final episode a week later. My sister and my daughter mixed her ashes in the patch of ground in which they had buried my father's eight years earlier. Afterwards my sister stood contemplating the spot and my daughter lit a cigarette. Which is not to say she was indifferent—she loved both her grandparents very much—merely that at times of emotion the young need a fag. □

ON THE ROOF
Geoff Dyer

Geoff Dyer (left); Brixton, Sunday June 22, 1986

Although I've written quite a lot about photography and photographers, I don't own a camera and hardly ever take photos. Apart from a few sexually explicit Polaroids, the only personal pictures I have are ones taken by friends, all crammed haphazardly in a folder in my filing cabinet. If I rummage around in this image-compost, I'm never sure what I'm going to dredge up. Last week I became convinced that I needed to see a photo of the sky-blue Vauxhall Victor my dad used to drive and in the course of looking for it (unsuccessfully), I came across this one, taken on the roof of a block of flats in Brixton, London, some time in the mid-Eighties.

I looked at it for quite a while, trying to remember more exactly when it was taken. Then I saw that, on the back of another one from the same afternoon (the same series, as photographers say), I'd written: 'Taken on the day England got knocked out of the World Cup by Argentina—Summer '86.' This meant that I was able to date the picture with absolute precision: Sunday June 22, 1986.

Back then my friends and I claimed to hate everything about England, including its football team, but I remember being pretty disappointed when Maradona single-handedly put an end to England's chances of making it to the semi-finals. Gutted, actually. Over the years this feeling—high hopes and nail-biting expectation culminating in the taste of ashes in the mouth—has become such a familiar part of watching England as to have taken on the quality of a national destiny. Not that anyone in the picture looks devastated or inconsolable. No, if it weren't for that caption you'd think this was just another afternoon on the roof of Crownstone Court. Brixton was a lot rougher then than it is now but the roof was like a waterless lido above the city. I loved it up there.

A friend recently said that, for as long as he could remember, his dream of perfect happiness had always centred around having a family (my idea of perfect misery). Perhaps I suffer from some kind of arrested development but my sense of perfect happiness has never progressed beyond a slightly archaic idea of bohemia. And it was in Brixton, in the Eighties, that this dream first came true.

Many people leave university with only a vague idea of what they might do for a living but I knew exactly what I wanted to do: sign on the dole. At Oxford, undergraduates reading English rarely went to lectures. The only thing you *had* to do was see your tutor once a week

115

(it might have been an obligation for the students but the tutor left you in no doubt that it was an unpardonable intrusion on his time). This set a precedent for the chore of signing on which, initially, also had to be done once a week. After a while, as the number of people out of work increased, this dropped to once a fortnight and, in Lambeth at least, to once a month. Thatcherism had ushered in an era of high unemployment but the safety net set up by the post-war commitment to the Welfare State was still just about intact. Housing Benefit paid your rent and Social Security gave you money to live on.

Mass unemployment might not be a desirable social or economic goal but it does mean that there are plenty of other people to hang out with in the afternoons. Before moving to Brixton I had lived briefly with a bunch of apprentice lawyers in a house in Balham. By nine in the morning they were all up and out and I was left on my own with nothing to do but lament my lot (i.e. my little). Then I moved into a house on Brixton Water Lane where only one of the six inhabitants was gainfully employed. The tables were abruptly turned: we felt sorry for her because she had to go to work. The rest of us did what we wanted all day. If Oxford had given me a taste for idleness, living on the dole in Brixton refined it. The difference was the quality of study—which, of course, was far higher in Brixton. Postgraduate work takes you down a path of greater and greater specialization (culminating in the supreme pointlessness of a PhD). In Brixton I went in the opposite direction: I read whatever interested me and, exactly as prescribed by the ardent young Sontag, I was 'interested in "everything"'.

It was an idyllic time and—such is the nature of idylls—it is now a vanished one. Students these days take out loans which oblige them to work part-time while they are studying and to start earning serious money once they have graduated (or at least after a gap year backpacking in Australia or South-East Asia). From this radically altered vantage point I see now what a privileged historical niche I occupied for the first twenty-five or more years of my life: free health care, free school, free tuition at university, a full maintenance grant and then—the icing on the cake—the dole!

I say 'free' but it was paid for, of course, by the sweat of my father's labour. My childhood memories of my dad involve him going to work and then coming home and working some more: on his allotment, on the garden, in his garage, on the house. Except for television (hour upon hour of it in winter) even hobbies like gardening had to take on the quality of an arduous chore if they were to be pursued with impunity. Work, like tidiness, was an absolute moral value. In common with many working-class parents mine hoped that after going to Oxford their only child might become middle class, but I went one better and became part of what Veblen termed the leisure class. Well, the low-income dosser class at any rate. If university taught me anything, it was that the world owed me a living. At Oxford I'd got used to doing pretty much as I pleased; on the dole I had even fewer claims on my time (signing on once a month soon came to seem a Herculean labour) and, in some ways, the situation has not changed since then.

I'd been doling it up for years when this picture was taken, but I had also managed to pull myself a few rungs up the ladder of welfare dependency: I'd moved out of the shared house on Brixton Water Lane and round the corner into a place of my own in Crownstone Court. The picture might well have been taken by one of the people who still lived back in the shared house, possibly by my friend P. J., the self-described 'dole wallah'.

It so happens that one of the people in this picture—Steve, the guy standing next to me—was not a doley (he was a solicitor, in fact), but if it had been taken on a sunny weekday rather than a Sunday there would have been an equivalent group of people up there, all of whom were unemployed and living within a mile radius, many of them (like Nick, the guy with his back to the camera) in the block itself. The roof was a form of what might be called Restricted Access Public Space (RAPS) where you could turn up without ever quite knowing who was going to be there. You could sit quietly on your own (reading, yoga) or hang out with whoever else was around. There was almost always someone up there you had never met before. But on any given day, though the individuals might have changed, the collective identity of the group remained more or less constant.

I say this and then, glancing through my diary for 1986, I see that the group ideal was already changing, dissolving, fragmenting. Steve's wife Sharon had left him and gone back to Chicago. The woman on his left was a new girlfriend whom I barely knew and she and Steve were together for only a few months. I was in the process of splitting up with Kate who I'd been going out with, on a freelance basis, for the previous three years. Which means that all sorts of people—most, actually—who were an essential part of the time and world the picture depicts aren't actually in it.

Steve was one of my closest friends. Then, as happens, we drifted apart. Actually, that puts it too passively. I came actively to dislike him. This happened much later, but by the time this picture was taken I'd already decided that I didn't like my old friend Scott—whom I'd known at school and university—any more either (he was always trying to sleep with my girlfriends) and by then he had certainly split up with Jessica (who I had tried to sleep with on several occasions). The more I look at this picture, in fact, the more conscious I become of the people who aren't in it. People such as Hannah (with whom I once had sex hours before having sex with Kate) and Nick's good friend Sally (who was probably downstairs having sex with Hannah), both of whom lived in Crownstone. 1986, 1986... I guess by then fear of Aids had made itself felt in the heterosexual world, but to me this picture evokes nothing else so much as the bareback heyday of unrestricted NSU.

To anyone looking at this picture it is probably hard to believe that someone with a physique (if we can dignify it with that word) like mine could ever have had the opportunity to contract any sexually transmitted disease from anyone. When I was fourteen my dad said I would thicken out when I got older and, at twenty-eight, when this picture was taken, I still hoped it might happen. Now I'm forty-four and realize it never will. Have you ever seen a leg like that outside of a famine-ravaged part of Africa? How does it function as a leg? How did it even keep me upright, let alone enable me to chase after these fit feminist chicks?

A clue is perhaps to be found on the ground, just behind the gnarled root of my right knee. I am referring, obviously, to my infamous home-made bong. Apart from my triumph at A Levels (three grade-As!) that bong was and will remain my greatest achievement. There are more elegant bongs in the world but few are more efficacious. I'm no longer in contact with anyone in the photograph, but I still have my loyal old bong. I made it from a chillum, a length of tubing and a coffee jar. The chillum is sealed in the lid of the coffee jar with candle wax but you can unscrew the lid and fill the jar with ice so that you're totally unaware you're smoking (or would be if you didn't start coughing your lungs up ten seconds later). I'm so glad that bong is in the picture. It played a decisive role in many of the key events on that roof. Listening to Miles Davis's *Sketches of Spain*, seeing a display team of parachutists drift into nearby Brockwell Park, playing tennis-ball catch with people on the roof of the neighbouring block... Without the bong they'd have just been great moments; that bong made them sublime, transcendental, timeless.

I wanted to preserve some of these stoner spots of time in a book, a kind of photo album with words instead of pictures. That's something else this picture doesn't record: that the skeletal figure on the left was possessed of a considerable desire to be a writer. When this photograph was taken I had already written an unbelievably boring book about John Berger, but what I really wanted to write was a book about the life I was leading then, a book, in fact, about that roof. Some of my contemporaries from Oxford had gone on to pursue successful careers; they had become yuppies, had a stake in the property boom, were part of the world imaginatively recorded by Michael Bracewell in his novel *The Conclave*. The flip side of this was the grim London of riots, unemployment and recession. That was the essential two-tone contrast of the Thatcher years. But there was also this in-between world of semi-creative idleness, of voluntary disenfranchisement. In some ways we had made a separate peace. It even seemed to me that there was a kind of aristocracy of welfare dependence, that a contemporary equivalent of the boundless leisure of the bright young things and the country-house novels of the Thirties or Forties or whenever it was could be found in the squats of Bonnington Square or Oval Mansions.

Most of the people in this scene harboured artistic hopes of one kind or another. Everyone wanted to be a writer, artist or film maker or something. In Britain, back then, the dole supported a whole generation of aspiring actors, dancers, writers. The dole was the equivalent of waiting tables in New York.

It is possible to have aspirations without having ambition—and vice versa. Whereas people coming out of university ten or fifteen years after me—Thatcher's children—combined the two, I had aspirations but was not ambitious. I liked the idea of writing because that was a way of not having a career. Those coming later saw writing *as* a career. And though many of my friends aspired to be artists not many of them had the will, talent, luck or stamina to stick at it. Some of them were just too lazy. That is the inevitable weakness of dole'n'dope culture. Not surprisingly, it was the dissolute models of Rimbaud or Kerouac (not Bukowski: we didn't sink that low) that appealed, especially the idea of a systematic derangement of the senses. A lot of people couldn't get beyond that phase of the artistic apprenticeship.

Let's suppose that, instead of me looking at the photograph fifteen years after it was taken, the younger version of my scrawny self was able, instead of just gazing out across the roof in his shades, to look fifteen years into the future. What has happened in the interim to the people who are in the picture and the people who should have been in it but aren't?

The same things that happen to everyone: home-ownership, marriage, a kid or two, disappointment, divorce, cancer scares, worsening hangovers, death of a parent or two, qualified success, school fees, depression, sudden rejuvenation following the discovery of Ecstasy, holidays in India or Ibiza, telly-watching, coming out (as homosexuals), coming in (as heterosexuals), going to the gym, more telly-watching, new computers, bad knees, less squash, more tennis, rewriting (and downplaying) of earlier ambitions to diminish scale of disappointment, fatal breast cancer, less sleep, less beer, more wine, more cocaine, hardly any acid, frightening ketamine overdose, total breakdown, more money, discreet tattoos, baldness, stopping going to the gym, yoga, even more telly-watching…

Some permutation of the above pretty well covers everyone. Me included—except that whereas many people my age are starting to feel worn down by the burden of obligations, responsibilities and commitments, it's the *freedom* that's getting to me. On Fridays I sometimes find myself thinking almost enviously of all those people who are coming home from work and looking forward to putting their feet up and having a couple of days off. That's the problem with having a lifetime off—you can never take a couple of days off. Yes, all those years of doing just what I want have started subtly to take their toll. Or perhaps it's just the first glimpse of middle age, the lure of television to which we all eventually succumb. But how could it have happened? How did I go from being interested in everything to not being that bothered about *anything*? When did the weather in the head cloud over like this? I am not only unsure how to describe this feeling, I am unsure exactly what I am describing. I certainly had no inkling of it—whatever it is—when this picture was taken, in 1986. But looking at the picture and its inscription, I realize it was familiar to me back then, that the taste of ashes in the mouth was as much a generalized premonition as a particular reaction to a football result. Destiny, I think, is not what lies in store for you; it's what is already stored up inside you—and it's as patient as death. □

THE SIEGE OF
MAZAR-I-SHARIF
Luke Harding

Mazar-i-Sharif, December 1, 2001

Of all the events from the three-day siege at the fort at Mazar-I-Sharif, in November 2001, the one I found hardest to forget was the request for tea: 'Could I have a cup of tea?' perfectly expressed in English. Then: 'We are very hungry. We have had nothing to eat.' I hadn't expected to find survivors—so much gun and rocket fire, at such close range, seemed impossible to survive—but in the semi-darkness of the shipping container, their temporary prison, I could see people who were definitely alive. From their looks and their dress, and from this request in English, I knew them to be Pakistanis. One was wearing a cardboard box over his head, perhaps in a feeble attempt to keep warm. Next to him, another shivered under a blanket. I could just make out, in the container's furthest corner, a man with almost no face. His nose and mouth had been shot away. His eyes shone out at me from the shadows.

We didn't know it then, but this was the end of the Taliban—their final surrender after what had been (though, again, those of us who witnessed it had no way knowing this at the time) the most significant struggle of the short war in Afghanistan. Was this final struggle intended? Was the slaughter inevitable? Or was it, as many armed conflicts must be, a long series of mistakes born out of vengefulness, ignorance and fear?

By the time I reached the Afghanistan border on November 17, 2001 it was clear that the Taliban were crumbling. Kabul had fallen five days before; Kandahar was looking wobbly; meanwhile, up in the north of Afghanistan, about 8,000 Taliban fighters were trapped in the town of Kunduz. Among them were an unknown number of 'foreign guests'—the Taliban regime's term for the thousands of Islamist volunteers who had poured into Afghanistan to support the Taliban cause. Most people in Afghanistan knew them as 'the Arabs', even though many of them came from Pakistan and the newly independent states of the former Soviet Union over the border to the north. Afghanistan wasn't new to me: as the South Asia correspondent for the *Guardian*, based in New Delhi, I'd made a couple of trips there in the era before September 11, when the regime was regarded as domestically oppressive rather than internationally dangerous. The year before, in Kabul, on one of these earlier visits, I'd seen a group of 'foreign guests', armed with Kalashnikovs and

Soviet-made machine guns. When they had sauntered into the restaurant where I was having lunch, the proprietor had ushered them into a private room. In a poor country their money marked them out, and, though their role then was mysterious, they were often said to be 'the real masters'. Now, at the border crossing at Torkham in the Khyber Pass, there was no sign of them or the Taliban. A mujahideen commander, who sat behind the iron gates smoking a large spliff, suggested he escort me through the darkness in an armed convoy to Jalalabad. 'The hills are still full of Arabs,' he said.

I spent a day in Kabul and pressed on northwards. The road to Kunduz led through the Hindu Kush mountains, already wrapped in snow. I walked through the Salang Tunnel—blown up, and partly blocked by ice and debris—and then took a taxi on through the newly liberated towns of Khinjan and Pul-i-Khumri. The next day I arrived at Aliabad, eighteen miles south of Kunduz and the front line for the Northern Alliance army which was intent on capturing it and defeating the Taliban. It was clear the Taliban's besieged northern army wasn't going anywhere. There was no way out. 'The Taliban are over there,' the Northern Alliance general, Haider Khan, explained, gesturing beyond a bleak brown escarpment. 'If they don't surrender we will kill them.'

Just round the corner, next to the river, an Afghan was leading his recalcitrant camel down a steep bank; another had halted his taxi and was trying—optimistically—to shoot ducks from the side of the road with his Kalashnikov. Refugees fleeing southwards from Kunduz in a succession of battered German tour buses brought harrowing stories. Two Talibs had shot dead a local doctor after he had failed to revive their wounded friend. Other Talibs had been gunned down by the 'Arab' troops among them when they had tried to sneak to safety across the front line. The siege had gone on for ten days. Everybody was terrified.

The Taliban were Pushtun, from the south, and Kunduz was one of the few towns in northern Afghanistan with a Pushtun majority. They had fled here to feel safe. This was an illusion. The mosque and the three schools where most of the Taliban were sheltering offered little protection against night bombing by B-52s. America had begun its air campaign against the Taliban on October 7, 2001. It had gone on for more than a month. By this stage nobody could be in any doubt about the Pentagon's determination to bomb its way to victory. A group of about 300 Pakistani volunteers who had been left behind during the Taliban's retreat had just been exterminated. They had been holed up in a school and were trying, it was said, to surrender when the school had taken a direct hit.

The Taliban had fled to Kunduz after abandoning Mazar-i-Sharif, ninety miles to the west and Afghanistan's most important northern city. It seemed to me that the fate of the Taliban who were still stuck in Kunduz depended on the man who now occupied Mazar-i-Sharif: the newly returned warlord-emperor, General Abdul Rashid Dostum.

I had heard about Dostum on previous trips; he enjoyed meeting visitors at his palace in the town of Shiberghan, where his garden had vines and peacocks. He was a bear-like man, a former plumber who had risen through the ranks of the pro-Soviet Afghan army and around whom a great personality cult had developed. During his fleeting public appearances he would wade through the crowds of well-wishers; troops paraded his framed portrait; women made carpets which lauded his heroism. And yet he was also, I would soon notice, scrupulous about his own security. He rarely left his palace without an escort of forty vehicles, including a tank and an anti-aircraft battery.

Dostum had risen, fallen, and risen again. He ruled a large chunk of northern Afghanistan for most of the 1990s until his deputy, General Abdul Malik, betrayed him. Malik gave Mazar to the Taliban in 1997. Malik then betrayed the Taliban just as he had earlier betrayed Dostum: his soldiers exterminated 3,000 Taliban fighters. The Taliban recaptured Mazar the next year. Now Dostum, their old enemy, was back and bent on recapturing his old fiefdom, with some new allies from Fort Campbell, Kentucky: the US Fifth Special Forces Group. They carried sophisticated communications equipment and wore desert khaki. Their apparent mission was to stick with Dostum wherever he went—to the gates of Kabul if necessary.

I decided to drive west to Mazar-i-Sharif to find him, and reached the city only a few hours before the arrival of an important emissary from Kunduz—the commander of the Taliban's northern army, Mullah Fahzel Mazloom, who had concluded that the Taliban's situation in Kunduz was hopeless. The only question was: to whom should he surrender, the Tajik forces to the east of Kunduz, or General Dostum's Uzbeks to the west? He seems to have believed that his best chance of securing a safe passage out of the war—and Afghanistan—lay with Dostum, an error that would eventually lead him to a cage in the American base at Guantánamo Bay in Cuba. Another Taliban commander, the multiply-disabled Mullah Dadullah, who cut the throats of his victims with his one good arm, had opted to stay behind in Kunduz.

The venue for negotiations between the general and the mullah was to be Dostum's personal fortress on the outskirts of Mazar—the Qala-i-Jhangi or Fort of War. This overblown baronial castle complete with towering mud ramparts and a theatrical moat had been built in the nineteenth century. It looked like something out of *Beau Geste*. All it lacked, it struck me, was a couple of buglers in kepis to blare out the reveille from its thick castellated walls. The Qala-i-Jhangi had served as Dostum's HQ before he fled to Uzbekistan and Turkey. It was now again the home of his Junbish-i-Milli-i-Islami, the National Islamic Movement militia.

Mullah Fahzel and his large escort of Taliban fighters arrived at the fort shortly before midnight on November 21. Several journalists and television crews were in the courtyard. We saw Mullah Fahzel, a short fat man with an enormous black turban and a green commando jacket, vanish upstairs with General Dostum. In the courtyard, two lots of troops stared warily at each other. While Fahzel and Dostum were negotiating over green tea and pistachios I wandered over to where Fahzel's guards were dozing next to their machine guns. They smiled. We shook hands. They were clearly delighted to be anywhere but Kunduz. At 2 a.m. the meeting ended. Dostum summoned us to his balcony suite to announce the terms of the deal: the Taliban's northern army had agreed to surrender without conditions. The fighters would give up their weapons. In the interests of Afghan unity nobody would get killed. There was a pause. What would happen to the foreign guests? Mullah Fahzel said: 'There will be no fighting. Nothing will happen. The Arabs and the Afghans are under my control.' Dostum added that the prisoners would be 'treated according to international law'.

On the general's lips, the phrase struck me immediately as odd; it was as if the general had said 'Blessed are the meek...' What could 'international law' mean in that place and at that time? How could it be applied, even if people agreed on what it meant? Afghanistan was a country brutalized by conflict, where the victors would sometimes massacre their enemies by cramming them into shipping containers. Later I thought of the phrase as a deceitful platitude. At the time I wondered where Dostum had got it from. The source was easily guessed. Earlier in the night a white Nissan jeep without registration plates had pulled into a corner of the compound. It belonged to Dostum's American advisers, who had entered the building via a back door, out of sight.

Two days later, with no sign of the surrendering Taliban, I set off from Mazar-i-Sharif with another reporter, Carlotta Gall of the *New York Times*. The road east was busy. We passed a checkpoint manned by Dostum's fighters, then dozens of jeeps packed with excitable soldiers. We kept going. And then—just ahead of us out in the desert—we saw hundreds of men wearing black turbans. They were sitting placidly among the dunes in neatly spaced groups. A few of them were dozing in the morning sunshine. 'Taliban!' our driver shouted. He spun the car round. We stopped for a moment and looked back. The men in the desert were clearly Taliban fighters, and they were still armed.

We talked to one of Dostum's local commanders, Gulam Sakhi. 'There are four hundred of them. Only thirty of them are Afghan. The rest are foreigners,' he said. 'Some of them are Pakistanis and Chechens. They came in their trucks overnight from Kunduz. They still have their weapons on them. They have agreed to surrender.' This, then, was the Taliban's foreign legion, which had been trapped in Kunduz for almost three weeks. They had arrived at 3 a.m. Their Afghan Taliban commander—who had been negotiating with his opposite number, Gulam Sakhi—tapped on our window. He was dressed in a blanket and a green turban and had dark, kohl-streaked eyes. 'He says it is time to leave,' Gulam Sakhi said.

The group we had blundered into was the first to surrender; thousands of other fighters would follow. With their collapse in the north, the Taliban were no longer a pan-Afghan force but merely a small provincial army which ruled over a rapidly shrinking southern empire. The Taliban's six-year reign was ending in a landscape of shimmering desert and telegraph poles. It was history, almost.

Still, I was surprised that the Taliban's foreign fighters had given up so easily. They were famous for their commitment to the Islamist cause, and for their willingness to die as martyrs. And, as opposition soldiers testified, they were adept at using all kinds of weapons.

In the afternoon, the round-up began. We followed Dostum to the top of a mound which gave him a masterful view of the surrendering army, and at the summit caught up for the first time with the US Fifth Special Forces Group. Five American soldiers—one wearing a woolly Afghan hat—were twiddling with a black communications aerial in a forward mud bunker. Some had grown beards to look more Afghan. They were not pleased to see us.

'Can you clear these guys away,' one of them grumbled. 'There are mines over there.'

They'd arrived in a small white van bearing the words BELL MATE COFFEE, perhaps as a joke or as a serious attempt at disguise. They were young and understandably nervous and warned us solemnly not to reveal their presence in Afghanistan ('I don't want a letter of anthrax,' said one). To say they were responsible for the disaster that was about to happen wouldn't be right, but their advice at this point played a crucial part in it. General Dostum had intended to take his prisoners to the damaged Soviet-built airport on the edge of Mazar, which would mean that they would be kept in clear view of their captors. His American advisers, however, said that the US military might need the runway. They suggested that the Qala-i-Jhangi fort was a better option. The fort was a complicated series of buildings, hard to police. Also, it was filled with weapons. But Dostum agreed. His militia cascaded down the hill and drove off in their jeeps towards the front line. We waited for three hours. Slowly, Dostum's soldiers collected their enemy's weapons: Kalashnikovs, machine guns and gleaming green piles of ammunition. We wondered what would happen to the prisoners. 'They will be taken to Mazar-i-Sharif. They will then be treated according to international law,' Dostum said again. 'Be careful,' he added with what turned out to be prescience, 'that they don't throw anything at you.'

It was Ramadan, when no food can be eaten between dawn and dusk. As the afternoon wore on, the Junbish guards began to tire of collecting and carrying weapons and escorting prisoners into trucks; they wanted to be back at the fort in time for sundown and five o'clock dinner. Five open trucks were now loaded with prisoners, but only in the loading of the first three had the prisoners been thoroughly searched. The guards waved the last two trucks forward and the convoy set off towards Mazar. The men inside the trucks looked sullen and hating. Some appeared to be Pakistani; all had wild beards; a few wore gold-embroidered prayer caps. I wondered where they thought they were going. Mullah Fahzel, I gathered later from talking to the few who would survive, had informed the 'foreign guests' that if they surrendered their weapons they would be allowed to go home. They were under the impression that their convoy would continue to the city of Herat, and from there they could travel south through the desert to Kandahar, then still under Taliban control. Fahzel must have known better, of course. He had betrayed them, knowing that the US authorities would want to interrogate them over their possible links with al-Qaida—and would in all probability lock them up.

With his prisoners out of the way, General Dostum now set off to organize the surrender of the rest of the Taliban army which remained ninety miles away in Kunduz. We followed him across the desert in a cavalcade of armoured personnel carriers decorated with mujahideen flags and 4 x 4 buggies containing US Rangers in goggles and balaclavas. As dusk fell, the convoy halted. The US Special Forces travelling immediately behind Dostum got out and posed for a picture with him, taken by an American officer. They seemed jubilant. In their enthusiasm to wrap up their mission, they had left only two of their colleagues behind in the Qala-i-Jhangi fort. Both were CIA agents: Johnny 'Mike' Spann and Dave Tyson. Their job was to screen the Taliban prisoners for links with al-Qaida.

I returned that night to the Red Cross compound in Mazar to recharge my satellite phone ahead of an uncertain trip into the desert. I had already decided that the following morning, Sunday, November 25, I would watch the Taliban surrender to Dostum's army rather than return to the Qala-i-Jhangi. Dostum had halted his army at Erganak, a mountainous ridge twelve miles outside Kunduz. His troops had taken up position on hills on either side of the road which plunged down into the haze towards the village of Chahar Darreh, a few miles away, where the Taliban army was encamped on the plain. By four in the afternoon Dostum's soldiers were hungry and looking forward to the hour when they could eat. Several of them sitting in a tank emplacement had already piled hunks of bread on to their Kalashnikovs, which lay flat on the parapet; others had killed a sheep and were cooking it in a metal wok. A few yards from where we stood an American officer was peering into his binoculars at a jeep which was advancing tentatively across the desert below and sending up rolling waves of dust.

'There's a Taliban dude there as well,' the officer said.

'Are they moving?' another soldier, sitting next to a large satellite aerial, asked.

'They are trying to make contact with the leaders on the radio,' came back the reply.

The vehicle stopped again. The soldier said: 'They are evil guys. They are quite prepared to die.'

Over on the other hill, where Dostum's gold-painted Landcruiser had been hidden in another tank emplacement, something appeared to have gone wrong. The Taliban were supposed to have surrendered by now. Instead their advance had been delayed and Dostum's commanders, it now appeared, had instructed them to stay put. It was getting dark. We climbed up, past unexploded US cluster bombs—deadly yellow tubes attached to delicate white parachutes—and the discarded wrappers of emergency meal rations marked: A GIFT FROM THE PEOPLE OF THE UNITED STATES. One of Dostum's aides explained that there was a hitch—a big hitch. There had been a revolt at the fort, he said.

In the days that followed I managed to piece together what had happened at the Qala-i-Jhangi on that day, November 25, and on the night before, after the Taliban's foreign fighters had reached the fort in their lorries.

The few boy soldiers left in the Qala-i-Jhangi had herded the new arrivals into the fort's southern compound, which had only one entrance and was surrounded by high parapets. It had a large courtyard. On the left-hand side next to the wall stood a stable block; in the middle an avenue of pines and a pomegranate tree concealed a bandstand; to the right lay a pink-painted military classroom; four shipping containers used as a weapons dump stood on its edge.

Dostum's chief of police, Nader Ali, had begun searching the prisoners soon after they arrived. One of them produced a grenade and blew Ali up. Several journalists caught the explosion on camera. A reporter for Independent Television News, Andrea Catherwood, had her leg pierced by a piece of shrapnel. Dostum's guards carried Ali away in a blanket, bloodied and dying. The guards regained control, but they abandoned the search for weapons. Later that evening eight Arab fighters, all of them dressed in tracksuits, sat in a circle in the stables and blew out their stomachs using more grenades. It was then, according to Amir Jan, the commander who had coordinated the surrender, that the guards realized that their prisoners were more than usually dangerous. 'We agreed it would be better to tie up their hands and put them in the basement.'

The prisoners spent the night in five underground rooms beneath the military classroom and next morning were marched one by one into the courtyard, where they were made to sit in straight lines with their arms tied to their sides. Several were badly injured; some groaned in pain. We know this, and what happened next, because an enterprising Afghan cameraman, Najibullah Qureshi, spent two hours in the compound that morning filming the events. His film shows the guards dragging selected prisoners to the edge of the courtyard, where they sit on a couple of grubby blankets to face interrogation by the CIA men, Mike Spann and Dave Tyson. Spann cuts a swashbuckling figure: dressed in light blue jeans and a black fleece, he carries a Kalashnikov slung across his back. He and Tyson, who can be heard speaking Uzbek, are trying to establish each prisoner's nationality. The film shows one unusually white prisoner sitting mutely on the ground, refusing to answer.

'Irish, Ireland?' Spann asks.

There is no reply.

'Who brought you here? Hey, who brought you here? You believe in what you are doing here that much, you're willing to be killed here?'

Spann snaps his fingers. A guard pulls back the fighter's floppy black fringe and Spann takes a picture with a digital camera.

'Hello. Wake up. Who brought you here? How did you get here?'

He turns to Tyson: 'He won't talk to me. We explain what the deal is.'

Tyson says: 'The problem is, he's got to decide if he wants to live or die, and die here. We're just going to leave him, and he's going to fucking sit in prison for the rest of his fucking short life. It's his decision, man. We can only help the guys who want to talk to us. We can only get the Red Cross to help so many guys.'

There are 400 prisoners at the fort. By 11.20 a.m. all but sixty of them have been tied up and dumped in the courtyard. Many look terrified. One prisoner claims he is a reporter with the Arabic TV station, Al-Jazeera. 'I am not a mujahideen,' he pleads in English.

The two CIA agents seem not to notice—or not to be bothered by—the fact that they are two Americans in a courtyard crammed with angry and confused Taliban fighters. They seem unaware of the provocation and the target that they offer. They begin chatting with an Uzbek prisoner from the revolutionary Islamic Movement of Uzbekistan (IMU), whose legendary leader, Juma Namangani, has been killed days earlier in an American air strike. Then Spann moves out of the frame. Then there is a commotion—a sudden explosion of shouting and fear.

Qureshi switched off his camera and ran.

Qureshi's film ends here, but not his testimony. The commotion off-camera was caused by two Uzbek prisoners who had run up the steps, shouting, '*Allah-u-Akbar,*' 'God is great'. One of the prisoners was the IMU's commander. He lobbed a grenade at the guards. They fell down. The two prisoners then grabbed the guards' weapons and started firing. It was then, according to Qureshi, that Spann 'did a Rambo'. As the remaining guards ran away, Spann flung himself to the ground and began raking the courtyard and its prisoners with automatic fire. Five or six prisoners jumped on him, and he disappeared beneath a heap of bodies.

Qureshi said: 'Mike defended by fighting and kicking and boxing. The Taliban seized Mike's Kalashnikov. But he took out his two pistols and managed to shoot six or seven guys. He got his weapon back and carried on firing. I then saw a Taliban fighter running at him. Then I heard an explosion.'

Other eyewitnesses claim that Spann was beaten up and then shot, probably with his own weapon. But by either account, his death was savage: the first American to die in combat in Afghanistan. The CIA's director George Tenet later described him as an 'American hero'. Tenet said: 'Mike fell bringing freedom to a distant people. We will continue our battle against evil with renewed strength and spirit.'

His partner, Tyson, managed to get away—by shooting dead four prisoners, including one who jumped on his back. Dostum's soldiers had already retreated in disarray into the fort's main building, 500 yards away. Several Taliban prisoners ran out from the compound, climbed into the pine trees and started sniping. It seemed that the Taliban prisoners were on the brink of capturing the entire fort. As they looted buildings for heavy weapons such as rocket launchers and mortars, civilians trapped inside the fort scrambled out. Two Red Cross workers jumped out of a window and left their jeep blazing in the courtyard. Many of the prisoners played no part in the revolt and took shelter from the crossfire in basements and ditches. Nearly every prisoner, however, was to share the same fate.

Dave Tyson, who had just seen his colleague die, borrowed a satellite phone from a German TV crew and telephoned the nearest US embassy, over the border in Tashkent. 'We have lost control,' he said. 'Send in helicopters and troops.' American military commanders, however, chose to respond in a more characteristic way. One hour after the mutiny began, the first American missile plunged into the stable area where many of the Taliban had been sheltering. A team of US 'combat air controllers' who were camping nearby in a hospital had scrambled to the scene. Lying flat against the parapets overlooking the Taliban's compound, they called in a succession of air strikes. High-flying fighter aircraft dropped at least nine bombs. Missiles smashed two brick houses and incinerated the shipping containers which the Taliban had looted for arms. An unknown number of prisoners died.

The American air controllers had two linked objectives, according to a journalist who sat next to them as the battle unfolded, and who listened to their radio conversations. The priority was to recover Mike Spann's body. But this meant killing all the prisoners. British troops joined their endeavour. Eight SAS soldiers arrived with the Americans. They pulled into the Qala-i-Jhangi in two white Land-Rovers. The British soldiers were casually dressed in jeans and jumpers and hid their faces with black-and-white checked scarves. At the time one of the Red Cross workers, who had served in the British army, told me: 'The SAS have been leading the firing at the Taliban's positions. You can tell they are Special Forces because their

Luke Harding

firing is more disciplined. They use single shots rather than bursts.'

That wasn't always true. Najibullah Qureshi filmed the British in action, and his film shows three SAS men firing repeated bursts from a heavy machine gun positioned behind a wall on the ramparts. One soldier, wrapped in a bullet belt, unleashes hundreds of rounds into the trees in the courtyard below. When the first bomb lands on the stable block, all three soldiers jump up and drill rifle fire towards any survivors who might be fleeing the wreckage. When dusk falls, they decide to leave.

'That's it, mate,' an SAS man tells the Americans.

When I got back to the Qala-i-Jhangi the next day, Monday November 26, the allies were still busy directing the Taliban's death rites. Their presence wasn't much of a secret. A Toyota jeep full of new American soldiers had pulled up earlier outside the fort's gates. Unlike the SAS, the Americans made no effort to hide their faces. An altercation with a TV crew, which filmed them, followed. One of the US soldiers cocked his weapon. The TV crew told him to fuck off.

We parked our car behind a high mud wall 500 yards away from the fort, and began advancing slowly towards it, through muddy fields of cotton. There was an explosion of gunfire—pop pop pop—and I ducked. A group of Afghans laughed: I hadn't recognized the sound of outgoing, as opposed to incoming, fire. A few seconds later a Taliban mortar came flying over the battlements, landing close to where they had been standing; no more laughter. The Taliban had improvised a mortar factory next to the bombed-out ruins of the kitchen, and were trying to blow out Dostum's HQ on the fort's southern wall. They weren't missing by much. Dostum's fighters, more numerous now and in control of the strategic high walls above the Taliban's compound, were firing away wildly. As I edged round to the outer ramparts, dozens of Junbish guards came streaming out of the fort in panic. 'The Taliban are breaking out,' someone shouted. We ran and collapsed panting behind a mud wall. But the Taliban, hiding in groves of willows and alders, were too pinned down to do much running.

Far above this fighting on the ground, B-52s glided serenely across a blue sky. They dropped one big bomb that day—a 2,000 pounder—which should have obliterated the remaining rebels. It missed the

136

compound, however, and instead destroyed an outer gatehouse occupied by Dostum's soldiers, and by the American forward air controllers who had called in the strike. Eight of Dostum's soldiers were killed, and all five Americans injured. (The error was one of several during the US bombing of Afghanistan. In this case, the pilot had received two sets of coordinates. One showed the intended target, the other indicated the position of the air controllers on the ground. The pilot may have punched in the wrong set of coordinates. Or the bomb may for other reasons have fallen short.)

It was a strange day. When I eventually got to the fort I met Angus Roxburgh, the BBC correspondent. 'We thought you were dead,' he exclaimed. While I was away at Erganak a reporter from *Time* magazine had filed a story claiming that the Taliban had dragged a *Guardian* journalist into their compound, and that he was now missing, presumed dead. The source was an Afghan commander who in the fighting of the day before had confused me with Spann. Spann's body, meanwhile, still lay sprawled in the courtyard. People said it was booby-trapped, that a grenade had been hidden under him.

Defiant bursts of gunfire came from the Taliban positions for the rest of the day. It was hard to know how many of them wanted to die and how many wanted to surrender or flee, and live. On the first evening three unarmed Pakistanis made a doomed attempt to escape by creeping in the darkness through the undergrowth along the route of a water channel. They got out of the fort, but not very far. One reached the nearby village, where local Afghans shot him dead. The other two scarcely got beyond the outer wall before being killed. They were all dressed in flimsy salwar kameez and carried nothing but a few crusts of bread.

Driving into the fort early the next day, November 26, I found a crowd gathered by the road. The bodies of three light-skinned Taliban fighters lay in the mud. Nobody was sure whether they had escaped from the fort during the early confusion, or had been holed up in an outbuilding for three weeks, following the Taliban's flight to Kunduz. They'd been shot the night before. We tried to work out where they were from. A traffic policeman suggested Chechnya.

Many Junbish soldiers were dying too. As the battle for the Qala-i-Jhangi entered its third day, Dostum's troops began carrying out the dead and wounded among their comrades. They lugged the dead out in grey blankets; the injured were bundled into taxis, dripping blood. A few Taliban prisoners—they must have been exhausted and dehydrated—were still firing at any target that presented itself. Then, in the afternoon, three suicidally brave Junbish soldiers jumped into the Taliban's compound in an attempt to kill a solitary prisoner hidden in a foxhole. He shot back. They fled but came back seconds later and flung a grenade into his hiding place. There was silence. It all appeared to be over.

Slowly and carefully Dostum's troops climbed down into the shattered courtyard and began to turn over the corpses. They found one badly injured Taliban prisoner lying on the ground, still alive. They threw a rock at his head. And then, perhaps predictably, five Taliban fighters emerged from a room in the stable block shouting, 'Allah-u-Akbar,' and firing randomly. The Junbish soldiers ran back up the sloping path that led to the upper parapets, and soon the compound was once again a blaze of gunfire. Several hours later Dostum's troops had another go. I watched a tank roll noisily through the fort's pockmarked gates. It fired several shells. The prisoners did not respond. By evening, it all appeared to be over again.

Early the next morning, Dostum's soldiers led us inside the Qala-i-Jhangi to survey the carnage. We had expected slaughter, but I was unprepared for its hellish scale. The first Taliban body lay sprawled in a ditch next to the front gateway. After a short walk through an avenue of splintered pines and outbuildings full of bullet holes, there were more bodies. Near the entrance to the citadel where the Taliban had been holed up, about forty prisoners lay covered in dust. The place smelled sweetly of decaying flesh.

A few journalists crunched around the debris while Dostum's soldiers got on with the more urgent business of looting. None of them showed any pity for their dead adversaries. I watched one soldier gingerly ease the trainers off a Taliban corpse and stick them on his own feet; another was trying to yank out a dead prisoner's gold tooth. By the afternoon there were no shoes left on any of the corpses. I talked to one of Dostum's soldiers—his name was Amanraj—about what had happened, and he was perfectly clear in his reasoning. 'If we had allowed the Taliban to surrender they would have simply started fighting again. We are sorry they were killed because they were Muslims, but we had no alternative but to kill them.'

Near the stable block a few fires still smouldered. The bloated remains of about twenty grinning horses lay in the scorched grass. One horse, a white one, had somehow survived and rolled helplessly on the ground. Dostum's soldiers gave it some oats, then shot it.

There were clues as to why many of the prisoners had preferred death to surrender. Several Koranic primers in Urdu and Arabic lay on the ground near the bombed-out remains of the pedimented house where the Taliban had been sheltering. Among the fluttering pages, one verse read in Urdu: 'Trust in Islam and there will be life after death.' It seemed probable that the Taliban volunteers had been alternately reading the Koran and lobbing mortars at the enemies who surrounded and finally engulfed them.

Next to the remains of the kitchen a rocket mounted on a tripod and a pile of fin-tailed mortars had been stacked neatly against the wall. The corpses of Arab volunteers lay all around, members of the Taliban's Arabic-speaking Ansar brigade. Even in death they looked better off than their comrades from Pakistan. One still wore his San Francisco 49ers football sweatshirt, another had a zip-up Dolce and Gabbana top.

After a few hours it was hard to take it all in. The dead and various parts of the dead (torsos, arms, penises) turned up wherever you looked: in thickets of willows and poplars; in waterlogged ditches; in storage rooms piled with ammunition boxes. One fighter had his arms thrown up in astonishment, as if his death were a surprise. I counted 166 corpses. The figure included seven or eight with their hands still tied behind their back (a photographer who arrived early said Dostum's soldiers had untied many other corpses).

As Red Cross workers started heaping the dead on to a tractor-drawn truck, General Dostum gave a kind of impromptu press conference from his debris-strewn balcony. About fifty of his soldiers had been killed and another 200 wounded, he said. The dead included three of his senior commanders and they had wives and children. 'We tried to treat the Taliban humanely,' Dostum said. 'We gave them a chance to wash and to pray, but they attacked us. We could have tied their hands and legs, but we didn't.'

How true was this? At no stage had Dostum or his American advisers attempted to negotiate with the Taliban rebels after the revolt broke out. Nor had they taken account of the fact that a substantial minority of the prisoners did not want to fight. Dostum's Northern Alliance and his British and American allies had only one plan: to kill all those in the compound. After an enormous effort and a three-day battle they had succeeded. But at the time it was hard to see what alternative Dostum had. The Uzbeks and the Arabs who started the fighting had no intention of surrendering. The next day British ministers and American commanders justified the slaughter. 'The situation had to be dealt with and you cannot be too squeamish,' a British government source told a colleague. A US spokesman in Islamabad, Keith Kenton, added, 'What happened at Mazar-i-Sharif was not a massacre. It was a pitched battle.'

The revolt was the Taliban's last stand; a final act of defiance before the regime sank into exile and oblivion. Surrounded by the carnage of the Qala-i-Jhangi it was clear to me—and probably to every other reporter there—that the USA's campaign against the Afghan president Mullah Mohammad Omar was heading towards total victory. Except that, even now at the fort, it wasn't quite over. As I prepared to leave, Dostum's soldiers beckoned me towards the shot-up classroom in the centre of the courtyard. Two Taliban volunteers were still down there and still alive, they said. At nine that morning a government soldier had peered down the stairs. They had shot him in the hand. Another soldier, Mohammed Asif, said to me: 'They are hungry and they are thirsty. But they are still fighting. We listened and they were speaking to each other in Urdu. We couldn't understand what they were saying.' He added: 'They are speaking right now. We are trying to kill them.'

Over the next three hours I watched from the battlements as Dostum's troops came up with increasingly ingenious strategies to finish them off. They poured oil into the building and set it ablaze. They rolled grenades down the stairs. They fired shots every few minutes—as a reminder, just in case the prisoners had somehow forgotten, that death was very near. Finally at 12.30 p.m. a genial commander, Din Mohammed, manoeuvred a six-foot rocket into a drainage chute that appeared to lead directly to the underground hideout. The rocket fizzed orange. Then it exploded, sending a furious back-blast of dust into the trees. Things went very quiet—it would be true to say there was a tomb-like silence.

'We are certain they are dead. But we will explode a few more rockets just to be sure,' Din Mohammed said.

I went back to the Red Cross compound, took a long shower, and filed my story.

The next day the guards who had been posted on either side of the classroom were stood down in the confident belief that everyone underneath was dead. Someone, though, had to carry out the bodies. Later that afternoon five Afghan workers from the Red Cross armed with only a torch ventured into the basement. They had taken twenty steps down when someone fired at them three times. 'I was shot in the arm. We hid in a corner of a wall and then we ran away,' one of the Red Cross men, Mohammad Karim, told me when I found him in hospital that evening. Only four of the five who had gone down came out alive, he said. The Taliban were surviving by eating a dead horse they had dragged into their chamber, he added.

The news that at least one prisoner was still down there brought the SAS and US Special Forces rushing back to the Qala-i-Jhangi. They spent the afternoon directing operations, as Dostum's troops levered yet more rockets into the basement.

Two days passed. I was puzzled by the discrepancy between the number of prisoners who arrived at the fort—400—and the number of bodies I had seen. A lot of prisoners were missing. Early on the morning of Saturday December 1, I decided to pay a valedictory trip to Dostum's ruined fort. Only a few guards were up and about; the main commotion was birdsong. As I walked through the rubble, a commander I didn't know waved me over to a shipping container, which he then unlocked and opened. There were thirteen Taliban fighters sitting in the gloom. They had emerged the previous night, the commander said, from the underground basement where they had been hiding for six days, surviving every rocket, bullet and grenade that had been flung at them. And now one of them made his request: 'Could I have a cup of tea?'

Of the thirteen inside the container, one man was Afghan and the remainder Pakistani. The prisoner who wanted the tea said he had tried to give up two days earlier. 'We wanted to surrender on Thursday. But there was a group of seven Arabs who wouldn't let us.' There were others still down in the cellar, he said.

I felt dazed. Everybody was supposed to be dead. I asked the commander if he could bring the Pakistanis some tea, but he shook his head and banged the container door shut. I ran back to my car, drove into town and went to the Red Cross. By the time I got back to the Qala-i-Jhangi forty minutes later, a spectral procession of Taliban prisoners was emerging from the basement into the winter sun. The guards were bringing them out one by one, searching them, and then sending them, shuffling and shoeless, towards us. A guard shouted out their nationalities in turn, in a tone that implied 'Look, none of these buggers is Afghan!'. 'Uzbekistan!' Pakistan! Yemen! Chechnya!' We shouted out questions. 'Where are you from?' 'What are you doing here?'

These were not the demons of Western imagining—they were sad, haunted-looking young men. Their nationalities, so far as we could tell, also included Sudanese, Somali, Saudi and Kuwaiti. One or two were Uighurs—from China's Muslim Xinjiang province. A young curly-haired prisoner, later identified as Yaser Esam Hamdi, told me that he came from a middle-class Arab family in Baton Rouge, Louisiana. But it was a scruffy figure in a black jumper who stood out most: a white man with a boyish face, long hair and a lank beard. I asked him where he was from. 'The Caucasus,' he mumbled. Later that evening a reporter from *Newsweek* had another go at him and the real facts emerged. He was John Walker Lindh from Marin County, California; a twenty-year-old US citizen who had converted to Islam at the age of sixteen, met the Taliban while he was a Koranic student in Pakistan, and who, the previous summer, had emailed his parents telling them that he was 'alive and well' and going 'somewhere cooler'.

Lindh was the prisoner Najibullah Qureshi had caught in his film six days before—the man who had so irritated his fellow Americans, Spann and Tyson, by refusing to answer their questions. He was the war's most compelling curio, and lucky to be alive.

After the unharmed prisoners came out of the cellar, it was the turn of the wounded and the dead. Several prisoners on stretchers lay dying in front of us in the cold. As a team from the Red Cross began to treat the wounded, I talked to a twenty-six-year-old volunteer from Uzbekistan, Abdul Jabar, about his reasons for being there. Why had he come? 'We are not against Americans,' Jabar said, 'but I believe that we should live by Islam and that the only real Islamic state is Afghanistan.' A nurse was dressing a bullet

John Walker Lindh, Qala-i-Jhangi, December 3, 2001

hole in his foot. Jabar described how he had survived by hiding in ditches when the first bombs fell, and then by fleeing into the basement. 'There are many dead people there. The commander said we would fight to the last bit of blood. We gave up because we had nothing left. We had no weapons and no ammunition,' he told me. They'd managed to endure the rockets and the burning oil but decided to surrender after Dostum's guards flooded the basement with freezing water. Even so, they'd spent twenty hours standing in the water before giving up.

After all that, his biggest fear was being sent back to Uzbekistan: 'It would be the end.'

The Red Cross team started handing out fruit. I put down my pen and fed an Arab prisoner a banana. He was unable to peel it: his hands were tied behind his back. Did he speak English? He didn't. His eyes beamed with gratitude. The prisoners had eaten nothing for a week.

Eventually, after a prisoner had been sent back into the cellar so that he could report back and declare it free of the living, I walked down the bombed-out entrance to the tunnel and peered into the dark. A chamber two feet deep in water led to a network of rooms. Water streamed from the roof; an upturned body bobbed in the filth; the smell of putrefaction rose to meet me. It had been a cold, terrifying and squalid extinction.

Outside, a large lorry carrying a blue shipping container pulled up. The guards started bundling the prisoners into it, including those who were gravely injured, and then the truck and its container rolled off towards the town of Shiberghan, where the remnants of the Taliban's once fearsome foreign legion were locked up in the town's tiny prison. Four of them died there that evening.

The Red Cross eventually recovered 237 Taliban bodies from the ruins of the Qala-i-Jhangi. Of the eighty-odd survivors, most did not remain in Shiberghan for long. US military planes flew them first to Kandahar and then to Guantanamo Bay. There, manacled and hooded, they began a new life in their metal cages, deprived of all legal rights. The Bush administration refused to identify or comment on any of the prisoners, but reports from Washington suggested that they had been of little intelligence value in the war against al-Qaida. In October 2002 John Walker Lindh appeared before a US court and apologized for fighting for the Taliban, though he said that during the entire siege he had not managed to fire his weapon. The court sentenced him to twenty years in jail. As for the Uzbeki, Abdul Jabar, General Dostum secretly returned him and nine other members of the Islamic Movement of Uzbekistan to the care of Uzbekistan's president, Islam Karimov. None has been seen since.

Nine months passed before I returned to Mazar-i-Sharif. The war was long over, but what had occurred during it remained debatable; for this reason, at my hotel in Mazar, I borrowed a spade. A few months earlier, in January 2002, a group of American physicians from Boston had discovered a mass grave in the desert just outside Shiberghan. Whose remains did the grave contain? The likeliest explanation was bodies from the Taliban army that had surrendered to Dostum at Erganak on the day the revolt at the Qala-i-Jhangi had broken out. We had returned to Mazar to witness the battle at the fort; those of Dostum's troops who remained at Erganak, had meanwhile rounded up several thousand Taliban prisoners and packed them into shipping containers for transportation west to Shiberghan. Nobody knew how many had perished on this journey—some estimates suggested about 900—but that many had died seemed beyond any doubt. Shiberghan prison still contained about 1,200 Taliban soldiers and I managed to talk to several of them through the bars of their cells. The conditions inside the containers had been terrible. A Pakistani, Irfan Ali, said: 'There was no air and it was very hot. There were 300 of us in my container. By the time we arrived in Shiberghan only ten of us were still alive.' The eighty-three-mile journey should have taken only a couple of hours; Irfan Ali had survived nineteen hours in his container.

Allegations of mass execution are easy to make but hard to prove, and I wanted to see the grave for myself. And so, with my spade and a photographer and a translator, I set off into the desert outside Shiberghan. Trying to find a mass grave in the desert wasn't as easy as we'd imagined. On the first day we dug in the wrong place. On the second day we went back with Najibullah Qureshi, the cameraman who had recorded Qala-i-Jhangi and who, after the siege, had interviewed on film the drivers who had driven the containers with the Taliban inside. They had given a grim account of the prisoners' final moments. Most had suffocated, though many also seem to have died when Dostum's guards shot into several of the containers while they were parked at Mazar. The dead, and a few who were merely unconscious, were loaded into lorries and taken into the desert, where Dostum's soldiers raked them with bullets to make sure there were no survivors. Then they buried them.

With Qureshi's help, we found the right spot near the village of Dasht-i-Leila. The evidence lay abundantly on the surface: tattered black turbans, charred shoes, a prayer cap, jaws, femurs, ribs. A bit of digging turned up most of a skeleton. We found teeth and thick human hair. The site was littered with spent cartridges. It was easy to imagine how these people had disappeared on that cold day in November 2001.

We poked about for a while among the debris and the indifferent sand, and then we left. □

ANOTHER AGE
Helon Habila

From left: Helon Habila, Odia Ofeimun and Tony Kan, Lagos 2002

The first time I saw Odia Ofeimun was at a party in Lagos. We came late, Toni Kan and I. It was a Friday, we had left the office and stopped at several barrooms on the way, and by nine o'clock, when we arrived at the party, we were tipsy. But we were in good company: almost everyone was high. There was an air of euphoria in the room; it was the same all over the country. This was November 1999. The country had just emerged from fifteen years of military dictatorship. Everyone was savouring that feeling of having survived a shipwreck, or a plane crash. The future looked bright, especially for the people gathered in this room: over a hundred of them, poets and writers and playwrights. In everyday life they were journalists and teachers and out-of-work graduates, a handful who had narrowly survived General Abacha's elite-exterminating agenda which saw a lot of pro-democracy intellectuals killed or exiled or compromised. Those who could not afford to go into exile during the reign of terror, and who refused to become turncoats, had lived in a sort of limbo, occasionally bringing out a book of poems or stories or essays whose oblique metaphors and idioms made sense only to other writers. Tonight these writers were being hosted by Maik, a novelist and journalist, and the booze was flowing. They were exchanging stories about fellow writers exiled in foreign capitals. Next to me two young men were arguing about a poet who had been found strangled in his car the year before.

'He sold out!' one insisted.

'Then why was he killed?' the other shouted back angrily.

'He refused to sell out, that's why!'

The poet's death is still a subject of controversy in Nigerian literary circles. He was found dead in his car in a ditch close to Omole Estate on the Lagos mainland. The car boot was full of poetry books. It is one of the many unsolved murder mysteries from the military era.

On the balconies, in the rooms, people came and went, talking about their latest works. Toni pointed out a slim, fair-skinned man in a corner. 'That's Chiedu, he won the MuSoN poetry competition last year. He's the hottest poet in the country right now.' The story was that after he had received the prize (awarded annually by the Musical Society of Nigeria), Chiedu and a group of poets had gone into the nearest bar with the prize money and emerged the next day, the money gone. Odia, perhaps the oldest man in the room, abstemious, avuncular, wearing his trademark batik *dashiki* and a matching cap, went from group to group, listening, nodding, putting in a word here and there.

Later, in my novel, *Waiting for an Angel*, I tried to recreate that occasion using the same mix of ingredients: poets, alcohol, camaraderie, euphoria—but in the book the euphoria is not of celebration and hope, but of panic and despair. I put the time back to 1997, the last days of General Abacha's reign of terror. Those were days of wanton killings, of activists shot in their cars in broad daylight, of student riots controlled by guns.

In the story, Lomba and James, a reporter and his editor, are running from Abacha's equivalents of the Tontons Macoute, and after going from one back street to another, all of them lined with dead bodies and queues of cars waiting for fuel, they finally end up at the house of a fellow poet and activist, Emeka Davies. A party is going on: two poets have been arrested at the Nigeria–Benin border and the party is in their honour. There are readings and speeches. Outside, soldiers roam the streets, and Tontons Macoute in their dark glasses patrol the back alleys, eliminating anybody who sees things differently from them. It is usually necessary to exaggerate and defamiliarize events in stories to make them captivating, but sometimes real events remain scarier than fiction.

In the story I made the soldiers knock on the gates of the house to be let in while the revellers, including Lomba, slipped out through a back door. In real life the headhunters were more subtle: they didn't knock on your gate when they arrived, and they didn't give you a chance to escape through the back door. In the novel I don't dwell much on the circumstances of the arrest of the two poets, but in real life it sent a big shock through the small community of intellectuals. It made them realize what other African writers, such as Ngugi and Dennis Brutus, had known long ago: that to these dictators a poem was as much a threat as a rally; that you might risk arrest or death or exile just by joining one word to another.

Back to the party at Maik's house. We stood at the door, Toni and I, weaving slightly, trying to see where the booze was. There were couples on the floor dancing to a Hi-Life tune from a huge CD player in the corner. Solitary figures were slouched against the walls, determinedly knocking back their beers. Toni shook hands. I nodded and smiled at the strange faces. I was new in Lagos and this was my first such literary party.

'Aha,' Toni said, 'Come, let me introduce you to Odia Ofeimun.'

'Odia Ofeimun!' I remember repeating it, following him, not sure if he was serious or not.

At that time Odia Ofeimun was probably the most influential and the most visible poet in Nigeria. He was something of a cult figure among young poets, and few poetry books were published in Lagos during the 1990s without his name among the acknowledgements. He had arrived on the Nigerian literary scene in the Eighties, first as the youngest poet in Wole Soyinka's influential anthology, *Poems of Black Africa*, then with his own collection, *The Poet Lied*. The poet he accused of lying was none other than the great J. P. Clark who, together with Chinua Achebe and Soyinka, had an almost oracular status in Nigerian literature at the time. It was a gutsy thing for a young poet to do.

When I was at school, Odia was a fixture on the syllabus. Our teachers called him 'the last great Nigerian poet'. By this they meant the very last of our poets to be published by a multinational publisher, in his case Heinemann, in the Eighties, before the great pull-out of foreign publishers began.

After 1985 the military regime systematically undermined the once-buoyant, fuel-driven economy of Nigeria. The country's infrastructure collapsed. There were no plans for industrial and technological recovery. Local manufacturers couldn't compete with the cheap foreign goods that were dumped daily on our shores: everything was imported, including toilet paper. Publishing was one of the businesses that was worst hit. What small market there had been, thanks to a pre-independence curiosity about African literature—which had encouraged energetic literary activity inside the country—fizzled out because ordinary people couldn't afford to buy books for pleasure. The big publishing houses disappeared, to be replaced by small-time hustlers moonlighting as publishers. If you add all this to the political tension and suppression of any intellectual activity by the military, you can understand why we aspiring poets held Odia in such high regard: he had reached a position which fate and circumstance seemed to have decreed that we never would.

'Helon Habila, a poet,' Toni introduced me to Odia.

'Sir,' I said tremulously, holding both his hands in mine, 'this is a great moment for me.'

'Call me Odia,' the great man said, patting me on the back. I was surprised to find he was no taller than me. He asked what I was working on and I told him: 'A novel.' We stood there: Toni my best mate, the great poet, and me. Toni and I couldn't help exchanging significant smiles.

We had both dreamed of such a moment since we first met at university about ten years before. Toni, like me, wanted to become a writer, and university was simply the means to that end: to get the necessary education and the necessary connections.

We'd become friends immediately. I was from Gombe State in the north, and Toni from Delta State in the south-east, and in Nigeria that meant we were supposed to be wary of each other. But our common aims proved greater than our different backgrounds. We had read the same books, admired the same authors and, when lectures started, we'd both read more than half the books on the reading list. Toni, like me, had never met a published writer. Whenever we heard of a lecturer who had actually been published, we'd say, 'Wow, how did he do it?'

Our friendship was underscored by rivalry: each of us wanted to be the first to achieve literary glory. We went in for the same BBC competitions, then hid the rejection slips from each other, claiming our manuscripts had been lost in the post. But in 1992, in our second year, Toni won an essay competition. The prize was a six-week trip to Britain. Of course I was happy for him, and depressed for myself: I'd entered the same competition. But then, a year later, one of my short stories was included in an anthology of Nigerian writing, *Through Laughter and Tears*. I was a published author. It would take a lot of trips to Britain by Toni to best that. But he did. He won a radio competition, and this time the prize was two weeks with a family in Switzerland. After that, try as I might, I couldn't win anything. The return of my manuscripts became almost routine. But one more defeat was still waiting for me: when we graduated, Toni got a 2.1, and I got a 2.2.

'It's not the kind of degree that matters,' I told myself. 'It's the use to which you put it.'

Toni was offered a job by a magazine in Lagos, the cultural capital of Nigeria. Before the end of the year a rival magazine had made him a better offer. He was a star.

And me? This was 1996, perhaps the toughest year in Nigerian history: the economy was in a shambles, we had just been suspended from the Commonwealth of Nations and had sanctions imposed by almost every country in the world. It was, among other things, a result of the hanging of the pro-democracy activist and author, Ken Saro-Wiwa, by General Abacha and his junta.

Graduates walked the streets looking for any kind of job, some turned to crime just to survive. I was lucky to get a post as a lecturer in a polytechnic in Bauchi, my state capital. I worked there from 1997 to 1999. It was a lonely period for me. Bauchi is a small town and there was no outlet whatsoever for my literary work, either in print or in conversation. My only escape was to continue writing, and reading. I read like mad. Friends would find me with five books on the table in front of me: I'd read a chapter here, a page there. They'd say, 'Take it easy, man.'

Toni was a household name by this time, and whenever I wanted to impress people, especially girls, I'd tell them, 'Toni and I were in the same class.'

There was plenty of opportunity during those two years in Bauchi to look deep into myself and ask whether I shouldn't forget this dream of writing and do something else. I could be a banker, for instance. Lots of young people were making it as bankers. But whenever I picked up a book, a poem or a story, I felt that this was where my destiny lay.

Then one day in 1999 Toni wrote me a letter. 'Come to Lagos. There's a place on the paper for you.'

He had become the editor of his magazine. In 1999 things had started to change in the country. Abacha had died the year before and his successor, General Abdulsalami, bowing to international pressure, had hastily organized elections. A retired general, Olusegun Obasanjo, an ex-military head of state and an ex-political detainee, was the new civilian ruler. I didn't hesitate. I left Bauchi in August 1999 without even resigning from my job. In Lagos I became a columnist and an editor on Toni's magazine, *Hints*. Toni introduced me to the Lagos literati, and told me which competitions to enter.

'The most important one,' he said, 'is the MuSoN poetry competition.' It was the biggest in the country, both critically and financially, worth 50,000 *naira* in cash, more money than I had ever held in my hands.

'The second place is worth 30,000 *naira*, and the third place is 20,000. You should aim for second or third,' Toni said, 'because I'm getting the first place.'

We set to work refining our poems. Winning became almost a matter of life and death for me. I needed the money. I wanted to prove once and for all to myself that I could win a competition, and that I was in the right profession. Besides, I'd burned my bridges in Bauchi.

Some of my friends advised me to get close to Odia Ofeimun, because in Lagos he decided who won which competition. I was shocked by this. For me it wasn't just about winning the competition, it was about being a writer. If Odia helped me win this time, what about all the competitions I'd have to enter in the future? I put my trust in my craft and in God. When the results came out my poem, 'Another Age', was first and Toni's, 'A Dying Man I Reflect', was third. The next day I was in all the papers and on television. But my most treasured memory from the whole night is this picture of Toni and me with Odia in the middle. Odia had come up to us and asked us to pose with him. 'I will treasure this picture of me and two great poets,' he said as it was taken.

This snapshot of us in the foyer of the MuSoN Hall has come to symbolize a lot of things to me. Our smiles seem to say that the worst for our country is over, we are gazing beyond the camera into a new and brighter future, where we could be poets without fear of arrest, murder or exile. We had cheques worth 50,000 *naira* and 20,000 *naira* in our pockets. But above all the picture is a confirmation of my deepest dream, that of becoming a writer. □

SOFT CORE
Joyce Carol Oates

'Why are you showing me these?'
'I thought you should know.'
'Should know what?'

They were two sisters of youthful middle age with three breasts between them and a history that might be summed up as *much left unsaid*. Maggie, the elder, who'd had a mastectomy eighteen months before, rarely alluded to the fact in her younger sister's company and spoke with an air of startled reproach if Esther brought up the subject of her health; as if Maggie's breast cancer were a symptom of a moral weakness, a deficiency of character, about which Esther had no right to know.

Eighteen months before, after the removal of Maggie's left breast, Esther had driven 370 miles to see her sister and was immediately rebuffed by Maggie's steely good humour, just as, when they were girls, she'd been outplayed on the tennis court by Maggie's remarkable cannonball serves and vicious returns. In her hospital bed, in the presence of Maggie's husband Dwight, Maggie had assured Esther, indicating the bulky-bandaged left side of her chest, 'Hey, sweetie, don't look like a funeral. It's no great loss, I wasn't planning on using it again.'

Was this funny? Esther had managed to smile, weakly.

Wanting to slap Maggie's face.

Now it was late spring of another year. The day following their elderly father's funeral. Four days after their elderly father's death. Esther had returned to Strykersville too late by forty-five minutes to see Dr Hewart before he died: of a heart attack, after a long, deteriorating illness.

Esther had returned to Strykersville hurriedly. Esther had returned, it had to be admitted, reluctantly. For twenty years, in fact for more than twenty years, Esther had avoided Strykersville as much as possible for no reason she could name, not wanting to concede even to herself *It's Maggie's territory. I hate Maggie.*

Of course, Esther didn't hate her sister. Esther was in terror that her sister would die and leave her, the surviving Hewart sister. About whom people would say *Oh but Maggie was the one we all loved. That Maggie!* In Maggie's presence Esther felt as undefined as a tissue soaked in water, yet when she was summoned into Maggie's presence she understood that there was something crucial at stake, and so she would shortly be defined, her role would become clear to her; her aimless tissue-thin life would acquire a new significance. When Maggie called Esther to say, in her mildly scolding/bemused elder-sister way, that drew upon their shared girlhood, yet resounded with the authority Maggie had acquired as head librarian of a dozen regional public libraries addressing her intimidated staff, 'Esther, it's time to be responsible. It's time for you to come back to Strykersville, to make the effort to be an adult,' it was Esther's cue to say quickly, 'Maggie, I know. It's...time.'

Cryptically Maggie had said, 'More than time.'

In middle age we discover that our parents have become, as if overnight, elderly. It's a discovery like sprouting hair and emerging breasts at puberty. It's a discovery that signals *A new era, ready or not*. Because Maggie had never left Strykersville, and lived with her family just across town from their parents, Esther had managed to avoid this new era for a long time. Though of course she'd felt guilty, all those years. Her visits to her former hometown were infrequent and often painful. Pilgrimages fuelled by the tepid oxygen of family duty, unease, guilt. The more Esther loved her parents, the more helpless she felt, as they aged, to protect them from harm. A moral coward, she kept her distance. The Good Sister would call the Other Sister in New York City if too much time was elapsing between visits, to remind her: 'Esther? Just to pass on, Mom and Dad are missing you. I miss you. Come see us!' This was not a command. This was not coercion. It was enough for Esther to be told that she was being missed: to be so informed, to be designated as *missed*, lacerates the heart, and there is only one way to remedy it.

When Mrs Hewart began to fall sick in her mid-seventies, Esther had shuttled back and forth between New York and Strykersville for months, feeling herself a puppet cruelly jerked about, exhausted and demoralized, for she was no longer a young woman and her life was careening past her and when her father was diagnosed with cancer and began his inevitable descent into weakness, dying, death, Esther had wanted to scream at Maggie that she'd had enough of Strykersville as you might have enough of a recurring flu—*No more! I've had it.*

Except of course Esther hadn't had it, entirely. There was more.

She'd returned, and when she had expressed a wish to leave the day after the funeral, Maggie had stared at her with a look almost of derision. 'Esther, really! We're not contagious.'

Half-consciously Maggie had stroked her left breast. What was now, foam rubber inserted into a specially equipped bra, Maggie's left breast.

Seeing this gesture, Esther blushed. She'd wanted to protest *Maggie, I didn't mean you.*

Since Dr Hewart had moved into a nursing home the previous year, the Hewarts' house had stood empty. It was made of sandstone and red brick in a dignified Queen Anne style but it was old, and in visible need of repair. Before the property could be put on the market it had to be cleared of household furnishings and the accumulation of decades. Esther felt faint at the prospect. So soon after her father's death she couldn't bear to help Maggie, she'd told her sister, she just couldn't. 'But why, exactly? Why, if I can bear it?' Maggie had reasonably asked. That reproachful smile, the calm assessing eyes, the voice that, when required, cut through another's voice like a wire-cutter cutting wire.

To this, Esther had no reply. It would not have been possible to say *But I'm the lesser Hewart sister. Everyone knows that.*

Sharp-nosed as vultures, local developers had been calling Maggie for months to ask about the untenanted old house. It came with seven acres of prime real estate, extending into Strykersville's most fashionable suburb and bordering a golf course. Each time, Maggie called Esther to gloat: 'Can you believe, they're offering two million dollars?'—'Can you believe, they're offering two point *five* million?'

Esther gripped the phone receiver tight against her ear and waited to feel some emotion. Was she elated, like Maggie? Was she sick with guilt, to profit from the collapse of her parents' lives, that seemed to her such good, decent, kindly lives? Or had she so long steeled herself against any emotion generated by news out of Strykersville, she was unmoved?

Anaesthetized, that was it. The wisest strategy.

She objected, 'Dad wouldn't want the property broken up. If that's what the developer is planning. He always said—'

In her wire-cutter voice, Maggie interrupted, 'Sweetie. This is us now, not Dad. We make the decisions now.'

Sobering to conclude, this was so. Maggie was fifty-two years old, Esther was forty-nine.

At the old house, Maggie briskly led Esther through familiar rooms that had become subtly unfamiliar since Esther's last visit the previous spring. Maggie's heels rang against the hardwood floors, where carpets had been removed. Esther, fending off a migraine headache, had an impulse to press her hands over her ears. She'd slept badly the night before. She'd been trying to talk to her father, a blurred figure with a face that seemed to have gone askew like melted wax, and though often in life, at least years ago, she'd had quite lucid, warmly engaging and intellectually provocative conversations with Dr Hewart, especially on the subjects of genetics and palaeontology in which he'd had an amateur's interest, Esther had not been able to speak to him now. *Daddy! It's me, Esther. You know me, Daddy—your daughter.* She blamed Maggie for the disturbed sleep. When she visited Strykersville she had to stay with Maggie because Maggie insisted and always at Maggie's she slept badly, and could not tell her sister; never could she have told her sister that she'd rather stay at a motel. And there were reasons for not staying in the old house, where her girlhood room was hardly changed, as if awaiting Esther's return. (Esther was determined not to make another sentimental visit to the upstairs room, she'd made so many over the years!) Maggie had had Dr Hewart's power of attorney for some time before his death, and had been in and out of this house frequently, so returning now after their father's funeral was no profound event to her; but Esther was feeling shaky, unreal. Waves of visceral horror swept over her repeatedly, *They're dead, they're not here, why are you here?* Though Mrs Hewart had died four years ago, yet it seemed to Esther that she must be somewhere in the house.

If not here in the house, where?

Led to the rear of the house, Esther was saying to Maggie's stolid back, 'Maggie, I've told you, I don't have room for much in my apartment. It's only five rooms. You should take whatever you want, and what's left over…' There was a flutter of panic in her throat. What was Esther trying to say? That she wasn't sentimental about their past, she didn't really want anything from her parents' household, she hadn't an ounce of healthy acquisitiveness in her bones? Maggie would disapprove, Esther knew. Maggie needed to believe that Esther coveted something of the past; something located only in Strykersville, nowhere else. All those years Esther had lived in New York, adrift in her own selfish life; her selfish, moderately happy life; her not-entirely-unhappy life; her life-in-exile from Strykersville, which was Maggie's territory; all those years she'd sent a stream of lavish greeting cards and a small galaxy of potted mums, poinsettias, cyclamens and tulips; she'd helped pay for live-in nursing care; she'd returned to visit when she could, which had not been often. Naturally you would think that the Good Sister had sacrificed her life to their parents while Esther, unencumbered as milkweed seed, had blossomed in more fertile soil, but quite the reverse was true. Maggie had her own rather wonderful family, she remained as popular in Strykersville as she'd been in high school; even after her mastectomy and chemotherapy treatments she was still an attractive, hearty woman, with flushed girlish cheeks and a habit of tilting her chin upward. Maggie was one who marched stalwartly onward while Esther seemed always to be stalling and reviewing her life, 'making a fresh start' in a new job, a new course of instruction— graphic design, public relations, a master's degree programme in math at the Columbia School of Education, to qualify her for private school teaching—or, in the cool clinical vocabulary of the era, a new relationship. From girlhood she'd been wanly pretty like a watercolour that begins to fade even as you examine it; she knew herself anaemic beside Maggie's ruddy skin, strong-boned face and pale-lashed penetrating eyes. As a girl she'd thought *I hate Maggie* but her truer thought was *I wish I was Maggie!* She'd resented Maggie's high-school popularity, which she'd been expected to inherit, like Maggie's position on the girls' basketball and field hockey teams, in which Maggie had excelled; she'd resented not her sister's marriage, family life, career, but the expectation that she should follow suit; failing this, she'd become increasingly unnatural in their parents' eyes, like a woman with a shrivelled limb.

Now they were adults. Their parents had vanished. Esther had only Maggie, to link her with them. She was in dread of losing Maggie. In dread of Maggie's scorn. *Esther, really! We're not contagious!*

Yet cancer is genetically determined, isn't it: in a way, contagion.

'...What's left over, we can sell. We can give away.'

OUR SUBSCRIBERS get *Granta* delivered to their homes, at big savings on the bookshop price. Why not join them? Or, if you're already one of our select group of nearly 70,000 discerning people from every corner of the world, give a subscription to a friend? It makes a great gift: unusual, thoughtful and lasting.)

➤ **YOU SAVE 25%** WITH A ONE-YEAR (FOUR ISSUE) SUBSCRIPTION FOR £26.95.
➤ **YOU SAVE 30%** WITH A TWO-YEAR (EIGHT ISSUE) SUBSCRIPTION FOR £50.
➤ **YOU SAVE 35%** WITH A THREE-YEAR (TWELVE ISSUE) SUBSCRIPTION FOR £70.

'ESSENTIAL READING.' Observer
'RECOMMENDED FOR ANYONE WITH A PASSING INTEREST IN HUMANITY.'
British Journal of Medical Practice

ORDER FORM

I'D LIKE TO SUBSCRIBE FOR MYSELF FOR: ◯ 1 year (4 issues) at just £26.95
◯ 2 years (8 issues) at just £50
◯ 3 years (12 issues) at just £70

START SUBSCRIPTION WITH ◯ this issue ◯ next issue

I'D LIKE TO GIVE A SUBSCRIPTION FOR: ◯ 1 year (4 issues) at just £26.95
◯ 2 years (8 issues) at just £50
◯ 3 years (12 issues) at just £70

START SUBSCRIPTION WITH ◯ this issue ◯ next issue

MY DETAILS (please supply even if ordering a gift): Mr/Ms/Mrs/Miss

Country   Postcode

GIFT RECIPIENT'S DETAILS (if applicable): Mr/Ms/Mrs/Miss

Country   Postcode

Gift message (optional):

TOTAL* £_____ paid by ◯ £ cheque enclosed (to 'Granta') ◯ Visa/Mastercard/AmEx:

card no: __ __ __ __ __ __ __ __ __ __ __ __ __ __ __ __

02LBG80

expires: __ __ / __ __ signature:

* POSTAGE. The prices stated include UK postage. For the rest of Europe, please add £8 (per year). For the rest of the world, please add £15 (per year). DATA PROTECTION. Please tick here if you don't wish to receive occasional mailings from compatible publishers. ◯

Return details:

POST ('Freepost' in the UK) to: Granta, 'Freepost', 2/3 Hanover Yard, Noel Road, London N1 8BR. **PHONE/FAX:** In the UK: FreeCall 0500 004 033 (phone & fax); outside the UK: tel 44 (0)20 7704 9776, fax 44 (0)20 7704 0474 **EMAIL:** subs@granta.com

DON'T MISS OUT ON MAJOR ISSUES!

GRANTA

There, Esther had uttered the words. She wouldn't take anything back with her to New York, she would give away what might be hers. All of it!

Maggie, striding ahead, like a team captain, gave no sign of having heard.

Esther followed slowly behind. She was feeling what a mistake this was, not to have driven off immediately, headed east on the Turnpike. Making her way through the house she'd always believed to be so imposing, so dignified among its neighbours, now she saw how small and cluttered the rooms, how dated the design, the narrow windows emitting a stingy sort of light. To be the daughter of a highly respected general practitioner in Strykersville, New York state, in the 1950s and 1960s was to be respected, too; in some quarters, envied. But all that was past, and could not be retrieved. Returning to this house was like descending in a bathysphere into a region of undersea shadows and darting shapes in which Maggie, the elder sister, always the wisest and certainly the most pragmatic sister, knew her way blind. In this fairy tale the elder, good sister leads the younger through a labyrinth of rooms crammed with elegant but old, fading furniture, chintz draw-curtains, dust-heavy rolled-up carpets. Quilts handmade by their mother. Cracked and chipped Wedgware china. Stained-glass objects, the most beautiful a Tiffany-style lamp in rich blues and greens made by their restless father in the stained-glass phase of his retirement. Seeing it, Esther looked quickly away. *There: something I could take back with me.* She hated the sudden greed, the desperation. She hated Maggie for bringing her here. She hated Maggie for being so brave about her cancer, not collapsing into a rag doll as Esther would have done.

'Maggie? I can't breathe here...'

Maggie heard nothing for Maggie was talking continuously. At the funeral home, close by their father's open, gleaming casket and his wonderfully composed if rather shrivelled monkey-face, Maggie had chattered. The good news was, two Buffalo-area developers were now in the bidding, which would drive the price up even higher. And where they could rent a U-Haul for Esther to attach to her car.

Dwight would help them load it, Maggie promised.

Esther wondered what Maggie, who'd rarely visited her in New York, imagined of the brownstone into which Esther had recently moved: five rooms in fashionable Chelsea on West 22nd near by a welfare hotel whose dazed residents sprawled on the front steps even in the rain. Esther's apartment was chic and spare, mostly neutral colours, her living room/dining room scarcely as large as the kitchen in this house. Esther said, pleading, 'I don't have space for heirlooms, Maggie. Clutter makes me anxious.'

It was true, her breathing had become laboured. Possibly the air was rife with pollen. As Maggie tugged a shroud off a sofa, dust lifted. Esther stared at a massive piece of Victorian furniture with claw feet, a scalloped back, a wine-coloured velvet fabric that, as a teenager, she'd compulsively stroked, like fur. Reversing the motion, running her hand over it backward, had made Esther shudder, and she shuddered now, recalling. Maggie said, rapidly, 'Things you like, that you don't have room for now, you can store. Some day you might want them. And if they're gone, they're gone forever.' She paused as if waiting for Esther to object. 'I'm going to be storing lots of things.'

Maggie too seemed out of breath. Her eyes glistened. Her tone was argumentative, yet shaky. Esther had no intention of arguing with her sister face to face.

'Esther, look here.' They were in their father's office at the rear of the house. Dr Hewart had had his professional office in downtown Strykersville, where he saw patients, but he had a work-related office at home, to be distinguished from his book-lined study off the living room. The home office was comfortably cluttered with an old roll-top desk, much-worn leather chair and hassock, several filing cabinets. Maggie and Esther were forbidden to enter this room as children unless Dr Hewart was in it, and unless he invited them the door was always shut. To push the door open so brashly, as Maggie had just done, seemed to Esther an insolent gesture, so soon after their father's death.

'These were in the bottom desk drawer. I think he must have forgotten them. I can't think he'd have wanted...' Maggie paused, unconsciously bringing the back of her hand against the left side of her chest. Esther stared at the faded Polaroids on the desk top, at first uncomprehending. Were these old pictures of her and Maggie? Why was Maggie behaving so strangely?

She saw, then. She gave a little cry and pushed the Polaroids away.
'Did you see who it is?'
'Maggie, I don't want to see.'
But Esther had seen: Elvira Sanchez.
Elvira!—Elvira she'd always been to them, not Mrs Sanchez—a
woman who'd 'helped out' Mrs Hewart with housework; a former
nurse's aide at Strykersville General—Esther seemed to recall this
background, though not clearly. This was sometime in the late 1970s
when Esther was in high school, and Elvira's daughter Maria was
in Esther's class, and so there was an awkwardness between them,
an air as of sisters who had no way of speaking to each other and
who, you might have thought if you'd seen them unavoidably forced
together, didn't know each other's name. Elvira had been a familiar
household presence at the Hewarts' for a few years, then abruptly
she'd disappeared, as often cleaning women, handymen, lawn crews,
snow-removal crews appeared and disappeared in the mysterious life
of the dignified old sandstone and red-brick house on East Avenue,
and none of this was questioned by the children of the house, nor
even much noticed.
'It must have been an oversight. He was forgetting so much. He
did destroy lots of "old boring things" he called them, in the fireplace.
I was afraid he'd burned legal documents, financial records...'
It angered Esther that Maggie was speaking like this. In a rapid
voice, with an air of being bemused.
Esther took up the Polaroids to look at them more closely. There
were about a dozen of them of them, and all were faded. Yet you
could see who it was, unmistakably. Elvira Sanchez: naked. A
stocky but good-looking woman in her mid-forties with enormous
breasts, berry-coloured nipples big as coat buttons, a bristling black
pelt of pubic hair. Elvira was lying lazily back, legs spread, on the
leather chair in this room; in another more extravagant pose, tongue
protruding between fleshy lipsticked lips as she fingered the fleshy
cleft between her legs, Elvira sprawled on the wine-coloured velvet
sofa in the living room. *In that part of the house*—Esther was
wounded, stunned. As if such behaviour in the living room was more
shocking than in Dr Hewart's office.
Esther fumbled the Polaroids, not wanting to see more.
'This one—' Maggie snatched it from Esther's fingers, to shove

into her face, '—it's their bed, see? Mom and Dad's. That's the ivory quilt Mom sewed.'

'Why are you showing me these?'

'I thought you should know.'

'Should know what?'

Maggie stopped to pick up the Polaroids. Her breath was agitated. Her face was warm, flushed. Yet she was trying to behave normally, considering Esther's question as if she might not have thought of it herself.

'Should know what Dad was. What Dad wasn't. I thought you might like to know, Esther.'

Tactfully not adding *Since you avoided knowing so much, all these years.*

'Did you think it would make me happy to know, Maggie?'

'I wasn't thinking of your happiness, Esther. Believe me, not everyone spends twenty-four hours a day thinking of your happiness, Esther.'

There, it was uttered. Esther recoiled in hurt, that her sister hated her, too.

Maggie held the Polaroids like a hand of cards she'd been dealt. She seemed tired. She seemed, in this moment, not-young and possibly ill. 'Maybe I didn't want to be the only one to know, Esther. Maybe I felt lonely.'

'Lonely! You!'

'Why not me? I'm lonely.'

Maggie spoke flatly as if daring Esther to believe her.

'You with your family. Your "good works".'

'Nothing is more lonely than fucking "good works".'

Esther laughed. Though she was shocked, disoriented. Maggie wasn't one to use profanities lightly, still less obscenities. There was something very wrong here.

She's sick, Esther thought. *The cancer has come back.*

Maggie said matter-of-factly, 'We'll burn them. In the fireplace. Dad would approve. That seems right.'

In the fireplace in Dr Hewart's book-lined study, which was already messy with ashes, Maggie burned the Polaroids.

Hesitantly Esther asked, picking at a thumbnail, 'Do you think Mom knew? About Elvira...'

Maggie shrugged. Maggie wasn't going to speculate.

Esther was thinking of Maria Sanchez. The shame of it, if Maria had known! That would explain... No, Esther couldn't bear to think so.

Maggie laughed. 'Remember we'd find Dad's magazines, sometimes? Those pulpy things like movie magazines, mostly pictures. The shock of it, in bright colours. Once I found, I guess it was only just *Playboy* under the front seat of Dad's car.'

Esther shook her head, no. She didn't remember.

'"Soft-core porn", it's called now. Nothing worse than what you see in movies now, or on TV, but it seemed shocking then.'

They were watching the Polaroids flare up, wan bluish flames tinged with orange. How curious fire is. How quickly evidence disappears, anonymous soot remaining.

With schoolgirl obstinacy Esther objected, 'Some of those were Dad's medical magazines. I used to look through those.'

Maggie snorted in derision. 'Not these, sweetie. These were not the *New England Journal of Medicine*, I assure you.'

'No, but there were others, with pictures, like—' Esther was confused: medical magazines with lurid juicy close-ups of surgical procedures? Childbirth? A bared, red-muscled heart, no more mysterious than meat in a butcher's display case? Was she remembering these, or imagining them?

They waited until the Polaroids were destroyed utterly.

Esther said, 'Now you tell me about you, Maggie. I deserve to know.'

Maggie turned a startled face toward her. Esther saw what looked like a glimmer of resentment, and guilt.

Here was a fact: Esther had been waiting since the night of their father's death for Maggie to confide in her. The claim of one sister upon another. *I knew you before your husband knew you. Long before your children knew you.* Esther waited for Maggie to confess to her what she hadn't yet been able to tell her husband and children: she was going to die. The cancer had returned. The cancer had— Esther hated this word, familiar from their parents' ordeals— *metastasized.* And how would Esther react? She wondered if she would begin to shake, as she sometimes shook in the cold of the mammography examination room, and Maggie herself would have to console her. *Oh sweetie! C'mon.* Or would she stare at Maggie, who'd been mysterious to her all their lives, as she was staring now, and feel nothing, nothing at all?

'Deserve to know what?'

'Your health. You never tell me...'

'My health.' Maggie ran her fingers through her short, springy talcum-coloured hair, that had grown back sparsely after her chemotherapy. She smiled roguishly at Esther. 'Strong as an ox. Ask my enemies.'

'Oh, Maggie. Don't be like that.'

'Like what? I don't have enemies?'

Esther pleaded, 'You would tell me if—wouldn't you?'

'If—if what?'

Maggie was mocking her but Esther couldn't retreat. She made a clumsy gesture with her arm, against her left breast.

'*That?* Oh, certainly. You'd be the first to know, Esther. As soon as my oncologist tells me, and before I tell Dwight.'

Maggie spoke sneeringly. Evidently she was angry.

Esther wanted to say *Fuck you, then. I don't need you.*

Esther apologized. She was sorry, she said.

'Maggie, forgive me? I'm only thinking of you.'

'Think of yourself, sweetie. I'm fine.'

They'd returned to the living room. Esther followed Maggie in a haze, stumbling into things. By this time her ice-pick headache was causing her eyes to lose focus. The chemical stink of the Polaroids! She wanted desperately to leave this place but she understood that Maggie wouldn't allow it, not quite yet. She would have to be punished further. She'd been summoned back home to be a witness, and to be punished. The dining room table looked like a table in a yard sale, upon which items were spread in the forlorn hope of attracting buyers. Tarnished silverware and candlestick holders, woven place mats with shadowy stains, more of Mrs Hewart's finery, that had been overlooked, apparently, after her death. Maggie nudged Esther to 'take something, for Christ's sake', but Esther stood numbed, unable to move. That boxy handbag: alligator hide? Esther shuddered at the thought of touching such a thing. She couldn't remember her mother carrying that bag.

Maggie said, annoyed, 'The lamp, at least. You can take that, can't you?'

Maggie meant their father's stained-glass Tiffany-style lamp. She pointed out the painstaking craftsmanship that had gone into it: the triangular pieces of glass, blues, greens, pale red and russet-red. 'It's beautiful. Your New York friends will admire it.' Again Maggie was sneering, but less angrily than before. 'It has nothing to do with— you know. That other.'

That other. Esther foresaw that, after today, neither she nor Maggie would allude to what they'd seen in their father's office, and burned together in his fireplace. Not even elliptically as Maggie was doing now, with the mildest embarrassment. *That other.*

They would not utter the name Sanchez.

Esther said, 'It is beautiful, Maggie. But...' She was groping through the pain in her head. She might have said nothing further but heard her voice continue. 'I don't like beautiful things.'

Maggie said sharply, 'Don't like beautiful things?'

'I mean—beautiful breakable things.'

As if to prove her point Esther made a sudden gesture toward the Tiffany lamp. Perhaps it was involuntary, like a tremor. Perhaps Maggie overreacted, shoving at Esther's arm. The Tiffany lamp fell from the end table, slipped through both the sisters' fingers and toppled over on to the floor. *Shattered into a thousand pieces!* But when Esther opened her eyes she saw no broken glass. The lampshade was wrenched around like a head on a broken neck, but the lamp had fallen against a rolled-up carpet. Maggie, trembling with indignation, picked it up and placed it back on the table, exactly where it had been, in a square clear of surrounding dust. 'You're right, Esther. You shouldn't take this lamp, or anything. You'd better go back home.'

Esther wanted to protest *But I am home!*

Instead she said, wiping at her eyes with a wadded tissue she'd found in her pocket, 'Well, Maggie. Now you know my heart.'

It wasn't true. But she hoped Maggie would think so, from now on. □

CONSCIOUSNESS AND THE NOVEL CONNECTED ESSAYS

DAVID LODGE

As the richest record we have of human consciousness, literature, David Lodge suggests, may offer a kind of understanding that is complementary, not opposed, to scientific knowledge. Writing with characteristic wit and brio, and employing the insight and acumen of a skilled novelist and critic, Lodge here explores the representation of human consciousness in fiction (mainly English and American) in light of recent investigations in the sciences.

The Richard Ellmann Lectures in Modern Literature / cloth

TO BE THE POET

MAXINE HONG KINGSTON

"To *Be the Poet* is Kingston's manifesto, the avowal and declaration of a writer who has devoted a good part of her sixty years to writing prose, and who, over the course of this spirited and inspiring book, works out what the rest of her life will be, in poetry. Taking readers along with her, this celebrated writer gathers advice from her gifted contemporaries and from sages, critics, and writers whom she takes as ancestors.

William E. Massey Lectures in American Civilization / cloth

STRANGERS TO OURSELVES Discovering the Adaptive Unconscious

TIMOTHY D. WILSON

"Know thyself," a precept as old as Socrates, is still good advice. But is introspection the best path to self-knowledge? What are we trying to discover, anyway? In an eye-opening tour of the unconscious, as contemporary psychological science has redefined it, Timothy Wilson introduces us to a hidden mental world of judgments, feelings, and motives that introspection may never show us.

Belknap Press / cloth

HARVARD UNIVERSITY PRESS
US: 800 405 1619   UK: 020 7306 0603   www.hup.harvard.edu

TWO FARMS: ONE BLACK, ONE WHITE
Lindsey Hilsum

Two Farms: One Black, One White

A few weeks before the Zimbabwean parliamentary elections of June 2000, I went to visit a white couple, Graham and Glenda Douse, at their farm near Harare. Nyagambe Farm is about an hour's drive south-east of the capital, beyond the small, neat country town of Marondera. Turning down the murram road that led through the farm, I passed rich, brown, ploughed fields on either side and a dam the Douses had constructed for irrigation. During the course of the next eighteen months, I would spend several hours sitting on the edge of the dam, watching dense white cumulus clouds mass and disperse in the blue arc of the sky, while small black swallows swooped and dived over the waterfall. On that first visit, labradors bounded up to the car as I approached the low, whitewashed farmhouse. Graham was tall, dressed in white shorts and long socks, with a tidy beard and the beginning of a paunch. Glenda, hospitable and energetic, worked as a pharmacist in the local hospital. They were both in their early forties. We drank tea on the veranda, watching the dogs play as the water sprinkler greened the lawn. This was the Africa of the white man's dream, where nature can be subdued inside the compound, but where the bush extends in its thrilling wildness just beyond the fence.

In the corner of the dining room, the two-way radio crackled— a security measure. 'War vets' had occupied most of the farms in the neighbourhood, including part of the Douses' land. President Robert Mugabe claimed that those seizing farms were people who had fought alongside him in the 1970s, when he led guerrillas fighting the white government of Prime Minister Ian Smith. Their aim, then, was to turn what had been a British self-governing colony called Rhodesia into the independent African republic of Zimbabwe. The cause was nationalist, the rallying cry was land. Black farmers had been pushed to the margins of existence in dry, dusty 'tribal' areas while white farmers had fenced off vast tracts of land that they turned into productive, commercial farms. Black men and women joined the struggle to get their land back, and the first guerrilla raids of the war were against white farmers on isolated homesteads.

But 'war vets' as applied to the people who occupied white farmland was a misnomer. They were unemployed youths, a mob for hire, not a force for liberation. Most of them were too young to have fought in the war. They supported ZANU-PF, Mugabe's party, because they hoped to be given land or money. According to Mugabe, whites

171

still owned seventy per cent of Zimbabwe's land. The Commercial Farmers Union, representing the farmers, said whites owned just twenty-six per cent of the surface area of Zimbabwe. Whatever the figures, the farmers remained the most easily identifiable, and historically most hated, group of whites in the country.

It appeared that everyone had reverted to wartime roles and language. The Douses were part of a network of white farmers who used the radio to 'keep coms', checking on the movements of the 'gooks' and making sure everyone in the community was safe. A new verb had been created: to be 'warvetted' meant to have your farm occupied.

I went with them to see their red-brick tobacco curing sheds, where the war vets had gathered the labourers for a *pungwe*, an indoctrination session, just as they had done with villagers during the war. The workers were sitting on the ground in two lines and singing in Shona, 'The land is ours, it doesn't belong to the white man.' Lookouts with knobkerries and sticks had been posted in a semicircle around the farm buildings to stop anyone escaping. I was with a cameraman trying to film, but we didn't stay long. When we raised the camera, they chased us away.

I was uncomfortable being associated with the white farmers in this way. I did not want to like the Douses. I had lived in Kenya during the 1980s and regarded southern African whites as racist diehards, with no connection to liberal white people like myself who lived in Africa out of choice and because we felt we had something to offer a beleaguered continent. At a dinner party in Harare I had come across a white farmer who fitted my image of the breed, ranting about the 'Afs' and pledging undying loyalty to a Britain which he had left half a century earlier. 'I support the Queen,' he had said, raising his whiskey glass in unconscious fulfilment of the old stereotype that Rhodesians were more British than the British. 'But I couldn't go back now. Too many Afs and Pakis there.'

On the Douses' bookshelves I found a collection of colonial literature, including a volume of poetry by Hylda Richards, a farmer's wife who had written popular verse for the *Rhodesian Herald* in the 1940s and '50s under the byline The Poems of T. The doggerel catches the mood of the time:

Oh I would go a-farming in the veld so wide and free,
Where the purple sheen on grasses, stretch around me like the sea.
Against the veld so wild, alone I'd set my hand;
Oh, I would go a-farming, for my heart is in the land.

The book, full of jokey rhymes about drought and crop failure and the impossibility of communicating with the natives, was entitled *Next Year Will Be Better*.

The Douses thought that next year would indeed be better, because they believed the opposition Movement for Democratic Change (MDC), of which they were members, would win the forthcoming election. When the MDC leader Morgan Tsvangirai visited the Marondera Country Club to meet farmers, Glenda Douse was impressed.

'We could never bear Mugabe and I didn't trust him,' she said. 'During the war, when I was working in Harare Hospital, I used to see atrocities committed by his men. Ears and lips chopped off. There was a war which had to be fought, but he was so rabid and extreme. After independence he toned down a bit, but in the last few years he's gone back to what he was. He hates whites.'

Glenda had been brought up on a ranch, a huge expanse of bush in what is still called The Midlands. 'I had a blissful, old-fashioned farm childhood. My brothers and I had 50,000 acres to wander around. Our nearest neighbours were fifteen miles away, and all through my childhood we never had electricity—just a generator, gas lights and candles.' The week before Christmas 1978, when the war was in its final stages and Glenda was away in Harare working in the hospital, her father was killed in an ambush.

'The gooks had come in before to hack the cattle's hamstrings. My father and both my brothers were on a routine patrol when they were attacked. They fired back for three hours. It was awful. The army was everywhere and there were bombing raids, but it was all too late. My dad's body was still lying there when I got home. Then my mother was injured hitting a landmine as she tried to move off the farm. The army told her the farm could not be defended, and she was trying to get the equipment away.'

It didn't dim Glenda's desire to farm, nor her belief that once the war was over, white and black could live together. She and Graham came from more liberal families than other farmers, and while many whites were educated overseas, the Douses went to Harare University where they met and made friends with the black elite, children of businessmen and aspiring politicians. But afterwards somehow the two groups drifted apart.

'The blacks we went to school and university with are now Zimbabwe's captains of industry or have left the country, and we're out here farming, so we don't move in the same circles,' Graham said. 'They're managing directors of banks, they have tea with Bob Mugabe and drive Mercedes.' His former running partner from university, a black Zimbabwean, went on to Oxford. 'We went to stay with him once and had supper at the Gridiron Club. It was a strange situation. He really attracts ridicule because of his anglicized attitudes—he talks with a plum in his mouth. I only speak Shona to him.'

After they bought Nyagambe Farm from Graham's father, the Douses slipped seamlessly into Zimbabwe's segregated social life. It was not very different from the life their Rhodesian parents had known: holidays in Beira on the Mozambique coast, where the beaches are clean and the lobster delicious. Weekends boating on Lake Kariba, or trout fishing and game spotting at Inyanga park. Two sons boarding at a private school. Worrying about the rain— too early or too late, too much or not enough—trying to develop new products, like paprika, and new markets in Europe.

The black people Graham knew best were his farm labourers. He tried to treat them with respect, providing decent accommodation and health care, but the divide between two ways of living was unbridgeable. When he took me down to the tobacco sheds, he spoke Shona to the foreman and workers, who were friendly and polite, but this was an essentially colonial relationship—the white *baas* was in charge. Graham had believed that land should have been redistributed, and that white farmers could have done more to help black farmers. He wished he had made the effort to integrate more with the black middle class, but he hadn't been able to work out how to start, and farming life was challenging and profitable, so he stopped thinking about it. It wasn't until they joined the opposition that the Douses found themselves mixing with the black middle class from Marondera town.

'At the hospital we all used to work together fine but we didn't socialize. It was them and us—they had their lives and we had ours, even the doctors,' said Glenda. 'But when it became known that we were MDC, we became buddies.'

'It's good for all of us,' added Graham. 'We remained very separate as a group of people, the farmers. We just didn't come into contact with other people. But now we've got a tremendous respect not for the black elite who we went to university with, but for the middle class—tradespeople and professionals.'

The Matibes, like the Douses, are farmers. Like the Douses, they are members of the MDC; unlike the Douses, they are black. Philemon Matibe bought Paarl Farm near Chegutu, Zimbabwe, in 1999, after years of working as a manager on white-owned estates. He planted barley, tobacco, sugar beans and wheat. His wife Pearl sat with the farm-workers' wives making strings with which to tie up the tobacco plants. She was everything the 'madam' should not have been—young, elegant and black. They lived in a colonial-style, thatched farmhouse with a swimming pool at the back, and sent their two children, Phoebe and Mpho, to private school. They bought a pony for Phoebe, and Phil even dared to think that Mpho might inherit the farm one day. When he walked into the Country Club, Phil's white farmer neighbours looked at him with suspicion—he was better educated and more westernized than the government ministers whom they would smile at in public and mock in private, but still they didn't feel entirely comfortable. They would talk of tobacco prices and the state of the economy. The Matibes agreed with the white farmers that Mugabe was running the country into the ground, and Phil decided to stand for Parliament as an opposition candidate. They were optimistic that a new government would allow black and white to work together, and so end the hostility and suspicion that Mugabe had fostered during his twenty years in power.

I first came across Pearl Matibe in the offices of the MDC, where I was waiting to interview someone and she was collecting material for her husband's election campaign. Her accent—tight and nasal like a white southern African's—intrigued me. The next time I visited Zimbabwe I looked her up. I was reporting news, and she was not representative of the mainstream, but I thought she might help me understand the ease with which Mugabe was able to pit one group against another. Zimbabweans seemed to live in boxes marked 'white farmer' or 'white liberal', 'urban population', 'rural population', but Pearl Matibe could not be so easily defined, and I felt that she somehow held a key to seeing why it was so hard for Zimbabweans to escape the identities history had visited upon them.

'Black people don't like me,' she said. 'They call me "Nose Brigade" because I talk through my nose.' We were driving to the Tobacco Sales Floor, just outside Harare, where Zimbabwe's tobacco farmers auction their crop to middlemen who supply the cigarette companies. The Matibes were among a handful of successful black commercial farmers. They had several hundred hectares at Chegutu, and this was their first tobacco of the season. On the way, Pearl explained that the success of her father's small chain of shops had enabled him to send his children to private schools.

'I went to a boarding school called Arundel in Harare from the age of five. It was quite proper and rather snobbish. There were only five black girls in the whole school, and just two in my year. I would spend thirteen weeks at a time there, so I suppose I just picked up the accent. I've ended up mixed really. I didn't really grow up in African society as such, because I was away at school so much of the time. I wouldn't say I feel uncomfortable in African society because I know how I'm supposed to behave. But I get a certain reception because I'm perceived as untypical.'

Pearl was feeling her way back into her ancestral culture. Partly as a hobby, and partly as a business, she collected artefacts made by Shona people and sold them in America. She studied the customs and history as if she were an outsider, but in the end it was marrying her husband that had really tied her in.

'There's no such thing as divorce. If the relationship isn't working, the only way to split up is if your husband gives you a penny; it's called a *gupura*. I have an extremely hard time with Phil's mother. She's very traditional. When I visit her house, I become her maid, her *morora*. I have to sweep and clean and cook, and when family decisions are made I'm not part of the decision-making process.'

We parked, and entered the vast auction house. The concrete floor was covered in neat bales of yellow leaf, and the damp aroma of a million unsmoked cigars hung in the air. White farmers in blue short-sleeved shirts and khaki shorts, their faces tanned from a lifetime in the sun, knees red and knobbly above long fawn socks, walked along the rows comparing prices. The buyers stood in huddles talking quality. It is a ritual unchanged since the days when Rhodesia began to export tobacco in large quantities in the 1940s: a group of men shuffles up and down the rows; the 'starter' proposes a price for each bale in turn; the auctioneer chants a high-pitched, rapid-fire sing-song of competing prices from the buyers; and each bale is assessed, auctioned and sold in as little as six seconds. These days, starters and auctioneers are usually black, buyers and farmers white. Pearl, a self-possessed woman in her early thirties, received particular courtesy, and then respect, as her best bales retailed for the highest price of the day. Gnarled white men with faces wrinkled like brown paper bags wanted to know where she farmed and whether her farm too was in danger of being 'designated', seized by the government.

It was a surprise for them to find a black person sharing the same problems, because they rarely mixed. 'The white community didn't make any effort before because of fear,' Pearl explained. 'Mugabe is very cunning, so he allowed very little documenting of what really happened in the war. Whites were seen as such bad people, they were not given time to speak of their experiences during the war. Even among themselves they never talked about it. People have never been open about what happened. You could never say, "I killed so many black people," because if you talked about it you might be victimized. There was no period of adjustment, and you can't emerge from prejudice overnight. So they kept quiet, because they didn't know how to behave. Everyone kept quiet.'

'*Houthop* means "woodhead", from the Afrikaans. *Munt* comes from the Shona word *muntu* meaning person. *Kaffir* you already know.' Phil Matibe was remembering the insults white boys at his secondary school had used for the handful of black boys in their midst. '*Af*, of course. *Toe-ee* because most black kids only had one pair of tackies, so their big toe showed through. And *floppy* because when they killed black people during the war their bodies went all floppy.'

'And what did you call them?'

'We didn't have those kinds of words. There was *murungu*, which means a white person, although in Malawi it actually means God and it's not an insult. And *bhunu*, meaning farmer, wasn't derogatory in those days, although it's used that way now.'

Phil, handsome and athletic, always eager to talk and argue, laughed. It struck me that under the joshing and flirting ran a clear current of aggression, carefully controlled and managed, like a river dammed and directed into canals to prevent it from bursting its banks. We were drinking tea in the reception-area lounge at the Meikles Hotel, a genteel Harare institution still run by the descendants of Thomas Meikles, who followed the pioneer trail to Rhodesia in 1892. The walls were decorated with sepia prints of hunting expeditions and scenes from the capital and other towns in days gone by: SALISBURY IN 1924, THE MEIKLES STORE IN BULAWAYO, 1933. The nostalgic representation of colonialism is for tourists— or it would be, if there were any tourists.

While living on a gold-mining compound, Phil's family was incorporated into what was called 'The Harmony Programme'. In 1978 Prime Minister Ian Smith, famed for saying that Rhodesia had 'the happiest black faces in the world', introduced a limited scheme of integration in order to fend off criticism that Rhodesia was an apartheid state like South Africa.

'It was the first experiment. Four black families were going to reside in the white area, and we were chosen by my father's seniority because he was in charge of paying black workers. My younger sisters were allowed to go to whites-only schools. But what was amazing was that we were made to live on the periphery of the white residential areas, and it was during the war, so we became a buffer zone—if the compound was attacked, we'd be hit first!'

They weren't, but the fighting beyond the boundary was never far away. In 1972, when Phil was five, the guerrillas made their first attacks on isolated white farmsteads. By the time he was nine, they were making regular incursions from Mozambique and Zambia. Young white men were conscripted, and black men were also recruited as soldiers on the Rhodesian side. Like all guerrilla wars, it was cruel: white troops would round up and ruthlessly interrogate peasants they suspected of feeding and helping the guerrillas, who would, in turn, torture villagers they regarded as 'sell-outs' to the whites.

The mythology of the war was strangely seductive to a young black boy, attracted to what looked at the time like the winning team.

'We had to caddie for the whites at the Country Club. I was paid one Rhodesian dollar and fifty cents, which went to the Dalny Mine school for development. But I would sneak out to the rifle range and pick up spent cartridges, and for a bag full of cartridges I'd get twenty-five cents pocket money. There was a fire force stationed at the police station, and I'd go and clean their boots. I saw the bravado, the helicopters, the dead freedom fighters—they called them terrorists or "terrs". We had a TV, so I saw the Rhodesian propaganda. I viewed the Rhodesians as the ones safeguarding us from communism. If the war had continued, I would have joined the Rhodesian security forces. I saw that the white side had all these amenities, and they seemed so polished—but all I saw of the other side was broken bodies, half-dressed and scruffy. I would never have joined them.'

When international pressure forced Smith to negotiate an end to the war, and white rule gave way to independence in 1980, thirteen-year-old Phil was sent to what had previously been a whites-only school. There might have been a new black government in Harare under Comrade Prime Minister Robert Mugabe, but it made little difference to schoolboys at Jameson. Blacks sat at the end of the dining table and ate from crockery marked with green paint. When Phil carried a white girl's satchel, he was beaten by a group of sixth-formers armed with cricket bats and hockey sticks. That was lesson one: never, ever be seen walking with a white girl.

'I started to feel I wasn't wanted, I was inferior. So I decided to be ten times better than any of them at anything. I did cricket, rugby, debating society, astronomy, swimming—everything.' It didn't work. The bullying got worse. One day he found his exercise book had been defaced with the words: WE ARE KAFFIRS, WE EAT SADZA. *Sadza* is the staple food of Zimbabwe, a stiff maize-meal porridge that few whites would ever touch. Phil began getting into fights with white boys. At sixteen, a week before his O Levels, he was expelled.

He still wanted to do what the white man did, but better. After independence, whites still grew most of the country's export crops and food. Common wisdom had it that only a white man could run a successful commercial farm, because blacks were too ill-disciplined and incompetent. Phil wanted to prove them wrong. He went to a crammer to get O and A levels, and won a scholarship to agricultural college in England.

He began to reflect on what made the races different from each other. Several of the men in his class at college were Zimbabweans—white Zimbabweans. In England, they were all foreigners together, but difference still had to be acknowledged.

'We became friends. But the fabric that makes me African makes me fundamentally different from you. I have never hugged or kissed my mother. In my culture it's unheard of. I hate playing in water, while you love swimming.' He also thought about the differences he saw within the same racial group.

'I found that whites in England were not the same as whites in Zimbabwe. In England I started to realize that something had gone terribly wrong with our white people. All this time I had thought it was impossible to love a white person, but in England I even dated white girls.'

On returning to Zimbabwe, he got a job as a farm manager. 'My grandfather fought for the British in Burma and Malaya, and when he returned to Rhodesia the colonial administration rewarded him with a bicycle. There was a white man called Leslie Edwards who did the same, and he was given a farm called Inshallah. When I got back from the UK, it had been passed to his son and I worked for him.' He found it hard not to be resentful. The white Zimbabweans who had been on the same course as Phil in Wiltshire inherited farms on their return. When he walked into the local Country Club, there was no hostility from them, just distance. He was not part of their world. Zimbabwe's white liberals tended to live in cities, and most farmers had accepted independence without challenging their prejudices or way of thinking. A *munt* was still a *munt*.

'I learned never to greet a white person, unless he greeted me first,' said Phil. 'I was embarrassed too many times.'

Phil eventually earned the money to buy Paarl Farm from running a successful business selling meat to the army.

'I joined the Country Club. I took out a life membership—just to annoy them.'

As parliamentary elections approached in 2000, the TV news grew hateful. Mugabe's equation was simple: to vote for ZANU-PF was to be patriotic and loyal to your racial group, while to vote for the MDC was to be a stooge of the white man—worse, of the white farmer, the most hated kind of white man. White farmers, like black opposition activists, were now being killed by Mugabe's thugs. 'You are now our enemies because you really have behaved as enemies of Zimbabwe, and we are full of anger,' he told white farmers in April of that year.

'The white man has not changed!' he bellowed at a parliamentary election rally I attended. 'The whites can never be our cousins. They are racists.' His statements in Shona were more radical. His audience, many of whom had not been born when Ian Smith was in power, listened as Mugabe raised his fist and denounced his former rival as if he were still a current force, not an eighty-year-old whom Mugabe himself was allowing to live out a peaceful old age on his farm. It was like watching an old boxer punch an empty bag, reliving the fights of his youth.

Phil Matibe continued his campaign for the Chegutu parliamentary seat. He lost by a handful of votes. Believing the election to have been rigged, he took out a petition against the ZANU-PF victor.

In London a few months later I opened the *Daily Telegraph* and saw a photograph of Phil holding Mpho, his three-year-old son. They had been given the same punishment as was being meted out to white farmers: they had been thrown off their farm. I called their mobile and got Pearl.

'We're on the border at Beitbridge. We thought we'd better go to South Africa for a bit.'

'Are you all right?'

'We're fine, we just grabbed what we could and left.' Phil explained that a few days earlier an envoy from the victorious ZANU-PF candidate had come to tell him that if he did not withdraw his election petition by the end of the week, the farm would be seized. Phil said no. Two days later, a group of 'war veterans' arrived accompanied by district officials and villagers.

'They had a hat full of numbered bottle-tops. The villagers had to pick a number, and that was the plot they were allocated,' he said. 'Maybe they'll leave,' he added, hopefully. 'We'll try to get back on the farm next week.'

The following week, their home (with most of their possessions still inside) was burned to the ground.

When I returned to Zimbabwe a few weeks later, Phil took me

round the wreckage of his farm. The irrigation pipes had been pulled out, and parched barley stocks dangled brown and ruined. An emaciated old man who had previously worked as a farm labourer scratched in the dried earth for sugar beans. It looked like a scene from the Ethiopian famine. We wandered around the blackened carcass of the farmhouse, and looked out over the charred ruin of the barn and a heap of burnt maize cobs.

'I've lost everything,' Phil said. 'All my life savings. It's gone.'

We drove down to the workers' compound. It could have been a village anywhere in Africa. Women sat breastfeeding outside clay and wooden homes, while barefoot children gathered excitedly to see the *murungu*. The men stood in the shade of the *msasa* tree while Phil tried to explain to them why they had not been paid. I could see a small, sullen group dressed in jeans and bomber jackets circling us silently around the edge of the compound.

'Those aren't my workers,' said Phil, quietly. 'I think we should leave.' As we drove away, one of the group chased after us waving what looked like a machete. Phil said, 'The worst thing is dealing with the workers. What can I say to them if I can't pay them?'

After visiting the farm, I went to see Zimbabwe's Home Affairs Minister, an affable man called John Nkomo who delights in showing journalists his novelty telephone which looks like a toy train and, instead of ringing, goes 'choo choo'. He explained to me the problem with the opposition.

'They're a sponsored group, the result of efforts by white commercial farmers who wanted to defeat our land reorganization programme.' I asked why Matibe, one of the country's most successful black commercial farmers, should be ousted from his land in a programme which is meant to turn white-owned land over to blacks. He replied: 'Anyone who becomes a tool of the colonial legacy cannot be safe'—he paused for a moment for the message to sink in—'from the programme of land redistribution.'

Phil rang me to say they had offered him a new farm if he withdrew his petition.

'I said no. If they give me a farm it'll just be one they've taken from someone else.' They found one which had not been confiscated and renewed the offer. As he rounded the corner to look at the proposed property, he was shot at by men positioned near the gate. Pearl started agitating to get the children out of the country. Local officials visited to say he could have two farms if he joined ZANU-PF.

A few weeks later, he rang me in London again.

'I'm struggling with the pressure. They've pressured me up to the point where the next solution if I don't conform is death. So I've withdrawn my petition. All I want to do now is make sure the family's safe and I can get by.' He sounded defeated.

By the time I returned to Zimbabwe to report the 2002 presidential elections, I couldn't visit the Douses' farmhouse either. It was surrounded by a drunken mob chanting, shouting and drumming all night. The war vets had set up a roadblock at the gate, which Glenda crossed twice a day to get to her job at the hospital in Marondera.

'They put rocks in the cattle grid. One day when they screamed and shouted at me I got out my camera and took a picture, which they didn't like. Another day they stopped me and asked for my ZANU-PF card. I said I had an MDC card. Some of them just started laughing because it was such a stupid thing for me to say, but others were kicking the wheels and banging the windows, so I had to reverse and go and stay somewhere else that night.'

A ZANU-PF campaign video repeated endlessly on state TV showed grainy footage—presumably from the war—of a group of whites setting an Alsatian dog on a black man, while the pop star Chinx Chingaire sang in Shona:

'You think they like you,
But they don't.
They only smile because they want something.
Underneath, they're devils.'

The strategy worked. Mugabe won the presidency. Six more years to add to the twenty-two he had already served as leader of Zimbabwe. The war vets celebrated, while the Douses at first reverted to type and did what Zimbabwe's whites always do when times are bad: they went to Inyanga for the weekend and lived the white African life, drinking cocktails and fishing for trout. They returned to a rented town house in Harare and hoped that the gooks who were going round assaulting MDC activists would not come for them. The white manager of the next-door farm was beaten so badly he was taken to hospital covered in blood. He and his young wife and baby left the country as soon as he could walk.

Graham has decided that Nyagambe Farm will inevitably end up being confiscated. He has been to Zambia to look for a new farm; if that does not work out, then he may try Australia.

Glenda, back on the farm, cannot bring herself to move, even though Graham is leaving, even though the triumphant war vets are more hostile than ever. Most of the black MDC supporters she has grown to know during the election campaign cannot leave the country, so why should she? 'The worst feeling after the election result is this anger and sense that people must hate us,' she says. 'All this time in the MDC we haven't felt that, we felt part of the struggle and the future, only now there's no future because they hate us. In my heart I think if we stay here it'll be okay sooner or later, but that's what my father thought and he got shot for it. But this is my home and I'm not going to leave. It's strange, but I feel I just can't go.'

Pearl has had enough. She has a brother in America, and the possibility of a university place in Britain. She can choose where she belongs, and is determined her children should have that choice too. They can be anyone they want to be. She says, 'I never thought in Zimbabwe we'd become like the rest of Africa.'

Phil wants to stay. His despair has turned to anger, and the pent-up frustration of his youth is propelling him towards an African destiny that he never envisaged in the years he was trying to work out who he was and where he belonged. After the election, twenty-six of his farm labourers sued him for failing to pay their wages. He told them to ask Robert Mugabe for the money, whereupon the police charged him on twenty-six counts of defaming the president, one for each worker who heard the remark. Other cases have been brought against him, and he travels with a bodyguard now. 'I used to brag that we were different Africans. I never thought it would come to this,' he says. 'I don't know what we have to do to bring change in Africa. You see me today as a democrat, but you realize that tomorrow I could be a warlord.' ☐

SCOUTING FOR BOYS
Paul Theroux

Paul Theroux (fifth from left, in sneakers); Michael Bloomberg, now mayor of New York (third from left, with badges), Medford Massachusetts scout troupe, 1953

Three figures came single file over a wooded hill of the Fells carrying their rifles one-handed and keeping their heads low. They were duckwalking, hunched like Indian trackers, with the same stealth in their footfall, toeing the mushy earth of early spring. I was one of them, the last, being careful, watching for the stranger, his black hat, his blue Studebaker. Walter Herkis and Chicky DePalma were the others. When we got to the clearing where the light slanted through the bare trees and into our squinting faces you could see we were twelve years old.

'Where?' Chicky asked, in a harsh disbelieving tone, keeping an irritated grin on his face. He had a brown birthmark like a raisin on his cheek. His hair, greasy from too much Wildroot, and his big nose and his yellowish Sicilian face made him look even more like an Indian brave.

'Wicked far,' Walter said. Worry settled on his scrubbed features whenever he was asked anything about the incident. He motioned with the muzzle of his gun. 'Up by the pond.'

Walter's saying it was far made us slow our pace, though we still kept off the path. When one of us stepped on a dry twig and snapped it, someone else said, 'Watch it,' because in the movies the snapping of a twig always betrayed a person's position to strangers. We wanted to be silent and invisible. We were not three boys, we were trackers, we were Indians. Certain words, such as sure-footed, and hawk-eyed, made us self-conscious.

'Skunk cabbage,' I said.

Dark red and black claw-shaped bunches of the glossy plant grew in the muddy patch near a mass of rotten wood and dead grass that was pressed down and combed looking from the weight of the snow.

'Them others are fiddleheads,' Walter said, stopping farther on, where the mud was thicker and wetter. Ragged veils of gnats whirred over its small smooth bubble holes. From the evaporated puddle, a slab of mud as smooth as chocolate, rose a clump of packed together ferns in sprays like bouquets, their coiled tops beginning to unroll and spring open. Fiddleheads was the perfect name for them.

'Vinny eats them,' Walter said. He lifted his rifle and poked the ferns and gently parted the stalks with the muzzle.

Chicky said, 'He'd get sick. Vinny Grasso is a lying guinea wop.'

'And you're a pissa.'

'Eat me, I'm a jelly bean,' Chicky said.

'Shut up,' I whispered. 'Someone will hear.'

'Fuckum,' Chicky said.

For emphasis, he stepped over to the tight green bouquets of new ferns and scattered some in one kick, then broke the ones that remained and tramped them flat, his boots squelching the mud and burying them.

Looking at the damage, he said, 'But my Nonna eats dandelions.'

Chicky's outbursts alarmed me, because they made him sound crazy, and his threats were sudden and scary, especially when he was trying to be funny. To act tough, he sometimes punted schoolbooks and kicked them along the sidewalk. I had never before seen anyone kick a book. He said: Who cares? I can hardly read, anyway, which was true, and as shocking to me as wrecking the books.

'Give me a freakin weed, Andy.'

'Coffin nails,' Walter said.

'Who asked you?'

'They're wicked bad for you,' Walter said, straightening himself with confidence.

'You're just saying that because they're against your religion,' Chicky said.

Walter Herkis was a Seventh Day Adventist. He couldn't be in our Scout troop, because Protestants weren't allowed to be Scouts at St Ray's. He wanted to join our Beaver Patrol, but he would have been shocked by our Scout meetings in the church hall, the prayers, especially, Father Staley—'Scaly Staley'—telling us to kneel on the varnished wood floor of the basketball court and raising his scaly hands, which was how he got his name, and folding them, and giving a sermon, or else saying, Let us pray. Walter went by bus to a special school in Boston, with other Adventists. Walter could not smoke, or eat meat, not even hot dogs, or tuna fish, and he was supposed to go to church on Saturday. He was playing hooky from church today, as he often did, though today was special: we were hunting the stranger.

'They stunt your growth,' Walter said.

Chicky snapped his fingers. 'Come on, Andy.'

I unbuckled my knapsack and found among the canvas pouches of bullets and the marshmallows and tonic, the crushed pack of

Lucky Strikes Chicky had stolen from his brother. I shook out a cigarette for him, and put the rest away.

'Luckies,' Chicky said. He tapped the cigarette on his knuckle like an old smoker, and said, 'Got a match?'

'Your face and my ass,' Walter said.

'Your face and the back of a bus.' I handed him a book of matches. 'You want a kick in the chest to get it started?'

Chicky lit up and puffed and wagged the match to put it out. He inhaled, sucking air with his teeth clamped shut, making slurping sounds in his cheeks. Then he plucked out the cigarette and admired it as he blew out a spray of blue smoke.

'You're giving it a wicked lipper,' Walter said.

'Stick it, goombah. You don't even smoke.' Chicky handed the butt to me.

I puffed without inhaling, snuffled a little from the smoke leaking up my nose, and covered my gagging by saying, 'Where was he?'

'Not here,' Walter said, and walked ahead. Pale and freckled, taller than either Chicky or me, Walter was skinny, and had long legs, his bony knees showing in his dungarees. He was such a fast runner we could not understand how the man had caught him—if he had caught him. Walter had not told us much of the story, only that we had to track the man down and find his blue Studebaker. He was round-shouldered hurrying ahead of us, and his spiky hair, his slender neck made him look lonely.

'I don't even freakin believe him,' Chicky said.

'Quit it,' I said. 'Walter doesn't lie.'

'He's a Protestant.'

'So what?'

'It's not a sin for them to lie,' Chicky said.

We followed Walter up the hill, away from the path, deeper into the woods. We passed Wright's Tower at the top of the hill, and climbed the urine-stinky stairs to the lookout: Boston—the Customs House—in one direction; the dark woods in the other. We descended and went deeper into the woods.

Even on this early spring day, there were mud-spattered crusts of mostly melted snow, skeletal and icy from softening to slush and refreezing. The woods looked littered and untidy with the snow scraps, with driblets of ice from the recent rain in the grooved bark and boles of trees, ice enamelling the sides of rocks, the old poisoned-looking leaves, curled and dead, brittle, black, thicknesses of them like soggy trash, the earth still slowly thawing, with winter lingering on top. Even so, spring was swelling, pushing from beneath, like the claws of skunk cabbage rising through the mud, and small dark buds on bush twigs, the knobs of bulbs and plants like fists thrusting up through softened soil, and the first shoots, white as noodles.

Walter was waiting for us at the bottom of the hill, at a cliffside and a boulder pile we called Panther's Cave.

'Was he here?' Chicky said, glancing at the cave entrance, a damp shadow falling across it, for it was already five and would be dark soon. The portals of the cave were two upright boulders, bigger than we were, scorched and smelling of woodsmoke.

'I already told you, no.'

'Tell us the story,' Chicky said.

'Shove it up your bucket,' Walter said, and peeled the cellophane from a package of Devil Dogs.

'Fungoo,' Chicky said. 'Hey, Herkis, I had dibs on them.'

'I'm hungry,' Walter said, poking a Devil Dog into his mouth, chewing hard, his voice sounding dry and cakey when he said, with his mouth full, 'Anyway, you got cigarettes.'

'Give me one or I'll whack your ass.' Chicky swung his rifle by its barrel like a bat at Walter.

'Let's go,' I said, because Chicky's quarrelling made me uneasy and this was all a delay in the darkening woods.

'He's a Jew,' Chicky said. 'Okay, if he's scoffing the Devil Dogs, I hosey the Twinkies.' He looked hard at Walter. 'Jelly belly.'

'Rotate,' Walter said, and raised his middle finger.

With his tongue against his teeth, Chicky chanted, 'My friend Walter had a pimple on his belly. His mother cut it off and made it into jelly.'

Walter, still chewing, staring at the ground, looked hurt, not for anything that Chicky had said but as though he was thinking about something worse.

'Come on,' I said. I had meant Let's go, but Walter took it to mean the story.

'It wasn't here,' he said.

'Where then?'

'I told you, wicked far.'

'Near the road?'

'No, past the Sheepfold.'

'Spot pond? The Rezza?'

'The other one,' Walter said. He was licking fudgey flakes and frosting from his dirty knuckles. 'Where you see cars sometimes.'

'Where we shot holes in that No Parking sign?' Chicky said. Then shouted, 'You had to eat all the Devil Dogs yourself, you fucking Jew bastard.'

'Doleful Pond,' I said. My father sometimes took me fishing there with my brother Louie. We caught small slimy fish there, pickerel, hornpout and kibbies, and removing the hook we sometimes slashed our fingers on the fishes' sharp fins.

Doleful Pond was so far, we did not bother tracking or whispering, but started off again, walking together on the bridle path, our rifles slung by their straps on our shoulders.

Chicky said, 'Walter's got a new girlfriend.'

'Quit it,' Walter said.

'Her name's Mary Palm.'

'At least I don't eat fur burgers like some people I know.'

'You gobble the hairy clam,' Chicky said. 'So does Andy.'

Chicky let the cigarette die. He lit it again and finished it, puffing it to a small butt, less than an inch, tweezing it between his fingertips. 'Look,' he said, and pinched the ashy tip off and began tearing at the paper and loose tobacco. He peeled the paper and flaked the tobacco and scattered it.

'That's called field stripping. My cousin showed me how. He was in the Navy in Japan. He brought back this wicked nice jacket with a dragon on the back. I'm going in the Navy.'

'The Navy gets the gravy, but the Army gets the beans,' Walter said. 'That's true, you know. The food in the Navy is really good.'

'I bet you've never seen one, Andy.'

'One what?'

'Twat.'

It was true, but I shrugged in a worldly way, as though the question was irrelevant.

'I've seen billions of them,' Walter said. 'My mother's always charging around the house bollocky.'

'That doesn't count,' Chicky said. 'She's too old.'

'I saw my cousin's,' Walter said. Though he sounded as though he was breathless from the memory it was from climbing the path, beating the twiggy bushes aside, kicking the snow crusts with his wet shoes. 'She was bollocky. She didn't even know I was looking at her.' He measured with his cold reddened hands. 'It was yay big. It even had some hair on it.'

'Like you'd know what to do with it.'

'I didn't have any Trojans,' Walter said.

'As if they make them that small.'

'Anyway, I wouldn't bang my cousin without a rubber.'

'She must be a nympho.'

'She's a virgin.'

'So are you,' Chicky said.

A silence entrapped us with the truth: we were each of us virgins.

'You Jew bastard, why did you eat all the Devil Dogs?'

'Hungry,' Walter said. 'This kid I know at school says to me, "A girl doesn't have to get pregnant. After she gets banged she can just piss it out—piss out all the sperm."'

Another silence and the crunching of dead leaves as we walked: each of us considering this, trying to imagine the process.

'What a shit-for-brains,' Chicky said. 'It's impossible.'

Though none of us knew why: in fact, it seemed logical.

'I would have known what to do with your cousin,' Chicky said.

'Sure. Every day and twice on Sunday.'

'Anyway, what's her name?'

'Cheryl.'

'Headlights?'

Walter nodded and said, 'She even wears a boulder-holder.'

Chicky said, 'I'd say, "Hey, Cheryl,"' and then do like the four Roman emperors. Seize 'er. Squeeze 'er. Pump 'er. Dump 'er."

'Did you really see her knobs?' I asked and thought what heaven it would be to behold such a miracle.

'Yeah,' Walter said. 'We was sitting on the glider, on her piazza. I was going to feel her up.'

'I would have,' Chicky said, ''cause I'm in the Four "F" Club. Find 'em, feel 'em, fuck 'em and forget 'em.'

Now the woods ahead were indistinct, though there was still light in the sky. The great thing about being in the woods at this hour was that there was rarely anyone else around: the woods were ours, and we were free in them. We walked on, into the thickening shadows.

2.

'Tell us the story again,' I said.

Walter clawed his damp spiky hair and sighed, having to repeat himself. He said in a mumbling way, 'I'm walking along the path near where we found the ripped-up magazines that day.'

'Doleful Pond,' I said.

'Yeah,' Walter said. 'Where you see cars sometimes and you wonder how did they get there?'

But I was thinking about the magazines, how they had been torn to pieces, but even so they were easy to put together. Each fragment was a part of a naked woman, and some pieces were so big there was a whole naked woman, the white of a smooth body so clear, almost luminous, or pale as sausage casing, breasts like balloons. They had seemed like witches to me, powerful and pretty, smiling sinners, representing everything that was forbidden.

'I'm walking past this blue Studebaker and I didn't even know this old guy was in it until he says, "Hey, kid," and reaches out the window. I looks over—he's smiling with these yellow teeth, and as I walks away I hear the door open.'

'Why didn't you take off?'

Walter could run faster than either Chicky or me, but he was slower witted, so he did not always know when to run.

'I almost shit a brick because he scared me. I didn't know what to do. I just kept walking, to show I didn't really care.'

I knew the pond and the road there, so I could easily see Walter marching stiffly away from the blue Studebaker, his little head, his skinny neck, his spiky uncombed hair, his baggy pants and scuffed shoes; trying so hard not to look scared he moved like a puppet.

'I thought he was supposed to have a boner,' Chicky said.

'That was later,' Walter said.

'When he chased you?' I asked.

'No. I looks back and he's back in the car, so I kept going. I knew he wouldn't drive on the path. There's a sign, the one we blasted with our guns. There's a gate. He couldn't get through.'

'Which path?'

'To the Sheepfold, like I said. I was going up there to build a fire and get warm.'

'What about your gun?'

'I didn't bring it.'

'You said you did.'

'No sah.'

'Yes sah.'

'My sister hid it, to be a pain.'

Chicky said, 'You said you aimed your gun at him and he freaked.'

'Knife. I had my hunting knife, so that I could make wood shavings to start the fire. I had it in my belt, in the sheath. I pulled it out as I was walking up the path, in case he chased me.'

'You said gun before. Didn't he, Andy?'

'I don't remember,' I said. Truly, I didn't. All I could recall was the blue car, the old man, his black golf cap, Walter being pestered.

'You told the story different before,' Chicky said. 'You said you saw him in the woods.'

'You didn't let me get to that part,' Walter said, in a wronged pleading voice, his eyes glistening so much I felt sorry for him. More softly he said, 'So I'm at the Sheepfold. There's nobody around. I whittled a stick and got some shavings. I try to start a fire, and I'm kneeling down and blowing on the sparks and I hear something.'

'What?'

'How do I know? Twigs. But I look around and the old guy is standing right behind me. He followed me somehow. He's saying, "Hey, kid." His fly is open. That's when he had the boner.'

'What did it look like?' Chicky said.

'He tries to grab me,' Walter said, hurrying his story. 'I screams at him but there's no one around, right? So then I starts running.'

'What about all your stuff, and the fire?'

'I just left it.'

'Anyway, you escaped,' I said.

Walter didn't say no. He frowned again and clawed his spiky hair. He said, 'Then, when I was out to the road and thought it was all over, this blue Studebaker comes screeching up beside me, and it's the guy again, and he's after me.'

When he said that, I got a chill. I could imagine it clearly, for sometimes in my worst dreams people kept showing up, I never knew how, to scare me or accuse me.

'Everywhere I go I sees the stupid guy.'

Chicky said, 'He's definitely a homo.'

Walter was silent, paler than when he had started the story, biting his lips.

'But you told it different the first time,' Chicky said.

'You think I'm bullshitting?'

'Sounds like bird-turd to me,' Chicky said.

'You believe me, Andy,' Walter said in a beseeching voice.

'Sure.' But he had told the story differently the first time. He had a gun. He had turned and threatened the man, who had fallen back and returned to his car. He had not said anything about the Sheepfold and the fire. Seeing the man again on the road, the car stopping—that was new.

'Wait till you see his car,' Walter said. 'Then you'll believe me.'

'Anyway, what did he want?' Chicky asked.

'He was a homo. You know what those guys want.'

But we had absolutely no idea, except that it was wicked and dangerous and we were unwilling. In my imagination, such a man would hold me captive in his car, all the windows rolled up, trapping me and threatening me. What he did was not anything I thought of as sex. These men were friendly at first, so that they could grab me and tie me up. In my imagining I was gagged and blindfolded. Then he would take some of my clothes off, and something happened, something that hurt. In the end, when I was naked, he would kill me, probably stab me.

'I don't get it,' Chicky said. He was still impatient and over-stimulated, flecks of spit in the corners of his mouth, blinking hard, his yellowish Italian face looking damp with confusion. 'He was bigger than you, right? So why didn't he just grab you?'

'He did grab me,' Walter said. 'I was fighting with him.'

'You didn't say that before.'

'You didn't give me enough time.'

Walter was looking breathless and wretched, yanking his hair.

'Did he touch you?' I asked.

'I didn't want him to,' Walter said, protesting.

'Where did he touch you?'

'I told you, the Sheepfold.'

That was new. I had not seen Walter struggling at the Sheepfold, only fleeing. Now I put him back at the Sheepfold, on the ground, the man grabbing at him.

'I mean, did he touch your nuts?'

Walter said, 'I was pushing him as hard as I could,' and as he spoke he was fighting tears.

'I thought you ran away.'

'I did run away. After.'

'What else did he do?'

'I don't know. He was feeling my pants. He was really strong and he had this moustache and was chewing something like a cough drop. He even tried to kiss me. He was snatching my hands.'

'Was he saying anything?'

'Yeah. "Don't be afraid, don't be afraid."'

'I would have shit a brick.'

'I was wicked scared,' Walter said.

He was quiet for a moment. His face was blotchy with red patches, he was remembering, his mouth quivering, trying to start a word.

'How did you get away.'

'Ran. Like I told you.'

'You never said he touched you.'

'I forgot that part.'

'How could you forget that, you freakin banana man?'

Walter lowered his head and said, 'When I screamed out loud he got wicked worried. He tried to put his hand over my mouth. His hand was really smelly. That's when I tried to stab him in the leg with my fork.'

'Your fork?'

'I was going to heat up some beans. The fork was lying there.'

'That's great,' Chicky said.

I said, 'I don't get why he showed up later.'

Walter kicked at the snow crust. This was painful, an awful story, much worse than the first time. I suspected it was true because it was messier, there was more of it, and the new parts were unpleasant.

'He was trying to tell me he was sorry.'

'Pretending to,' I said. 'He was just trying to trick you. If he had caught you he would have killed you.'

'He said he wanted to give me some money. Ten bucks.'

'That's bull for one thing,' Chicky said. 'Ten bucks!'

Walter reached in his pocket and pulled out a little ball of paper and flattened it and smoothed it: a five-dollar bill.

'Jeez,' Chicky said.

Five dollars was more money than we ever saw, and it could only mean that Walter, who never had money, might be telling the truth. But it was five, not ten.

'Where's the rest?' Chicky said.

Walter opened a flap of his knapsack and took out a box of bullets, and slipped out the paper drawer, showing us the fifty tightly packed bullets. I had a little envelope of bullets for my rifle, Chicky had the same. But this was ammo.

'Vinny sold them to me for a fin,' Walter said. 'I want to find this guy and sneak up on him. And scare him like he scared me.'

'Like how?'

'I don't know.'

'Kill the bastard, maybe,' Chicky said.

'Maybe we should tell the cops,' I said, because whenever Chicky talked about killing someone it made me nervous. He had never done anything so violent, but it seemed that he was always trying to nerve himself for something that bad, and that one day he would succeed.

'Don't be such an asshole,' Chicky said.

'The cops wouldn't even believe me,' Walter said. What kept us from asking any more questions was that we both knew that Walter was going to cry.

'I would have blubbered,' I said, because I could see Walter's eyes getting wet.

Hearing that must have made Walter feel better, because he sniffed and wiped his nose on the sleeve of his jacket and didn't look so tearful.

'I mean, especially if some old guy put his hands on me,' I said.

I thought it would help some more but it made it worse, because when I mentioned the hands Walter got tearful again.

'I'd like to kill him,' he said in a fearful, helpless voice.

'Let's all kill him,' Chicky said, smiling wildly.

'I don't even care,' Walter said. 'If he was standing right here I'd shoot him in the nuts.'

Chicky loved that and started to laugh, his face growing yellower at the thought of it. Seeing Chicky laugh, Walter's anger left him, and he laughed too, but harder, angrier, his whole face brightening. But there were tears in his eyes and stains of tears on his cheeks— smears of wetness and dust. He wiped his face with his arm, smearing it more, looking miserable.

'I will,' he said. 'In the nuts!'

But the day had gone cold and dark had come down on us without our realizing it, a dampness rising with it from the dead leaves and rotten earth, and so we headed home with darkness pressing on our heads.

3.

'There were three boys,' Father Staley was saying at the Scout meeting in the over-bright church hall of St Ray's the following Wednesday. He was giving a sermon, one of his stories from the Navy, about a captain who was trying to find the smartest boy to do a job. 'Three boys' made me think of Walter, Chicky and me, and as Father Staley spoke I saw each of us in the story.

'The captain gave each boy a keg of nails. "There are five thousand nails in each keg," the captain said. "There is also a gold nail in each keg. The first one to find the gold nail will get the job."'

Father Staley paused and let us picture this, but the pause was too long and when we began fidgeting after a little while Arthur Mutch, the scoutmaster, said, 'I'm going to be handing out demerits!'

'What would you do if you were in those boys' shoes?' Father Staley said.

'Find the freakin gold nail,' Chicky said, much too loud.

'DePalma—one demerit!'

Father Staley then explained that the first boy picked through the nails in his keg, pushing them aside, looking for the gold nail. While he was doing this, the second boy began removing one nail after another from his keg, trying to see which one was gold.

'The third boy asked the captain for a newspaper,' Father Staley said, and paused again to enjoy our puzzlement.

Chicky covered his mouth and muttered, 'And he read the

freakin newspaper while the other dinks found the gold nail.' When he looked up Arthur Mutch was staring at him.

'The boy spread the newspaper on the floor and dumped the whole keg of nails on to it, all five thousand of them,' Father Staley said. 'He saw the gold nail at once. He picked it up and then funnelled the nails back into the keg. And he got the job. What lesson does that teach us?'

We said nothing. We had no idea, though I saw the story clearly: the wooden kegs, the boys, the glittering gold nail in the pile of iron ones.

'Sometimes you have to take drastic action,' Father Staley said. 'And sometimes, to save your soul...'

As soon as he uttered those words, *save your soul*, I stopped listening, and so did Chicky, because afterwards when we were in our circle of folding chairs, the patrol meeting, Chicky said, 'What was the point of that freakin story?'

Arthur Mutch approached us and glared at Chicky, and said, 'Beaver Patrol, at ease.' Then, to me, 'What merit badge are you going up for, Andy?'

'Campcraft,' I said.

'What have you done about it?'

'Took a hike last Saturday.'

'Name some of the essentials you had in your pack?'

Mossberg .22, twelve bullets, Hostess cream-filled cupcakes, bottle of tonic, stolen pack of Lucky Strikes, book of matches. I said, 'First Aid kit. Flashlight. Canvas tarp. Some rope. Canteen. Pencil and paper. And some apples.'

'I think you forgot something.'

Since none of what I had told him was true, it was easy to remember the missing item required by the badge for a hike. 'Um, compass.'

'Good,' Mr Mutch said. 'Engage in any activities?'

Killed a toad, chased a squirrel, listened to Walter Herkis's story of being molested by a man in a blue Studebaker. But I said, 'Knot-tying. Cooking. Tracking.'

Tracking was not a lie: we had headed towards Doleful Pond with Walter before it got too dark to go farther.

'What did you cook?'

'Beans and franks. And afterwards we doused the fire and made sure the coals were out.'

More lies, but once—months before—I had done just that, and I considered that it counted.

'What knots and what did you use them for?'

'Sheepshank for shortening the rope. Half-hitch. Square knot. Propped up the tarp with them to make a shelter.'

'Know the bowline yet?' Mr Mutch asked.

'I'm trying.'

Behind me, a voice—Father Staley's—said, 'I think I can help you with that, Andy.'

'Thank you, Father.'

Mr Mutch, satisfied with me, turning to Chicky, said, 'DePalma, what badge are you going out for?'

'Civics.' Chicky blinked and as his yellow face grew pale his brown birthmark got darker.

'Civics? DePalma, tell me, what is a bicameral legislature?'

Chicky twisted his face, to show he was thinking hard, and said nothing. His fists were pressed in panic against his legs.

'You don't know, do you?'

Chicky shook his head, his springy curls glistening. No, he didn't know.

'How many merit badges have you earned, DePalma?'

Chicky muttered something that was inaudible.

'Louder, please.'

'None,' Chicky said in a hoarse humiliated voice.

'You're still a Tenderfoot after a year and a half in the Scouts,' Arthur Mutch said.

Father Staley said, 'Try a little harder, son. Do some homework.'

'I could go out for car maintenance, Father, but do they have a badge for it? No.'

'Any other ideas?' Father Staley said.

'Maybe Indian Lore.' Chicky's eyes were shining with shame and anger. 'Maybe Campcraft.'

'What makes you think you can earn them?'

'I went on a hike with Andy.'

'And did you cook franks and beans, too?'

'Yes, Father. And capacol. Guinea sausages.'

'Well, that's a start.'

Father Staley stepped over to me and smiled and lifted my chin with his hand, saying, 'You pick up the lame and the halt, don't you?'

'I don't know, Father.'

He looked pleased, having asked me a question I could not answer; and he followed Mr Mutch to the next patrol group.

Under his breath, Chicky said, '"How many merit badges have you earned?" Mutch is an asshole.'

'You'll get millions.'

'I'd get one if they had car maintenance, engine repair, some shit like that,' Chicky said. He stood, round-shouldered and discouraged. 'I got gatz.'

As Chicky said gatz, Father Staley, at the front of the hall, said, 'Let us pray,' and blessed himself slowly, using the tips of his scaly fingers, 'In the name of the Father, and the Son and the Holy Ghost.'

The woods were full of wonders, full of occurrences that only happened in the woods. Some people parked at the edges, but they didn't walk far from their cars; others used the bridle paths; no one but us wandered the woods—or if they did, we never saw them. We hiked beyond the roar of traffic on the Fellsway—past Panther's Cave all we heard was birds chirping, the rustle of squirrels and the wind in the boughs up top.

There were still snow scraps now, but wetter ones; more fiddleheads, redder skunk cabbage, bigger buds. We looked closely at them, as self-conscious Scouts and woodsmen, and we took pains to hide ourselves from anyone on the path. That was why, near Doleful Pond, we avoided a fisherman who was fussing with his rod and line on the shore, slashing it like a whip.

'Is that the homo?' Chicky asked.

'No,' Walter said.

Nor was there a blue Studebaker parked behind him, but rather an old black Pontiac; still, because we had rifles, we kept to the bushes by the side of the pond.

'Hey, you kids, is there a fire station around here?' As he spoke he was holding his fishing rod.

Somehow the man had seen us. He had asked a pervert's question: perverts often pretended to be in trouble. Once a pervert had said to Chicky, 'There's a rock under my car. Help me get it out.' A rock under my car was just a lie to get his hands on Chicky, but Chicky had run away. This question about a fire station made us speed up and shoulder our rifles so that he could see we were armed and dangerous.

'He's waving something at us,' Chicky said under his breath.

The fisherman had put his rod down and was waving his spread-apart hand. He said, 'Hooked my thumb!'

He showed us his thumb, and it was true—a dark wire stuck out of the meaty part of his thumb muscle, like the loop on a Christmas ornament. I was thinking: Maybe a man would deliberately stick a hook into his thumb in order to look helpless, so that he could trap a boy.

'What do you kids think you're doing with those guns?' he said. He just glanced at our guns but he went on frowning at the embedded hook.

'Boy Scouts,' I said. 'We're allowed.'

'I was a Boy Scout. I never learned how to use a gun.'

'Hey, did you learn how to use a fishing rod?' Chicky said.

'What are you, a wise guy?'

'Because, hey, you hooked your thumb—don't look at me,' Chicky said.

'It's not funny, I need to get this fucking thing out.' He wiggled the hook and winced and swore again.

I said, 'You can't pull it out, because of the barb. You're supposed to push the hook in deeper, and twist it to get the barb through the skin, so it sticks out. Then you snip off the barb and you can just slip the smooth part out. Got any pliers?'

'So you're a wise guy, too. I'm going to tell the cops about your guns. Them are illegal, you know.'

What I had told him was in the First Aid merit badge handbook, three stages in removing a hook: push, snip, pull. Snip it with pliers, the handbook said, but he did not want to hear it. The hook in his thumb looked just like the one in the picture illustrating the hook-removal technique.

'Where's the emergency people?' he said angrily. 'Where's the fire station?'

'And you need a tetanus shot for tetanus toxoid,' I said, to irritate him, because he refused to do what the book told him to do. 'You could get lockjaw.'

The man stooped and groaned and gathered up his fishing tackle with his left hand—I could see a pair of the right kind of needle-nose pliers in the tackle box. He held up his right hand like a policeman signalling to stop traffic, his fingers spread out, his thumb hooked.

'This hurts like hell—it's throbbing,' he said. 'As if you give a shit!'

And he threw his tackle box and rod into the back seat and reversed down the narrow road, the car bouncing.

'Getting pissed makes your heart beat faster,' I said. 'The poison spreads.'

'He's not even supposed to drive here, the stupid bastard,' Chicky said. He mocked the man, saying, 'It's thrawbing!'

'This is where the other guy was,' Walter said.

'The homo?' Chicky said.

Walter sucked on his lips, probably so they would not quiver and show how upset he was, and we looked at him, feeling sorry for him, standing on the spot where the strange man in the blue Studebaker had—what?—fooled around with him. No one said anything for a while.

About twenty feet from where the fisherman had parked his car there was a barrier gate, just a horizontal steel pipe, hinged to a post on one side and padlocked shut on the other. Above it, the sign with our bullet holes in it, NO PARKING—POLICE TAKE NOTICE. Chicky unsheathed his hunting knife and shinnied up the pole and scraped away at the T, so that it said, POLICE TAKE NO ICE.

'Bastards,' he said.

Farther along the shore of the pond, in the water, beyond a scooped-out embankment, there were scraps of paper curling and bobbing beneath the surface. Making sure the fisherman was gone, we put our guns down and broke off branches from the low bushes. We stood at the edge and used these, dragging the branches, to fish up the fragments of paper. The women in the torn pages were alone, some sitting, or lying down, some in bathtubs, half hidden in a froth of bubbles, heavy breasts and dark nipples. We knew these dripping pages were from girlie magazines, ripped squarely in large pieces. On one was a large breast, on another a bare leg, a shoulder, the woman's head: bouffant hair, big lips, black-and-white photographs of naked women from a magazine. They seemed much wickeder soaking wet.

'I like this one,' I said.

'She's wearing socks,' Chicky said.

'She looks more naked that way.'

'You're nuts.'

Chicky found the cover, all in colour, *Naturist Monthly*, two women playing tennis, seen from the rear, a nudist magazine. We pieced some pages back together and saw naked people putting golf balls in a miniature golf course, others playing ping-pong, some swimming, and oddest of all, a family eating dinner at an outdoor picnic table, Dad, Mom and two little flat-chested girls. Mom was smiling: droopy tits and holding a forkful of droopy spaghetti.

'You can't see the guy's wang,' Chicky said, 'but lookit.'

Naked children frolicking in shallow water with naked parents, a whole bare-assed family. And even though one of the teenaged girls was being splashed I could see her breasts and a tuft of hair between her legs.

'I bet she's not a virgin,' Walter said. And then, grunting, 'I've got a raging boner.'

'Give him some saltpetre,' I said.

That was the remedy we had heard about, to prevent you from getting a hard-on. People said that in some schools the teachers mixed it with the food, to keep the kids out of trouble.

We trawled with the branches, hoping for more thrown-away magazines. There were certain secluded places at the edge of the woods, or near the ponds, where cars could park, where we found these torn-up or discarded magazines. They were always damaged; we had no idea where anyone could buy them. Without being able to explain it, we knew that men took them here, as part of a ritual, a private vice, to look at the forbidden pictures and then destroy the evidence.

And we did the same, piecing the wet pages together, and gloating over them, and then, feeling self-conscious, we scattered them and kicked them aside, and walked on.

We left the bridle path, and crouched, ducking through the budded bushes, traversing the hill. We trod on the balls of our feet, 'sure-footed,' as though in moccasins, like the Indians we saw in movies who were indistinguishable from the bushes and the mottled light of the forest.

Walking along the margin of the bridle path, we came to a clearing, the meadow of the Sheepfold, some scorched stone fireplaces and picnic tables, and stumps to sit on. The place was empty this cold afternoon: all ours. We gathered wood and started a fire, warmed our hands, piled on more wood, and I whittled a stick to roast the hot dogs.

Walter said, 'Those things have shit in them, real pieces of shit.'

'You're just saying that because you don't eat meat,' Chicky said. 'Because of your religion.'

He unpacked some Italian sausages, bright red meat and pepper, speckled white with fat, and held tight with filmy sausage casing that looked like a Trojan. These he penetrated lengthwise with a sharp narrow stick, and held them over the fire, letting them sputter and burst.

'I'm going up for a cooking merit badge,' Chicky said.

Walter ate a chocolate bar, while I burned my hot dog and, trying to toast it, burned the roll I had brought. Chicky nibbled the burned end of one of his sausages, and roasted it some more over the fire.

'It looks like a boner,' Walter said.

'Hoss cock,' Chicky said.

Back in the woods, heading home the long way, over the hill, off the path, we saw a squirrel, and chased it, throwing stones at it because a gunshot would be heard clearly so close to the road. And chasing it, the squirrel leaping from bough to bough, pushing the branches down each time he jumped, we came again to the margin of Doleful Pond, without realizing how we had got there, and losing the squirrel in the darkness.

That was when we saw the headlights, so bright the glare of them obscured the shape and colour of the car.

'That's him,' Walter said.

'Bull,' Chicky said, because it was just a pair of yellow lights.

We crouched down and watched the car reverse, moving slowly, and where the road was wider, the car stopped and made a three-point turn, lighting the bushes, illuminating itself, a small blue car, sitting high on its wheels, a Studebaker.

So Walter Herkis, who sometimes fibbed, was telling the truth after all. He did not gloat about being right—he didn't even seem glad that now he had us as witnesses to the blue Studebaker, the man inside. He even seemed sorry and looked as though he had eaten something bad and wanted to throw up. He looked more worried than ever, even sick, which seemed like more proof that he had not been lying. And maybe the truth was even worse than he had admitted. Certainly he had been very upset and we were not quite sure what had really happened, what the man in the blue Studebaker had done to him at Doleful Pond. We asked again but this time Walter did not want to talk about it.

The man had driven past us. He was not a blurry villain any more, but a real man in a shiny car, and looked strong. We had not seen his face—we were on the wrong side of the car, hiding against the pond embankment. He had driven fast, in the decisive way of a person who had finished something and wanted to get away; not on the lookout for anyone, not noticing anything, like a man in a hurry to go home, someone late.

The way the man was leaving fast seemed to make Walter angry. His eyes were glistening. He held his gun in his arms tightly as though he was cold. But he was clutching his stomach and retched, started to spew, a moment later bent over he puked into the bushes, and paused, laboured a little, and splashed some more, coating the leaves with yellow slime and mucus.

He wiped his mouth with the back of his hand, and said, 'I'd like to kill the bastard.'

'Yeah,' Chicky said. 'Let's kill him.'

I did not say anything. I was retching myself, my mouth full of saliva from having watched Walter. I was also afraid of the word; and they knew it, they noticed my silence.

'Andy's chickenshit.'

'Yah. Let's get him,' I said. I could not say the word kill without feeling unsafe. 'You all right, Herkis?'

Walter nodded. He was not all right. He was pale and pukey-looking. But he was angrier than ever, and his anger excited Chicky and touched me too. The anger gave us a purpose that was better than going out for merit badges but involved the same concentration. We had found the car, we had glimpsed the man, we had to find him again and do something. We were not Scouts, we were soldiers, we were Indians, we were men, defending ourselves.

'Kill him' was just an expression but one that frightened me. Walter and Chicky were not so frightened of it—Walter was angry, Chicky was excited. We did not explain what killing meant to each other but I wanted to think it was stalking him, trapping him, not firing bullets into him.

'We'll put him out of commission,' I said, so that they would see I was on their side, because they thought of me as the sensible one, the cautious one, the chicken.

'Even if we really do kill him, no one will know,' Chicky said.

That was the way we reasoned in the woods—getting away with something made it all right. If we killed a squirrel, or started a fire, or shot bullets into a sign, and no one caught us, we felt we had done nothing wrong: nothing to explain. If we found money we kept it. 'What if we discovered a dead body in the woods?' Walter had said once, and Chicky had said, 'What if it was a woman and she was bollocky!' In the woods we were conscienceless creatures, like the other live things that lurked among the trees. Even so, Chicky's excitement disturbed me—he was jabbering to Walter now—because talk of killing, even in a reckless jokey way, made me uneasy. My hesitation was not guilt, not even conscience—I was afraid of getting caught and having to face my parents' fury and shame.

'They'll never catch us. They'll think it's some big murderer. They'll never think it was kids.'

'Let's shadow him first, and then see,' I said, dreading their conviction.

Walter said, 'Chicky's right. Kill him.'

'We can track him. We're good at that,' I said.

Lurking, hiding, hunting; scouring the earth for footprints, tyre tracks, clues; the lore of our scouting was real and useful.

The sky had gone grey, some of the clouds as dense as iron, and as black, with streaks of red and pink between them, like hot iron that had begun to cool. And not only that but more, because the evening sky was always a mass of unrelated marvels—above the iron were vast decaying faces, tufts of pink fluff in a soup of yellow. The light in the sky was all the light there was; the woods were dark, and so was the surface of the pond at this low angle, and not even the path was clear.

'We should head back,' I said, and started walking.

'I don't even freakin care,' Walter said, but from the way he said it I knew he was glad to go, a bit wobbly and gagged from puking.

Chicky said, 'We could wait till he parks his car, then cut a tree down. It falls across the road, he can't drive away, we nail him.'

'Or dig one of those big holes and put sticks across it, and leaves and stuff, so that it looks like the ground,' I said. 'He walks right in. We could say it was an accident.'

'Or just shoot him in the nuts,' Walter said.

Talking this way in the darkness of the woods seemed unlucky and made me nervous about bumping into a stranger, maybe that very homo. The others might have felt that way too, for although they were talking big, they held tightly to their rifles, bumping shoulders and sometimes stumbling. When we heard some cars, and saw the lights of South Border Road, we walked faster and were relieved to be out of the woods.

Chicky started across the Fellsway alone, walking stiffly to conceal his gun. He turned around and took out his comb. 'Anyway, don't do anything I wouldn't do,' he said, tilting his head, raking his hair with his comb. 'Or if you do, name him Chicky.'

Walter and I turned towards Foss Street. He was silent, except for his puffing—winded and sick from the experience of having seen the man—a big boy out of breath, his whole body straining as he plodded up the hill.

'We'll get the guy,' I said, to reassure him.

'Who cares?' His voice stayed in his mouth and sounded awful, as though he couldn't swallow. When we got to the Fulton Street fire station at the top of the hill he said, 'My mother thinks I went to church.'

The special Saturday church of a Seventh Day Adventist made it sound pagan and purposeless, just an empty ritual on the wrong day.

Looking miserable, saying nothing except 'See ya,' he turned and headed down Ames Street towards his house.

4.

The next time we went was milder, mid-March now, some forsythia in blossom at the edge of the reservoir, and purple azaleas already starting to show. I knew their names from the flower book that Mr Mutch had loaned me. We waited for Walter, who was later than usual. His mother had found out that he was skipping church, and forced him to go. But he was loping along with his gun when he caught up with us at the stone pillars at the entrance to the Fells.

'I took it to church,' he said. 'No one even saw me.'

'That's wicked great,' Chicky said. 'I'm going to do that.'

I tried to picture it, sitting in a pew at St Ray's with my rifle lying under the kneeler.

'I still don't get why you have to go to church on Saturday,' Chicky said, as we walked into the woods, making our usual detour through the trees.

'Because it's the Sabbath.'

'Bullshit,' Chicky said. 'Sunday is.'

'Saturday,' Walter said. 'Jews go then, too.'

'That's why they're Jews. You're not a Jew, except when you're hogging the Devil Dogs.'

'Cut it out,' I said, seeing that Walter was getting pink-faced and a little breathless, as he did when he was upset.

But Chicky was annoyed because we had waited most of the day for Walter, and he was so late there were only a few more hours of sunlight. Chicky had even said, 'Let's go without him,' but I argued that we needed Walter—to be a team, to act together, and so that Walter would see the man's face.

'Yeah, we don't want to kill the wrong guy,' Chicky said.

Walter trudged ahead of us, as though compensating for being late. From the way he was silent and thoughtful, his shoes flapping, I knew that he envied us being Boy Scouts. But Scouts were forbidden by his church, like coffee and tuna fish.

'We're supposed to be tracking,' Chicky said. 'Get down low.'

'I'm a tracker,' Walter said. 'No one can see me.'

We glided through the woods like wisps, like shadows, alert to all the sounds. Blue jays were chasing a squirrel, harrying the creature from tree to tree the way we might have done ourselves if we had not been so determined to conceal ourselves. We were off the path, and the dead leaves were flatter and wetter these days, not like the brittle crackling leaves of winter. We moved hunched over in silence.

More buds made the trees look denser, and the tiny bright green leaves on some bushes gave the woods a newer greener feel, hid us better and helped us feel freer. The sky was not so explicit, the boughs had begun to fill out with leaves as delicate as feathers. And a different smell, too, the crumbly brown decaying smell of warmer earth and tufts of low tiny wild flowers.

Once again, Walter pointed out some fiddleheads, the only wild plant he knew, though most of them had fanned out into ferns. The skunk cabbage was fuller and redder. There were insects and some far-off frogs. We wanted to be like these dull-coloured creatures and wet plants, camouflaged like the wildest things in the woods.

Because it was so late there were no horseback riders on the bridle paths, no other hikers, no dog-walkers. They must have all left the woods as we had entered: the wilderness belonged to us now.

We cut around Panther's Cave, climbed the hill behind it, and kept just below the ridge line, parallel to the trail, listening hard. The light was dimming, and the sun was behind us, and below the level of the tree tops.

'I can't see squat,' Chicky said. 'It's all Herkis's fault. Fucking banana man.'

'My mother made me go,' Walter said, in an urgent tearful whisper.

'Let's hurry,' I said, hoping to calm them.

'How can we track anyone in the dark?'

'We'll learn how,' Walter said. 'Indians track people in the dark. Indians stay out all night. No one expects to be followed in the dark. We'll get good at it. Then we'll be invisible.'

'I have to be home for supper,' I said.

But we kept on and the gathering darkness did not deter us, it was a challenge, and a kind of cloak, a cover for us in our tracking, as we crept unseen below the ridge line.

And walking this way we made a discovery, for cresting the last hill behind Doleful Pond to reach our foxhole we saw that the water still held some daylight, the smooth surface of the pond reflecting the creamy grey of the sky.

The shore was dark, the woods were black, we saw nothing on the road. Instead of lying there in the shallow trench whispering, we made our way down the hill, as slowly and silently as we could, as though moving downstairs through many large darkened rooms of a strange house. Even so, I could hear Chicky breathing through his fat nose, and Walter's big feet in the leaves, clumsy human sounds that made me feel friendly towards them.

Before we got to the road, Chicky said, 'Look,' and swung his arm to keep us back, liking the drama of it.

At the very end of the road, there was a car, but so deep in the trees we could not see the colour or the make.

I put my finger to my lips: No talking—and took the lead, duckwalking to the edge of the pond, where the little trail encircled it. The others followed, keeping low, and still watching the car, trying to make it out. Closer we could see it was small and compact.

'It's the Studebaker,' Chicky said, whispering fiercely.

Walter knelt and slid the bolt of his rifle. 'Let's kill him.'

'Yeah,' Chicky said. He too knelt and fumbled with his gun.

'Wait a minute,' I said. I could not think of any way of stopping them, nor could I put my worry into words. We had bullets, we had our guns, only mine was not loaded: the other guns were cocked. In the darkness of Doleful Pond, having achieved our objective, there was nothing to stop us.

'We'll surround him,' Chicky said. 'We'll just gang up and shoot from all sides. He won't have a chance.'

I felt sickening panic fear and wanted to vomit. Until that moment it had been unreal, just a game of pursuit, Indian tracking, and I had enjoyed it. But we had succeeded too well and now I dreaded that we would have to go through with it. I saw in this reckless act the end of my useful life.

'Maybe he's not inside.'

The car was dark. I hoped it was empty.

'My mother's going to kill me if I'm late,' I said.

'Andy's chickening out.'

I was afraid. I thought: If I do this my life is over. I also thought: I cannot chicken out, I can't retreat.

'We should call the cops.'

'They won't do anything,' Walter said.

'Just take our guns away!' Chicky said.

The car moved, not visibly but we heard it, the distinct sound of a spring, the squeak of metal under the chassis, as though it was settling slightly into the road, for there was another accompanying sound, the crunch of cinders in the wheel track from the tyres. A weight had shifted in the car.

That sound stiffened us and made us listen. The next sound was louder, not from the springs but the crank-creak of a door handle, and with it a light came on inside the car, the overhead bulb.

We saw the man's face briefly as he turned to get out of the car and leaving the door open the light stayed on. Another shape barely bulked in the front seat—it could have been a bundle, or a big dog, or a boy's head. There came a spattering sound, like gravel on glass.

'He's taking a leak,' Chicky said.

'Shoot him in the nuts,' Walter said, in a husky sobbing voice. 'Shoot the bastard.'

'Hold it,' Chicky said, and I knew what he was thinking.

The man was not a blurry villain any more. He was a real person and that was much worse. He wore a black golf cap and buttoned to his neck a shapeless coat that looked greasy, the way gaberdine darkens in winter. Slipping back into the car, he flung out his arm to yank the door and we got another look: big nose, small chin, a pinched mouth and a face that was so pale his moustache was more visible, a trimmed one. He looked like a salesman in the way he was so neat, like someone who put himself in charge and smiled and tried to sell you something.

When the light went off, Walter raised his rifle, and Chicky pushed it down hard, saying, 'Quit it.'

I thought the man might hear but the door was closed, the engine had started, the gear shift was being jiggled and jammed into reverse. The brake lights reddened our faces.

'We can't do it now,' I said. I was giggling, but still panicky.

'I'm gonna,' Walter said, and tried to snatch his rifle from Chicky's grasp.

'Tell him, Chicky.'

'It's freakin Scaly,' Chicky said.

5.

In the woods we were free to do anything we liked. We knew from what we saw, the torn-up pictures, the tossed-away magazines, the used Trojans, the bullet-riddled signs, the couple we sometimes watched making out in their Chevy by the lake, even the fisherman with the hook in his thumb, that other people felt that way, too. We could make our own rules. We thought of the woods as a wilderness.

It was ours, it was anyone's, it was why we went there, and why Father Staley went there. No one looked for you there, and if they did they probably wouldn't find you: you could be invisible in the woods.

But we were Scouts, we were trackers, we could find someone if we wanted. We had found the man who had bothered Walter, maybe molested him, though I did not have any clear idea of what molested meant, other than probably touched his pecker. 'He tried to kiss me' didn't mean much. We talked wildly of sex all the time, but none of us had yet kissed a girl.

Walter would not tell us what the man had done. But the man was Father Staley. We could not explain how important that man was; how we could not even think about harming him. On the way home that night, walking at the edge of the woods among the low bushes, so that none of the passing cars would see our guns, Walter was upset.

'Stop crying, Herkis,' Chicky said.

'I'm not crying.'

'What's wrong then?'

'What's wrong is, I saw him. That was the same guy. You thought I was lying. I was telling the truth!'

He was screeching so loud he sounded like his sister Dottie, who was almost his age and had the same pink cheeks and pale skin.

'I don't get what you're saying,' Chicky said.

'I saw the freakin homo!' Walter said.

What he seemed to be saying was that by seeing the man he remembered everything that had happened. That had upset him all over again.

'We'll get him, don't worry,' I said. But I was glad the moment had passed, that none of us had fired our guns at Father Staley. The woods were free but we would have been arrested for killing a Catholic priest, and would have been disgraced and been sent to jail forever. It could have gone horribly wrong, for at that point our pretending had become real—pretending to be Indian trackers, pretending to be hunters and avengers, following the tracks, carrying guns. We had talked about what we would do when we found the man but I hoped it was just talk, that We're Indian trackers was the same as Let's kill him and Shoot him in the nuts, words we said to ourselves for the thrill of it.

Chicky would have shot if it hadn't been Scaly; Walter had wanted to fire, and was angry we hadn't let him.

'You both chickened out,' Walter said. He sang off-key, 'Chicken-shit—it makes the grass grow green!'

'We'll do something,' Chicky said. 'Something wicked awful.'

'No suh. You're chicken because he's supposed to be a priest. You actually know the guy.'

Even thinking of a priest as a 'guy' was hard for us, because he was a man of God, powerful and holy. Because Chicky and I were Catholics, and Father Staley was a priest, we felt responsible for him. It gave Walter another reason to dislike Catholics. We knew that the Seventh Day Adventists said bad things about Catholics, just as Catholics said, 'This is the True Church. Protestants are sinners. They're not going to heaven,' and 'Jews are Christ-killers.'

'He's a homo,' Walter said.

That hurt, but it was true.

'He's a percy, he's a pervert,' Walter said. 'He was trying to make me into a homo.'

'He's still a priest,' Chicky said. 'He's chaplain to our Boy Scout troop.'

'Big deal.'

'It is a big deal. We can't shoot him,' Chicky said. It sounded strange to hear Chicky being solemn and responsible, his close-set eyes, his yellow skin, his big nose, his picking at his birthmark as he spoke. 'But we can do something. Beaver Patrol to the rescue.'

'Just don't broadcast it,' I said.

They stopped walking and stared at me. We had come to the Forest Street rotary and were standing under a street light. Cars were rounding the rotary, going slowly, so we stood holding our rifles upright against our side, the butt tucked under our arm like a crutch, while keeping the muzzle off the ground. They were querying what I had said by being silent.

'Because we could get into trouble,' I said.

They saw that I was right. It was certain that if we had reported Father Staley to the police he would win and we would have to answer all the hard questions: What were you doing in the woods? Why did you each have a .22 and a lot of live ammo on you? You were lying when you said you were going on a cookout? Why were you fooling around near Doleful Pond with those dirty pictures? Staying out after dark we were up to no good. We had no answers.

Father Staley, a Catholic priest in a long black cassock, could not lose. He would say Walter was lying: people would believe him, not us. And no matter what happened, we would be known forever as the boys involved in the Father Staley scandal, wicked little fairies and tattletales. We would never get a girlfriend. Other kids would tease us and pick fights. We would lose.

'We'll figure something out,' I said.

6.

At the next Scout meeting, Chicky and I stuck together, not saying anything, but looking at Father Staley when his back was turned. He wore a black cassock with a hundred black buttons on the front, and the skirt-like lower edge of it touched the toes of his black shoes. Now the thing seemed like a dress to us.

When he looked at me, I felt he knew something—he smiled in a suspicious way, pinching his moustache. Being near him made me quiet, and fluttery inside: I couldn't think of anything to say.

But Chicky was more talkative than ever in a bold mock-serious voice. He looked straight into Father Staley's face and said, 'I'm going up for my First Aid merit badge, but I'm having some problems.'

'Maybe I can help,' Father Staley said.

'Father, hey, I'm not sure what you do if a snake bites you.'

'Get straight to the hospital, son. That's what you should do.'

Chicky said, 'Um, some people say you're, um, supposed to suck out the poison.'

It was the thing we always joked about. What would you do if a snake bit a girl on her tits, or a boy on his pecker, or his ass? Suck it out. Even the word suck sounded wicked to us.

'You only do that if you're in the woods,' Father Staley said.

'But, hey, that's where all the snakes are, Father,' Chicky said.

He was trying to get Father Staley to talk about sucking out the poison. Father Staley put his hand on my leg—his hand had never felt scalier—and said, 'You've got a First Aid merit badge, Andy. What would you do in a situation like that?'

I hated being asked. 'In a situation like that,' I said, and hesitated. Then, 'You cut the wound with a sharp knife, making an X. And when it bleeds, you kind of, um, suck the poison out. And I forgot to say, maybe put a tourniquet on the person's arm between the snake bite and his heart.'

'If he's bitten on the arm,' Father Staley said, and his eyes glittered at me.

'Yes, Father.'

'Very good. So there's your answer, DePalma,' he said, walking away.

I said to Chicky, 'You're such a pissa.'

Pleased with himself, Chicky said, 'I just wanted to see what he'd say. I know Scaly's a homo now. He was trying to feel you up.'

'Beaver Patrol,' Corny Kelliher said, calling the group together.

We scraped the wooden folding chairs into a circle and sat there, waiting for Corny to lead the patrol meeting.

'Let's talk about tracking. Anyone?'

'We done some tracking the other day,' Chicky said. 'Me and Andy.'

Father Staley came over to listen.

'Want to tell us about it?'

'Oh, yeah. We were in the woods,' Chicky said. 'We seen some tracks. We kind of followed them.'

Nothing about tracking down the pervert, nothing about our guns, nothing about Walter Herkis, nothing about our spying from the hill, nothing about Father Staley and his blue Studebaker—and who even knew he had a Studebaker, since none of the priests even owned a car?

Arthur Mutch handed us each a sheet of paper, saying, 'I just mimeographed these. I want each one of you to take it home and study it.'

The heading at the top of the smudged sheet was 'Elements of Leadership' with twenty numbered topics. The first was: Inspiring respect by setting an example.

As he passed by, Mr Mutch said to me, 'Andy, you should be asking yourself why you're not a patrol leader. You've got the ability. You just don't use it.'

Hearing this, Father Staley said, 'Mr Mutch is right. You pick up the lame and the halt.'

I faced him. I couldn't answer, I knew my face was getting red.

'People like that just drag you down.'

I wanted to say: What did you do to Walter Herkis? But I knew that if I did I would have to pay a terrible price for talking back to a priest.

'You know what I think?' Father Staley said, because he still wasn't through, and now he was so close I could smell the Sen-Sens on his breath. I knew that smell: we sucked Sen-Sens to take away the stink of cigarettes, when we were smoking. 'I think you enjoy hiding your light under a bushel. That's just plain lazy. It's also a sin of pride.'

I wanted to shoot him in the face. Shoot him between the eyes, we always said. I located a spot between his eyebrows and stared at it with a wicked look. The other members of the Beaver Patrol were pretending to read the 'Elements of Leadership' but were really sneaking glances at the way Father Staley was scolding me. Buzzy Dwyer, John Brodie, Vinny Grasso. And Chicky's yellow face was twisted sideways at me.

'Shall we talk about leadership and taking responsibility?' Father Staley said to the others when he was finished with me.

Homo, I thought.

Corny Kelliher said, 'That's a good idea, Father.'

'Or we could practise some knots,' Chicky said. 'I'm trying to learn the bowline. Maybe go out for the Knot-Tying merit badge.'

'I might be able to help you with that,' Father Staley said. 'You know I served in the Navy?'

'I want to go into the Navy, Father.' Chicky was smiling at him, and I knew he was deliberately choosing things to say to Father Staley, even trying to please him in a way, like a small boy dealing with a big dog.

Picking up a short length of rope and extending his scaly fingers so that we could see his movements, Father Staley slowly tied a bowline knot. With a little flourish, which seemed to me a sin of pride, he presented it, dangling it in our faces. I hated his fingers now.

'Now you do it,' he said. He picked the knot apart with his fingertips, then handed the rope to me.

My hands went numb because as soon as I started to tie the bowline, Father Staley lowered his head to peer at my fingers for the way I was tying the knot. His head was sweet from cologne, and I

Paul Theroux

could still smell the Sen-Sens. I made several false starts, then tied
the bowline.

'DePalma?' Father Staley handed the rope to Chicky.

Chicky started the knot slowly, his tongue clamped between his
teeth. But then he bobbled the rope and tugged on the ends and the
knot became a twisted knob.

'That's a granny knot,' Father Staley said.

He got up and crouched behind Chicky and put his arms around
him and taking Chicky's hands, which held each end of the rope, he
guided Chicky, pressing on his fingers, tying the knot using Chicky's
hands.

'See?' His head was in back of Chicky's head, his breath on
Chicky's neck.

Squirming free of the priest, and looking rattled, Chicky said, 'I
think I get it, Father.'

In the Navy you learned many different knots, Father Staley told
us. He had been stationed in Japan. He tied a knot on Vinny Grasso's
wrists and said, 'Japanese handcuffs. Go ahead, try taking them off.'
But when Vinny yanked on them he grunted and his hands went
white. Instead of untying Vinny, Father Staley used more pieces of
rope to tie Chicky's wrists and mine. I left the rope slack, because I
thought from Vinny's reaction that the knot would tighten if I put
pressure on it. Instead, I made my right hand small and it was so
sweaty I managed to slip it out of one side, and untied the knot.

Father Staley saw I had freed myself and smiled and put his scaly
fingers out for the rope and said, 'Want to try again?'

His friendliness made me so nervous I couldn't speak. I watched
him untying Vinny's wrists. Afterwards, Arthur Mutch told us to line
up and stand at attention. Father Staley made the sign of the cross
and said, 'Let us pray,' and my pressed-together hands got hot, for
when he prayed I was more afraid than ever.

'Dear Lord, make us worthy of Your love...'

On the way home, I thought Chicky would talk about Father
Staley hugging him and holding his hands to tie the bowline, but
instead he said in a trembly voice, 'Scaly thinks I'm dragging you
down.'

'He's full of shit,' I said.

'We should get the bastard.' Kicking the pavement, scuffing his

218

shoe soles, he was thinking hard. 'Know what we should do? Wreck his stupid car.'

'Like how?'

'There's billions of ways,' Chicky said.

I remembered how he got angry because there was no Car Maintenance merit badge. He knew everything about cars.

Before we parted that night, he said, 'I think you drag me down, because you're such a fucking banana man.'

We went to Walter's house after school the next day and hid behind a tree, waiting for him to come home. After a while, a car stopped in front of his house and Walter got out—a car full of kids, more Seventh Day Adventists, more bean eaters, who never danced, who went to church on Saturday. So many of them made the religion seem stranger.

Seeing us lurking near the tree, Walter looked around and then sidled over and whispered, 'What're we going to do?'

'Kill his car,' Chicky said. He loved the expression. He licked his lips and made his yellow monkey face. 'Kill his car.'

Chicky put himself in charge, because cars were the one thing he knew about. He said, 'Andy's the head tracker. And you're the head lookout, Herkis. But you've got to do what I say.'

'No guns,' I said.

'Why not?' Walter said.

'Because if we get caught they'll take them away.' But my worst fear was that if they had them they would use them and would kill Father Staley.

'How are we going to kill his car, then? I thought we were going to shoot bullets into it.'

'That'll just make holes and dents. We're really going to wreck it wicked bad, inside and out.'

The next Saturday we spent in the woods, lying on our stomachs in the foxhole on the wooded bluff above Doleful Pond, watching for Father Staley's blue Studebaker. He didn't show up, though others did—fishermen, lovers, dog-walkers. We watched them closely but stayed where we were, and we were well hidden by the leafy branches, for spring had advanced. Twice during the week we made a visit: no Scaly. Maybe he had given up?

When we did not see him at Mass, we asked Arthur Mutch, Chicky saying, 'Father Staley was supposed to teach us some knots.'

'Father Staley is on a retreat.'

'What's a retreat?'

'It's what you should do sometime, DePalma,' Arthur Mutch said, sternly, because he didn't like Chicky. 'Go to New Hampshire, to pray. Lenten devotion.'

Whispering to me at the Beaver Patrol, Chicky said, 'I bet he's not praying. Five bucks says he's whacking off.'

We did not see Father Staley until just before Easter, saying the Mass on Holy Thursday. We reported this to Walter, who sort of blamed us for Father Staley.

'We'll look for him tomorrow,' I said.

'You going to church again tomorrow?'

'Good Friday. Holy Day of Obligation.'

'I don't care what you say, that's worse than us.'

The Good Friday service lasted almost three hours, and the priests wore elaborate robes and faced the altar, but midway through the incense ceremony, one of the priests turned and swung the thurible at the congregation, waving a cloud of incense at us, and Chicky nudged me, whispering, 'Scaly.'

Attendance at church was not required on Holy Saturday. We didn't expect to see Father Staley by the pond, but we had the whole day for tracking, and it was a cold sunny day, with some flowers in bloom, and so we were glad to head into the woods. Even if Father Staley didn't show up, we would have more chances, for the following day was Easter, the start of a week's vacation.

Walter was early. He said, 'I was in this Bible class. I put up my hand and said, "Excuse me." The teacher says, "Okay." So I just left. He thought I was going to the john.'

Chicky wasn't listening. He said, 'If we kill his car we'll put him out of commission.'

We stopped and had a snack at Panther's Cave, sitting out of the wind, in the warm sunlight.

'What have you got?'

'Bottle of tonic. Some Twinkies. You?'

'Cheese in a bulkie. Bireley's Orange.'

'I ain't eating, I'm smoking,' Chicky said, lighting a cigarette and, with smoke trickling out of his nose, looking more than ever in charge.

The day was lovely, even as it grew darker, the woods so much greener than on that first day, when Walter had told us his story. We had been cold then, and the goosebumps of fear in our bodies too. Afterwards, frightened by the thought of the man chasing Walter we had stumbled through the woods, not knowing where to go or what to do. Now we knew. The weather was warm, the ground was dry, the woods smelled sweet.

'What did you bring?'

Walter had taken off his knapsack. 'Couple of bricks.'

'I've got the rope,' I said. 'About fifty feet. Chicky?'

Chicky kept his eyes on the pond. He said, 'A potato. A bag of sugar. A couple of tonic bottles. Pair of pliers. Usual stuff.'

He had always been talkative before, but now that he was in charge he liked to be mysterious. He wasn't good at school work, but he knew how to fix things, and was even better at breaking them.

'Someone's coming,' Walter said.

But it was the Chevy, the lovers. We watched closely.

None of us saw the blue Studebaker appear. All we saw was its rear lights winking as it braked, sliding into the shadows at the end of the road. Its rump-like trunk was blue, though just a few minutes after it parked, even while we were staring at it, we could not make out the colour.

Each of us had one job to do. Walter's was first—to get Father Staley out of the car and up the road, chasing him, long enough for Chicky and me to do our jobs.

'There's someone with him.'

'Probably some kid.'

'Maybe someone we know.'

'Like they say in Russia, tough shitsky,' Chicky said.

'What are you going to do?' Walter said.

Slow-witted and sly, liking the mystery, Chicky said, 'I got my ways. Just make sure that bastard is out of the car and up the road for a few minutes to give me time.'

'If he sees us, we're screwed,' I said.

'He's only going to see Herkis,' Chicky said. 'Herkis is Protestant!'

'Let's put on bandannas,' I said. The word was from the cowboy movies. I took out my handkerchief.

'You mean a snot-rag,' Chicky said, and shook out his own and tied it around the lower half of his face, as I was doing.

We crouched in the foxhole on the bluff, watching the car. The sun sank some more, the temperature changed, the woods grew cooler, damper, darker, while the pond held the last light of the day.

'What's the bastard doing?' Chicky said.

The end of the road where the car was parked was so shadowy a person passing by would not even have noticed the car. After it had parked it had seemed to darken and shrink and disappear, even as we had watched it.

'I can't see him,' Walter said.

Chicky said in his conspirator's whisper, 'If we wait any longer, he might take off. So let's go. You're dumping the bricks, Herkis. Andy, you're doing the bumper.'

'What about you?'

'You'll see. Meet back here, after.' Chicky then put his finger to his lips: no more talking.

Keeping low, we descended through the bushes single file to the edge of the pond. We used the thick brush at the shore to hide ourselves. Approaching the car by the rear we could not see anything of the people inside. We were sure it was Father Staley's car, but where was his head? Now we were kneeling.

Chicky turned and poked Walter's arm and as he did so, Walter snorted air and looked alert. With a brick in each hand Walter rocked back to a squatting position, sort of sighing as he did so. I could see how angry he was from the way his head was jammed between his shoulders and the sounds of his shoes when he crossed from the dirt path to the cinders.

We heard nothing but his shoes for a moment and then two loud sounds, one of a brick hitting the metal body of the car, the other the crunch of a brick against a windshield. Just after that, a complaining two-part shout that was so long that the first part was muffled inside the car, and the second part a very loud protest as it was released by the car door swinging open.

Father Staley stumbled out, pulling at his clothes, and Walter screamed, 'Homo!' as he ran into the woods, and he was gone, hidden by darkness, before Father Staley had stumbled twenty feet. But Father Staley was still going after him.

My hands trembled as I tied the bowline knot on the front bumper. The other end of the rope, another bowline, I tied to the nearest tree. While I was tying the knots, Chicky rushed from the rear of the car where he had been doing something, to the side where he was fussing with the flap that covered the gas cap. The last sound I heard was the smash of glass, the tonic bottles under the tyres.

Passing the car door, which was still gaping open, I saw someone inside, a boy, huddled in the seat, his head down, his knees up. I was glad I could not see his face. Then I was off.

Chicky kicked the car recklessly, making it shake, and ran, flinging his feet forward, and crashed into the bushes by the pond. He was right behind me, running hard, feeling the same panic that frightened me, the going-nowhere running of a bad dream, skidding on the soil that was cool and moist from the end of day, like running on fudge. We were running in darkness but after all the stake-out time we knew where we were going, and when we got to the look-out boulder on the bluff I knew we were safe, because I saw the car's headlights switch on, blazing against the green leaves.

'He's taking off.'

Chicky said, 'Did you see me kick the freakin car? I didn't even give a shit!'

The blue Studebaker was still stationary, its lights dimming each time the engine turned over.

A noise behind us startled us but before we could react, Walter flopped down and said, 'I wrecked his window!'

'Lookit,' Chicky said.

The car grunted and roared, the gear shift grinding, the engine strained against the rope I had tied—strained hard, making no progress, trying to reverse. When the rope snapped with a loud twang I expected to see the car shoot backwards, but it had not gone ten feet before the engine coughed and died. Chicky was laughing. The engine groaned to life again, Chicky said, 'Hubba-hubba, ding-ding,' and then it gasped and died again. But seconds later it was stammering, the intervals shorter and shorter, the engine noise briefer until at last there was only silence.

'Car's freakin totalled,' Chicky said.

And gloating, combing his hair, Chicky explained: my rope had made the engine rev; he had jammed a potato into the tailpipe to delay

the car in case the rope broke. He had put a pound of sugar into the
gas tank, and that was now in the fuel line, gumming up the pistons.
The engine was destroyed, the car was a wreck. Father Staley was
stranded in the woods with whoever he had brought there.

After we left the darkness of the woods, there was one last thing,
and it was I who raised it. I said, 'What about confession?'

Chicky said, 'Was that a sin?'

'We were helping Walter,' I said.

'Maybe it's a sin if you're helping a Protestant,' Chicky said.

'Not a mortal sin,' I said.

'What's the difference?' Walter asked.

'If it's a mortal sin you go to hell.'

The next day, Easter, we performed our Easter Duty, sitting at Mass,
Walter the unbeliever between us in the pew, not knowing when to
kneel or pray—skinny, round-shouldered, blotchy-faced with
embarrassment when he stood up, surveying the priests in their
starched, white lace-trimmed smocks, and whispering, 'Where's
Scaly?'

Scaly was not on the altar. The pastor's sermon that day was
about the meaning of Easter, Christ slipping out of his tomb, being
reborn, pure souls. That was true for me, the holy day reflected
exactly how I felt, and made me happy. The smell of the church was
the smell of new clothes. When the singing started I shared the *Sing
to the Lord* hymn book with Walter who mumbled while I sang
loudly,

> Christ is risen from the dead,
> Alleluia, Alleluia!
> Risen as He truly said,
> Alleluia, Alleluia.

Father Staley had vanished. All the pastor said was, 'Reverend Staley
has been transferred to a new parish.' People said they missed him.
At Scouts, Arthur Mutch talked about Father Staley's contribution
to the troop. His hard work. 'He was a vet.' But Mutch wasn't
happy. The blue Studebaker we destroyed was his: Scaly had
borrowed it. The thing was a write-off.

'Banana man,' Chicky said. That night he said he was quitting the Scouts.

No one knew Father Staley, and we never found out who the boy was—maybe a Protestant, like Walter; a secret sin. That was also the mystery of the woods. We had discovered that, going there as Scouts. The woods might be dangerous but the woods were free, the trees had hidden us, and had changed me, turned us into Indians, made us friends, so we couldn't be Scouts any more, because of Walter. When I quit the Scouts my mother said, 'You'll have to get a part-time job then,' and I thought: Great, now I'll be able to buy a better gun.

We had made Staley disappear. We had made ourselves disappear. No one knew us, what we had done, what we could do, how close we had come to killing a man. I was glad—it meant I was alone, I was safe, now no one would ever know me. ☐

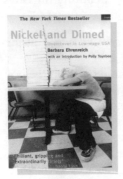

KING'S GIRLS
Lindsay Watson

Four of the first women to be admitted to King's College, Cambridge, 1972
From left: Caroline Davidson, Mary Newton, Lindsay Watson and Bridget O'Connor

M y relationship with the other three girls can best be defined in negative terms. From my point of view, it is only now that our lack of common interest can be partially explained and to some degree lamented. But surely it's better to admit that than to beatify ourselves or glorify that time, as some of those ghastly Old Girls' Society magazines do, where everybody is so darned virtuous, has been married to Ian for twenty-four years and has Jessica, twenty-two, and Josh, twenty, and sings in the local choir and does charity work and still regularly sees Lizzie and Julie...

But here we are on September 30, 1972, at King's College, Cambridge, completely unknown to one another, unconnected by anything except, perhaps, the desire to connect. The only trait that drew us together, briefly, for the photograph, was being female, in what had been until then an uncompromisingly male institution. Mary-Anne, as you might guess from the photograph, was secure, relaxed, and, as several of our male contemporaries noted, carried her insignia clearly before her. She was the only one I talked to in any depth that day. She was a Natural Scientist, while I was to read Modern and Medieval Languages—poles apart already. I remember she talked enthusiastically about being a Roman Catholic, which, since I have been staunchly secular since the age of fourteen, presented an immediate point of non-identification. I also remember the description of her happy and supportive family. At this point I started to cry, made my excuses and walked off before she noticed. The fact of my own ruptured family filled me with shame and the idea of hers filled me with envy. It wasn't that I disliked her. It was, as with the other girls, that I just couldn't find an opening, a familiar point of contact. As far as I know, Mary-Anne married a Kingsman and I would imagine they have been successful in a Darwinian sort of way.

Oh, that photo and its consequences. My mother had it copied and framed and sent it to me 'with the united love of your parents'. My father hadn't spoken to her for six months, and hasn't done since. A pervert wrote to all four of us elaborating on his bizarre sexual preferences, and sending samples of semen. I think the police became involved. I don't remember receiving any respectable proposals of marriage or offers of film contracts.

What I do remember is pushing myself forward to be in the picture. I wanted so much to be part of whatever was happening, even if it

Lindsay Watson

included three girls I'd never met before and have scarcely spoken to since. The traces of self-confidence and opportunism that existed then were to be shaken over the next three years. Looking at the picture thirty years on, I obviously had no qualms about posing before the nation dressed in home-made clothes and badly in need of a haircut and a good night's sleep. But here I go again: a new chance to settle scores with a difficult history, trying to wrest some psychic treasure from a painful experience.

Biddy is still an enigma. I don't think we ever exchanged more than a couple of sentences, though I saw her a few years ago at a King's event. Perhaps if we talked now, some of the imaginary differences might disappear: I never really understood why we couldn't find anything in common.

Caroline is the only one of the three I have had any contact with since we graduated. We've met at King's functions and exchanged phone numbers, but nothing has come of it so far. We didn't know each other at all as undergraduates. She seems interesting and urbane, maybe a notch or two above me socially. I'm fairly sure she went to public school. Class differences have troubled me since I was a child, when it was more often me who was called a snob or posh by those from even lower orders.

Caroline read History and Biddy read English, so we should have had some common interests. But I suppose there was a tribalism about what we studied. If so, mine was a tiny tribe containing enormous disparities. I was the only female Modern and Medieval linguist in King's that year. There were, I think, just four males: Nick, Peter, Steve and Bruce. Nick was a mature student, affable, but largely absent apart from the odd tutorial; he had a home and family to go to. Peter was doing Russian and Czech and we hardly spoke until after we graduated. Steve was a brilliant scholar, very serious, and in his second year moved on to Law. Bruce became a dear friend. We discovered we'd been born in the same hospital, just months apart, which gave us a deeper bond, and we both came from troubled backgrounds. But Bruce was part of what was known then, semi-affectionately, as the God-squad—C-of-E with an evangelical flavour—so again that disparity in ideology obviated a deeper relationship. I'm sad to say he disappeared from view about ten years ago.

We probably all tried to find a current in the King's ethos that we could comfortably swim along with. Religion was out of the question for me, though it was a major factor in college life for others. There was politics, of course. Feminism, socialism, communism, revolution were enthusiastically debated and exercised. I took part in sit-ins and went on all sorts of demos without necessarily understanding what the real consequences would be if, for example, the NLF (National Liberation Front of Vietnam) triumphed, as I once claimed ardently to wish. I leaned to the left in an old-fashioned socialist way, but by the end of the first year some of the student politics began to seem naive, grandiose and frankly mad.

King's in the early 1970s was supposed to be the centre of the East Anglian drugs trade and a fair few kilos of dope got smoked around me, though not by me. This excluded me from another peer-group subculture. One of my male friends honoured me with an introduction to the Chetwynd Society, an ancient college drinking club where the meetings culminated in pissing rituals, for which the female body was not well adapted. One night there was more than enough.

The effeteness of a small number of King's students was fascinating to me at first, then repellent, and before long completely uninteresting. They dressed in peculiar clothes, talked in silly voices and appeared to me to be living caricatures of the human race. At times I longed for some familiar ordinariness and found it with boys from other colleges who introduced me to football and pool and pubs. There were groups that gathered under various sporting banners, rugger buggers and boat club types. I joined a women's rowing team, but a six a.m. start and the single line of verbal contact, 'Are you ready? Row!' delivered by a small virago, gave me no incentive to hang around to see if anything developed. I began to think it was a lost cause to look for any groups at all to identify with, so I put my energies into one-to-one relationships, and that in itself had its drawbacks.

It was a confusing time sexually. As well as being a den of narcotics, King's was also, reputedly, a hotbed of homosexuality—which put women in an odd place, labelling them somehow redundant. Female homosexuality was not something I was particularly aware of at the time. Sex was, of course, a quick and irresistible way of bonding, practised by many, we may say, endogamously, since quite a few of the first female intake married Kingsmen. I was betrothed to one myself for a time. He tried thoughtfully to time his 'Dear Jane' letter so that it would arrive after my finals, but, alas for my results, it arrived in the middle.

I often wondered what on earth had possessed me to apply to a men's college in the first place. I'd given myself a choice: King's or a £10 assisted passage to Australia. I'd been seduced by the beauty of the college architecture on a pre-A-level visit and frankly thought that setting myself such an impossible target might see me safely out of academia for good. But there was also, I have to admit, a huge excitement at the prospect of being suddenly among men, lots of them, ten to every woman.

I'd been to single-sex schools throughout my education and had actively chosen the last one, Mary Datchelor Girls' School in Camberwell, London, because of its emphasis on personal freedom and responsibility. It was one of my teachers there, Kay Clay, among the first women to graduate from Girton in the 1930s, who made me believe I had a chance of getting into Cambridge at all. But I always felt I'd got into King's under false pretences. My original intention had been to study Law. To the King's interview, quite unselfconsciously, I wore a knicker-grazing bottle-green corduroy dress and powder-blue kinky boots. I had a matter-of-fact discussion with Dr Ken Polack about my wavering desire to join the law faculty. As no linguist was available to interview me that day, I had a charming conversation with Geoffrey Lloyd (the eminent classicist, now Professor Sir Geoffrey) about the poems of Jacques Prévert, about which he mercifully knew less than I did. It had all seemed so low-key, non-threatening, welcoming. Even so, I almost passed out when I read the letter offering me a place.

Of the women who arrived at King's that day, I still have two close friends. Both were state-school educated like me, and both came from complicated backgrounds. Both lean politically to the left. Both are secular in their outlook. Neither is particularly conventional, though one works as a trust lawyer in the United States and the other has her own technical-writing company in London. I think we were all bewildered as to how we had arrived at King's, wondering if we were in some way token, if we were undetected frauds.

Now that I think about it, most of my close friends there were from foreign countries and a lot of them were postgraduates. The two serious boyfriends I had during college years were, consecutively, Indian and Australian. Both had divorced parents, which was far from commonplace then. It is hard to believe today, but there wasn't much of a discourse on race. So I gravitated towards people from unfamiliar, exotic backgrounds, free from the more local prejudices of education and class.

The class divisions were the most shocking to me. My lower-middle-class meritocrat father generously paid his recommended supplement to the grant and there was enough for food and rent, a modest amount of clothing, books, and the odd pint of bitter. Restaurants were mostly out of the question and trips out of the sometimes stifling atmosphere of pre-M11 Cambridge were usually only possible if I could find somebody to hitch-hike with. It was hard to be mixing with contemporaries who had their own flats, houses, cars, expensive clothes, private incomes—not that I particularly wanted those things, but such huge material differences were confusing, especially as it seemed to have a great deal to do with being ignored. I doubt this inequality has significantly diminished over the years, as the nation still suffers the idiocy of the private–state school divide with its resulting material and social chasms. A friend's daughter who started at Oxford last year reports much the same difficulty.

In 1972 King's was a confluence of too many differences, minor and major, for it to be comfortable for all but the robust: too many classes, too many political and religious factions, and a huge weight of history—four centuries—from which women had been deliberately excluded. The introduction of the second sex meant a radical disturbance of the status quo and the repercussions have taken years to work through. The college feels much more ordinary now, with a ratio of roughly 50:50 men to women. In 1972 there were strong undertows of misogyny as well as a perpetual and wearing curiosity about what we women might be, do, think and feel. It was hard just to get on with it.

Thirty years on, I am still trying to bond with my contemporaries and with the college itself. It seems to be going better at last. I occasionally buy wine from the King's cellar, attend events I am invited to, especially the Provost's seminars, or anything involving eating and drinking. I seem to have been dropped from the guest list for fund-raisers, though, probably because I haven't yet rewritten history sufficiently to feel I want to give something back.

I don't blame the college in the least for the tribulations of that time. It was my choice. Much later in life I spanned another fault line by joining the first group of Lacanian psychoanalysts whose training was sanctioned by the UK Council for Psychotherapy. Once again I was greatly outnumbered by men. Once again it was difficult and frustrating, but also, this time, exhilarating.

There were two significant academic mentors whose influence has continued to work over the last thirty years. One was Geoffrey Cubbin, who inspired me with his passion for the German language and introduced me to a lifelong preoccupation with the powers of speech and propaganda in particular. The other was Robert Bolgar, who died some years ago before I was able to thank him. His kindness sustained me through emotional deserts and offered a glimpse into the world of true scholarship. He guided me patiently through the pangs of producing a dissertation on 'The concept of character in *Les Liaisons Dangereuses*', which must have foreshadowed the later involvement in psychoanalysis, dealing as it does with the unconscious substrate of character and with the aftermath of dangerous liaisons.

On the basis of my analytic training I can find some conceptual comfort in what I once construed as a failure of the group experience. In psychoanalysis, retroactivity, strictly speaking, applies to an event becoming traumatic *post hoc*, when newly acquired (sexual) knowledge puts it into a new perspective. In a more ordinary way, things may make a different sort of sense after a process of working through, and may cease to be traumatic. In the case of my college experience, I am still working to reconstruct it as a positive force in my life.   □

THE ELK'S FUNERAL
Todd McEwen

The Elk's Funeral

Some Elks Lodges glitter like country clubs; this one used to be a motel with a pancake house attached. In the parking lot, stretching after the hot drive, there is a pretty girl in a black dress. Not one of you. But she must be, no one but your party, the party assembled for your uncle's funeral, is wearing black to the Elks Club at three o'clock today, in eighty-degree California weather.

The bar your only foyer. It's filled with the smoke of a few afternoon drunks. After all, the Elks, The Benevolent and Protective Order of Elks, raised themselves in the face of the temperance movement, so that men might drink. Skewed portraits of flyblown guys, the officers, look down at you. They are photographed at odd angles, as though they were wearing party hats, but they aren't; as if the hot parking-lot sunlight you've just admitted yelled *Hey shut up you guys* and they're chastened, maybe even a little ashamed. Most of them sport big glasses from mall opticians above their plump, sallow cheeks. A woman of sixty stands by the guest book. Suddenly, you recognize her. His first wife.

A Calvert Reserve blackboard both points and blocks the way to the service. You walk by acres of tables set for dinner. Not his, not ours. The glasses are clean and the napkins starched; there are cigarette butts in the corners of the room.

The big ballroom of acoustical tile and old linoleum. You choose from the people gathering here the few identities you know. By her severely drawn eyebrows you find Sallie, by the hairline receding even in youth you guess Herb. But where is the remembered suntan, the back that was once so straight? One fluorescent light is giving up the ghost where the ceiling is damp. An exit door stumblingly enjoins the brothers NO DRINK'S IN THE PARKING LOT. Yes, Elks know when to leave it be. As their departed brother has done.

Against each wall stands an ornate throne—junk, dark Victorian junk, pulled by crowbar twenty years ago from the old lodge in the doomed downtown. Sitting on each is a battered looking Elk in a frayed tuxedo or black suit, his shoes cracked as the skin around his eyes. You feel sure they will sleep, and soon. They wear silver chains about their necks, which makes them look like sommeliers. An ornate table, another past glory of the lodge, has flowers and a few family pictures. Your uncle young, in his uniform. *Come sit with us, in the family chairs*, says the second wife. *Don't introduce us,* says your father, *we're not really related.*

Even now, here, you are going to try to sidle away from death?

The chief wine waiter, the Exalted Ruler, rises and begins. First a Bible will be presented to the widow. In a royal-blue suit, perhaps a tuxedo demoted for bad behaviour, a little man gets up.

I didn't know our brother long, but you could set your watch by him. Every day at three o'clock I'd have his glass of wine on the bar, with his little straw in it, and in he'd come. There was a lotta wisdom coming out of that man, a lotta wisdom. And it's my pleasure to be able to present this Bible to his widow. And thank you all.

He hands her the Bible, in a cedar souvenir-ware chest. Bemusement of the guests, supplanted by the realization that the dead Elk's sons have *asked* the barman to speak. Later, driving home, away from the valley, you're moved by this. From miserable thoughts of this Bible in its Trees of Mystery box, you turn with a jolt to his third wife's genuine grief. And it is not the grief you are selfishly feeling: what if your funeral were to be like this?

Now we are gifted a look at the mysteries of the Elks, when they are at their most vulnerable. Behind the words of the service, which might have been written by Sinclair Lewis on a bender, behind the lamely intoned honorifics, *Exalted Ruler, Recording Knight,* you hear Art Carney's voice, faint, filled not with satire but with precisely the solemnity of Elks and Masons and Moose, all these people who know there exists something noble, something mysterious, something *important about something,* but do not know what it is or how to find it.

The Recording Knight stands up and in his best Kent-filtered, Calvert-reserved voice calls the name of our departed brother. Alas, he can answer no more, he has passed into the shadows. He is not at the bar either. He is in the Lodge of Sorrow. The Exalted Ruler, who has his own parking space, invites us to listen to the tolling of eleven hours on the great Clock of Elkdom, which begins to bong like a doorbell when he touches a button. The hour of eleven is the hour of remembrance for all Elks, when the great heart of Elkdom swells and throbs. Sprigs of ivy will now be placed on the table, ivy the symbol to all Elks that brotherhood is undying, and the Exalted Ruler shakes his head, no no, you guys are coming forward with your plastic sprigs before your cue. Their sense of lodge ritual has not been out of bed at three in the afternoon for some time. But it doesn't matter and nobody minds. The Exalted Ruler calls for spontaneous testimonials and remembrances. A man gets up, gives his name, says he'll never forget him. A woman was at his birthday party in the fourth grade. All those years ago. And, silence. Especially from the hardbitten Elks, who would be raising the first drinks with him now. Most are thinking too hard, derailed by the flashing clock, to muster a clear idea of their departed brother. Somebody lights a cigarette. This lack of words for him—after all, what does one say? *He helped my children. He gave me some folders about Guadalajara. He used to have a few drinks.* All of this is beside the point.

People get up and smile. The janitor begins replacing the big ceremonial furniture of the lodge; it's mounted on castors. He looks around at all the chairs he set up, and the flowers. You can see beer and a cigar in his eye. Over the altar (Bible, flag and antlers) there hangs a large glass star, suspended from an electric motor. You catch your pretty cousin's eye—you're both guessing its role in mysteries you will not know. *Come on over to the house,* says the third wife. *It's not far.*

In a house dimly remembered you look at each other, you who have not spoken or seen one another for twenty years. Your insurance cousin has been schooled in drink by the deceased. Your policeman cousin tensely displays his pectoral development under his off-duty jacket. And your young bicycling cousin is now grey and a grandfather.

What did he die of? *He thought he had cancer.* What did the doctor say? *He didn't go to the doctor. He didn't have it, but he died.*

No one has had much of anyone's news. We assume so much from what we barely remember. Mistakes are made but of course forgiven. *Oh, the restaurant burned down in 1987. I'm selling carpet tile now. It's all 'Red Lobster' around here, there's no future for fine dining in this valley.* □

GRANTA

SEMINARIANS
Marcos Villatoro

Davenport, Iowa, 1980

There are problems with this picture. One, we're not all there, and two, the photo itself is impure. The man in the middle, without a hat, is a Yankee, somewhere from Peoria or Des Moines or one of the right-angled states of the Midwest. He was a friend; but he was not one of us. We were from Tennessee—East Tennessee. Flannery O'Connor's world. Nashville and everything east of it, that was our stomping ground. And, like Flannery, we were Catholic, which already made us strange back home, living in a state where only one half of one per cent of the population tipped their hat to the Pope. Others in Tennessee thought a great deal about the papacy, no doubt even more than we did. John Paul II and, before him, Paul VI and John XXIII all got hauled over the pulpits of many an evangelical chapel in small Appalachian towns. Antichrist. Satan's pawn.

Living in Tennessee made your Catholicism stick to you. And in the fall of 1980, something strange happened in the Volunteer State: fourteen young men, just graduating from high school, thought, 'What the heck—let's hand in our testicles, put on white collars and black shirts and join the priesthood.'

We were enrolled at the college of St Ambrose in Davenport, Iowa. Richard Geiger, our medieval history professor, took this picture in his home. I can't remember where we were going that night, though it must have been somewhere fancy, as my blue-striped tie pulls together so perfectly the blue pants and white jacket. The five-gallon cowboy hat is, admittedly, a bit much. Professor Geiger served us drinks (Scotch for me—I had a true vocation to the priesthood; Scotch and soda for Paul, the gapped-tooth lad second from the left; whiskey and cola for the rest). There we were: Chris Corby, Paul Froula, Pat McHenry, Larry Morlan (the good Yankee), Chris Noel and me. Where did the hats come from? And where were the rest of the boys?

Because as Southerners most of us hung together. Not for protection, for there was nothing that threatened us in the blistering cold of Iowa except the cold itself. More for the reminder of who we were, and how exotic we appeared to the Midwesterners around us. We drawled more in Davenport than we ever did back home. Girls, we figured, liked that. We had been sent to St Ambrose by our bishop, who had graduated from there back in the Thirties. In his rapture at having such an explosion of priestly vocation in his diocese, he somehow missed the fact that his alma mater had gone co-ed.

Marcos Villatoro

The seminary building, parked smack in the middle of the campus, looked west to Davis Hall (women), south to another women's dorm building, and east to the vocationless, unharnessed men of Beast Hall. What did they expect, with so many earthly reminders of flesh around us? Out of the fourteen young men who discerned the call, few, very few, made it to ordination.

But we tried. We followed the post-Vatican II rules as best we could. There weren't many: morning and evening prayers every day, a community supper on Thursday nights, and oh yes, that little caveat on sexual relationships. Here it is, from the seminary rule book of 1980: 'Your relationship with women should reflect a serious commitment to the consideration of celibacy and not of marriage.' I don't know if they've updated that yet, to say something like 'Your relationship with *anybody*.' I doubt it. The Catholic seminary, like the US military, holds to the wisdom of 'Don't ask don't tell'.

Before we all started to fall away, losing the celibacy marathon, we were a force on campus. We filled all the photos taken at parties, dinners, high masses. We were the loudest in class. The local Midwesterners liked having us around. They called us the Tenneseminarians.

At morning prayers we were an eclectic lot. Some of us would walk into the side chapel dressed for the day, ready to take the eight o'clock class after matins. Father Ed Dunn, our rector, was always the first there, sitting in the forward corner, to the left. He was a handsome man: a silver beard and moustache and long silver hair, with a tight turtleneck that stretched over ribs wrapped in muscle, a sports jacket over that.

In we came, one at a time, quiet, our breviaries in hand. Chris Noel from Knoxville had an eight o'clock; he carried his jacket with him, ready to go straight to the cafeteria for a quick bite before logic class. Joe McCain from Chattanooga bounded quietly down the steps like a gymnast. He had been a wrestler in high school, and in seminary was the centre of a mutual lust fest. A girl I liked from Missouri named Emma Simonezzi summed it up one evening after night prayers (open to all students), 'Man, he can wrestle with me if he wants. Yessir. Put me in a thigh hold any time.'

A number of us barely pulled in at seven-fifteen. Some rose from their beds, tossed on their robes, and shuffled into their pews with their eyes still caked with sleep and their hair tossed like stringy salads. Pat McHenry was of this group. He's the young man in the middle of the photo, wearing a floppy panama hat. Pat would later become our wise old godfather. Each time one of us left the seminary for a woman, we understood that, for the marriage to work, we had to receive a certain approval from Pat. He just somehow knew which relationship was good and which was bound to fall apart. His rules were pretty simple: 'You nice to her? She nice to you? Like being around her? She around you? Mm hmm...' He made us nervous. But we couldn't get through life without his say.

In seminary Pat wore a robe that reached his ankles. He was a rendition of Le Petit Prince, his dark brown hair curled like exploding black sunspots over his head. Pat hated mornings as much as he abhorred the Iowa winters. 'There's nothing quite as satanic as lauds,' was how he put it.

Jim Hannon was always one of the last to arrive at morning prayers, though it wasn't because he'd overslept. He was a few years older than the rest of us. He would turn up at lauds already dressed in his overalls, flannel shirt, leather work-boots and Jack Daniels baseball cap. Yes, he was from Tennessee. The breviary looked uncomfortable in his large, calloused hand. He was more accustomed to carrying crescent wrenches, vice grips and OHM meters. He would have been up since the crack of dawn, drinking coffee and smoking cigarettes. Jim wouldn't miss class, but he would have preferred to spend the morning under his sixteen-year-old Chevy truck, checking its timing belt. He worked on all our cars as well; our mutual debt to him in auto repair savings ran up into the thousands.

Now, at prayers, Jim (pronounced 'JI-yum') stubbed his Camel cigarette into a short metal bin of sand next to the door, dabbed holy water on his forehead, stomach and shoulders, and found a seat next to me. 'Hey Peeker,' he said. I do believe he coined me that nickname.

We all liked Jim immediately. If the rest of the Tennesseans had brought a certain Southern Comfort Manliness to the seminary, Jim ratified it. He was not your usual pre-cleric. 'Hey Peeker, how the hell you use this thing?' he asked, opening the breviary. Its spine cracked with newness. I showed him the multicoloured ribbons, how they kept your breviary updated: one ribbon on the Canticle of Mary ('My soul proclaims the greatness of the Lord, my spirit rejoices in God my saviour, for he has looked with favour on his lowly servant'), another ribbon, of course, on today's date (Tuesday of the fourteenth week of Ordinary Time, segment three), a third on upcoming Saints' days, a fourth in the hymn section. I showed him how to flip between sections, tossing chunks of pages to one side to read a doxology or a psalm. He just looked at me; he needed a smoke. 'Why the hell don't they have it in order? Just one prayer after another?' Those first few mornings Jim made frantic flips through his shiny new breviary, trying to keep up with the rest of us. From the middle of the group, between everyone quoting in unison, 'Forgive me oh Lord, for my sins, in your kindness wipe out my offence,' you'd hear, from one pew, 'Shit…dang…oh there it is… Now where'd we go?'

About every third week, David, the psalmist, got spiritually frisky, and hauled off with an explosion of praise,

> All the heavens, bless the Lord.
> All his angels, bless the Lord.
> All his armies, bless the Lord.
> Sun and moon, bless the Lord.
> Stars in the sky, bless the Lord.
> Mountains and hills, bless the Lord.
> Orchards and forests, bless the Lord.
> Snakes and birds, bless the Lord.

This went on for a long time. It was one of our most loathed psalms, boring in its repetition, and nothing less than a joke coming forth in the drone of our early-morning, pre-coffee voices.

After lauds, a collection of Tenneseminarians walked down the hall together. 'Fire hydrant, bless the Lord,' said Pat, raising his robed arm toward the hydrant in a blessing. 'Monkey plant, bless the Lord. Staircase, bless the Lord.'

This, of course, got everyone in on it. Coffee mug, bless the Lord. Broken clock, bless the Lord. Cinder block wall, bless the Lord. All through the seminary we looked for monotonous chants. Key to my room, bless the Lord. Dirty laundry, bless the Lord.

Jim was already down the hall, a cup of hot, black coffee to his lips. He turned to us and struck a rapturous pose, his jacket opened to show the faded oil stains on his overalls. He belted out, 'All you cocksucking motherfuckers, bless the Lord!'

Father Dunn's head leaned out from the corner of the hallway, his curtain of silver hair falling to one side. He just stared at Jim. The rest of us skittered away.

Jim would leave the seminary after a couple of years, but not because Father Dunn wanted him to. It was the rector's hope that people like Jim would stay in. Father Dunn's goal was to let psychologically healthy men loose on the world to serve as priests. That would rarely happen. Almost all the Tenneseminarians left, either marrying women or men from the area or simply returning to their homes in Nashville or Chattanooga or Cookville, having realized that the celibate life was not for them. Jim fell in love with Kathy Lucksetish from Dubuque. They settled down in Davenport and raised four boys who learned how to fish and hold a shotgun and string a bow, just like their old man. Pat studied for a year in a major seminary until he realized that the church life full-time was not for him. He got a PhD in English, married, and settled in a Georgia university where, among his many skills, he later edited a number of my manuscripts. Phillip James met a young man named Martin Lessening and they moved to Chicago, where both became lawyers. Chris Corby, entrepreneur, married Mary Brown, the Marilyn Monroe of our class. They have three kids. Paul Froula is now married with two kids and a successful career as an opthalmological surgeon. I mention these men for they are some of the healthiest people I have ever met (unlike the sad state of the seminary today: a walled-in correctional facility for sexually adolescent, homophobic, misogynous Catholic fundamentalists. I admit to some subjectivity, though recent scandals reveal that I am not too far off the mark.)

I walked out as well in the end. I remember the night I realized I was going to, over pizza and beer, all those fallen Tenneseminarians drinking the cold Iowa night away. 'I'm in love, Patrick,' I said. 'Oh really? Peeker in love. Another one bites the dust. Who is she?' I said her name, Michelle Menster, my voice dreamy with beer. I showed him her photo. 'Oh, I know her. Pretty lassie,' said Pat. 'And nice too. Yeah. She's good.' I breathed easier. I look around my house now, at the four children, at my wife who is working on her pottery in the next room. Pat got it right again.

Fourteen men joined. Only one was ordained. Father Mark Beckman is doing very well in Nashville, though he's stretched, with so few priests around any more. Our bishop recognized this problem of losing men to that pesky human condition called sexual drive, and he acted on it: he sent no more seminarians to St Ambrose. That campus held just too many distractions. Instead the bishop sent them to a monastery closer to home, where there are no women, and the isolation makes for few interruptions in the contemplation of priesthood. Men in a large building together, away from the world. Traditional. Pure. □

WHAT FRANCO DID FOR ME

FOR ME

Stuart Christie

Carabanchel prison, Madrid, 1967

The photograph on the facing page was taken on January 6, 1967 in the rotunda of Carabanchel prison in Madrid. I am on the left in the white Aran-knit jumper. With me are three Londoners, Jeff on my left and two others whose names have gone from my memory. The man crouching is Alfredo, an Argentinian.

The occasion was the Hispanic Roman Catholic fiesta of *Los Tres Reyes Magos* ('The Three Wise Kings'—Epiphany), a day when prisoners' children were allowed behind the prison's barred gates and high walls for a few precious hours to enjoy the company of their fathers and brothers, and to open whatever small gift these loved ones could conjure from their limited resources.

I was in my third year of a twenty-year sentence, having been convicted of 'banditry and terrorism' in 1964, when I was eighteen. I had been arrested in Madrid with explosives and detonators in what was to be the last of some thirty attempts to kill the last fascist dictator, General Franco. This particular plot involved targeting Franco in Madrid's Santiago Bernabeu stadium, the home of Real Madrid, where Franco was due to present his personal trophy to the winners of that year's football cup final.

What I didn't know was that Franco's secret police, the *Brigada Político Social*, had infiltrated the anarchist group behind the operation, the *Defensa Interior*, and were waiting for me when I arrived at my rendezvous in Madrid. My contact, the 'facilitator', a Spanish carpenter and fellow anarchist by the name of Fernando Carballo Blanco, was sentenced to thirty years.

We were the lucky ones; the ultimate penalty the court could have imposed was death by *garrote-vil*, a manually powered medieval device that strangled you and broke your neck at the same time. The previous year, the same drumhead court martial had ordered the garrotting of two young anarchists, Delgado and Granado. A few months before them, a communist, Julián Grimau, had been marched out from his prison cell in Carabanchel to a 'noble' death before a firing squad (as opposed to a 'vile' death by garrotte; 'vile' and 'noble' deaths being military and judicial distinctions).

Carabanchel prison, which no longer exists, stood on the slopes of Carabanchel Alto, a southern suburb of Madrid. Built in the 1940s to contain the defeated victims of the newly victorious military-fascist-clerical regime, it played a pivotal role in the Francoist penal system. After the Spanish Civil War ended in 1939 at least 100,000 men and women were executed—some estimates are far higher—and many of them spent their final hours behind those walls.

By 1964, however, Carabanchel was considered a 'model' prison with none of the brutality and near starvation of the 1940s and 1950s. Its warders, the *funcionarios*, had nearly all been recruited from the ranks of the fascist *Falange Española* and from veterans of the 'Blue Division' which had fought alongside the Germans at the siege of Leningrad. Most had mellowed by the time I arrived.

At the time the photograph was taken, I had recently completed three A levels by correspondence course (I left school in Blantyre, near Glasgow, aged fourteen, without any educational qualifications) and had one of the least arduous jobs in the prison. As the *practicante*, the orderly nurse-practitioner responsible for the medical administration of the prison's fifth gallery, I was the doctor's general factotum. I had the use of the doctor's consulting room and also a limited amount of freedom to move around within the prison, provided I could convince any official who chose to challenge me that I was on medical business.

My next-door neighbour was the gallery clerk, or *escribiente*, Miguel de Castro de Castro. His job was to keep a record of each prisoner's details and provide an official point of contact between prisoners and the regime. Miguel, a cultivated old gentleman, was my prison mentor, a wise adviser on the art of the possible. I suppose our relationship was similar to that between the old convict Fletcher and the young and naive Godber in the British TV series, *Porridge*.

Miguel was also one of the finest forgers in Spain; commissions for passports, ID cards, driving licences and other official documents were always being smuggled in from the world outside, and the results smuggled out. I would sit by him for hours, chatting, while he applied his graphic arts to every conceivable document of state and commerce. Regular searches meant he couldn't keep the commissions or materials in his cell. This was where I came in. The surgery was never searched so when Miguel finished his day's work I would hide the documents inside the cushion of the doctor's chair, and his materials—wax, dental plaster, talcum powder—in the medicine cabinet.

There was little violence in the prison. In fact, I don't recall any serious incidents other than a child murderer being pushed over the rails to his death from the fourth-floor landing. I don't remember ever feeling particularly angry with a Spaniard, or any genuine anger being directed towards me, other than from the secret police at the time of my arrest. Sometimes we would shout at each other when arguments over the morality of bullfighting became particularly heated.

By 1967 I had developed a deep sense of kinship with the Spaniards. In terms of cheerful temperament and generosity of spirit they seemed to me on a par with the Irish. They took pride in their individuality, were full of delightful paradoxes and contradictions, and were naturally antipathetic towards officialdom. Spanish lights were not hidden under bushels. No other nation on earth was, in Spanish eyes, so inventive or so rich in history and culture. (Until then I had understood that the Scots, of whom I am one, had been the driving force of modern civilization.) But although they were aggressively patriotic and proud of their common culture, with all its faults and animosities, it also seemed to me that they were intrinsically parochial; they defined themselves primarily not as Spaniards but in terms of their own village or parish, the *barrio*.

My associates were big redoubtable 'hardmen', wee 'flymen' and picaresque rogues from every part of Spain, and beyond. They were people I could never have met under any other circumstance. I never came across anyone I could describe as a Moriarty or criminal genius. Most of the men were opportunist small-time crooks, arrested for minor offences. The few British prisoners were in for smuggling cannabis from Morocco or, like the two young Londoners on the far right of the photograph, bouncing cheques. Jeff, the young lad on my left, had, however, been charged with attempting to murder his girlfriend. The two had had an argument and she went for him with a kitchen knife. Jeff said that he'd grabbed her arm and she'd stabbed herself. The girl told the police and magistrate that this was how the injury had happened, but they took a long time to believe her story, and it was several months before Jeff was released.

A few of the villains were imaginative and had been involved in the more creative and larger-scale crimes such as fraud, embezzlement, bank robbery and cigarette smuggling, but none had been clever enough to avoid eventual capture. They tended to be victims of their own overreaching temperaments, poor planning, or sheer bad luck. The murderers were the sorriest bunch. Most had killed someone they loved in a moment of madness or rage and now

Stuart Christie

had to live with their consciences as best they could.

Until I went to prison my world view was simple, clear-cut, black and white; a moral battleground in which everyone was either a goody or a baddy. In fact that was why I, a young Scottish anarchist, was in Spain with explosives—to help finish what the allied armies had failed to do after the Second World War, eliminate the tyrant Franco and focus the attention of the world on Spain's political prisoners. But the ambiguities in the people I came across in prison made me uneasy and I began to question my assumptions about the nature of good and evil.

After my trial I was released from solitary confinement into the general prison population. My youth, naivety and lack of Spanish meant it took me a little time to discover who my new companions were and why they were in prison. Some, such as Miguel de Castro de Castro, were genuinely kind people whose solidarity, company and guidance gave me a focus and direction that made prison life bearable. But there were others with more complex, darker characters, whose past behaviour seemed beyond any philosophical or psychological explanation that I could find.

Thus, in the early days, after a satisfyingly intelligent conversation in the yard with a new acquaintance, I would think I had made friends with a nice chap, only to discover that he was an SS or Gestapo officer awaiting extradition to Germany, France or Belgium on charges of mass murder, or an OAS killer, or a South American hit man (such as Alfredo, the chap crouching in the photograph), or a professional assassin, arms dealer, rapist or pimp.

In June 1967 I was involved in a botched escape attempt at Carabanchel and was then transferred to the high-security penitentiary at Alcalá de Henares, thirty kilometres north of Madrid. I spent three months there, until Franco unexpectedly pardoned me. Within a few days I was on a plane to London. I remember driving into the city from Heathrow through the streets of Earls Court and Chelsea, and the exciting sight of girls in buttock-hugging miniskirts and thigh-length boots. This was a different Britain from the country I'd left in the summer of 1964: wilder, younger, more free—the promise of a new world. But in my pocket I had a photograph of five people thrown together by *fortuna* and Franco to remind me that an older world still persisted. □

PRISONERS OF CONSCIENCE APPEAL FUND

Providing relief for non-violent victims of religious, ethnic and political oppression

No matter who you are, what your nationality is or to which religious group you belong, if you are reading this it is almost certain that you are able to celebrate Christmas, Ramadan, Hanukkah, Diwali or any other religious festival without fear of persecution.

You have the freedom to gather with your family and friends and hold your chosen celebrations, in your own way, whenever you like.

But there are many people to whom this is an unimaginable luxury. There are governments, armies, security services and police forces that make it far too dangerous for the ordinary people of their countries to have any hope of the freedom that we take for granted.

Many of those suffering under repressive regimes are not only prevented from celebrating their religion as they would like to but are persecuted for their ethnic origin—simply for being who they are—and for their political beliefs. The Prisoners of Conscience Appeal Fund exists to try and alleviate some of this suffering, wherever it occurs.

We rely on your donations. Please help.

The Prisoners of Conscience Appeal Fund
Thomas Clarkson House—Unit 3,
The Stableyard, Broomgrove Road, London SW9 9TL
Tel: 020 7738 7511   Fax: 020 7733 7592
E-mail: info@prisonersofconscience.org
www.prisonersofconscience.org

Registered Charity No. 213766

NOTES ON CONTRIBUTORS

Christopher Barker is a photographer. His pictures have been published in *Portraits of Poets* (Carcanet) and are in the collection at the National Portrait Gallery, London. He has recently moved from Soho to Norfolk.

Stuart Christie is a contract and online publisher (www.christiebooks.com) who specializes in unusual literary, political and historical works, mainly from a libertarian perspective. His most recent book, *My Granny Made Me An Anarchist*, is the first of a three-volume memoir.

C. J. Driver retired as Master of Wellington College in 2000. He has published four novels, five books of poetry and a biography of Patrick Duncan, and has recently finished a new novel, *Love & Death*, and a memoir, *My Father's Son*.

Geoff Dyer's novel of Brixton life in the Eighties, *The Colour of Memory*, is published by Abacus. His short-story collection, *Yoga For People Who Can't Be Bothered To Do It*, will be published next year (Abacus/Pantheon).

Tim Guest is writing a memoir about growing up in the communes of the Bhagwan Shree Rajneesh. He writes for the *Guardian* and the *Daily Telegraph*.

Helon Habila was the literary editor of the *Vanguard* newspaper in Nigeria. He is currently a writing fellow at the University of East Anglia. He won the Caine Prize for African Writing in 2001. His novel, *Waiting for an Angel*, is published by Hamish Hamilton in the UK and W. W. Norton in the US.

Luke Harding is the South Asia correspondent for the *Guardian*.

Lindsey Hilsum is the diplomatic correspondent for Channel 4 News. She has reported extensively from Africa and the Middle East.

Liz Jobey is associate editor of *Granta*. 'Snaps' is taken from a book she is writing about how photographs have influenced people's lives.

Angela Lambert novels include *A Rather English Marriage*, dramatized for BBC television with Albert Finney, Tom Courtenay and Joanna Lumley. Her most recent novel is *The Property of Rain* (Black Swan). She lives in London and France.

Todd McEwen's novels include *Fisher's Hornpipe* and *Arithmetic* (Vintage). His new novel, still to be titled, will be published by Granta Books in summer 2003. He moved to Scotland from California and now lives in Edinburgh.

Susan Meiselas has been a member of Magnum Photos since 1980. Her best-known books are *Nicaragua* (Writer & Readers) and more recently, *Kurdistan: In the Shadow of History* (Random House). She is currently working on a revision of her first work, *Carnival Strippers*.

Joyce Carol Oates's most recent novel is *I'll Take You There* (Fourth Estate/ Ecco Press). She lives in Princeton, New Jersey.

Paul Theroux's new novel, *The Stranger at the Palazzo D'Oro*, will be published by Hamish Hamilton in the UK in 2003.

Marcos Villatoro's most recent novel is *Home Killings: A Romilia Chacon Mystery* (Arte Publico Press). 'Seminarians' is based on a work-in-progress titled *The Priests: A Sexual Memoir*.

Lindsay Watson studied Modern and Medieval Languages at King's College, Cambridge 1972–75. She is now a psychoanalyst in London.